Extended Reality Performance

Performance + Design is a series of monographs and essay collections that explore understandings of performance design and scenography, examining the potential of the visual, spatial, material and environmental to shape performative encounters and to offer sites for imaginative exchange. This series focuses on design both for and as performance in a variety of contexts, including theatre, art installations, museum displays, mega-events, site-specific and community-based performance, street theatre, design of public space, festivals, protests and state-sanctioned spectacle.

Performance + Design takes as its starting point the growth of scenography and the expansion from theatre or stage design to a wider notion of scenography as a spatial practice. As such, it recognizes the recent accompanying interest from a number of converging scholarly disciplines (theatre, performance, art, architecture, design) and examines twenty-first century practices of performance design in the context of debates about postdramatic theatre, aesthetic representation, visual and material culture, spectatorship, participation and co-authorship.

Series Editors

Stephen Di Benedetto, Joslin McKinney and Scott Palmer

Scenography Expanded: An Introduction to Contemporary Performance Design
Edited by Joslin McKinney and Scott Palmer

The Model as Performance: Staging Space in Theatre and Architecture
Thea Brejzek and Lawrence Wallen

The History and Theory of Environmental Scenography: Second Edition
Arnold Aronson

Contemporary Scenography: Practices and Aesthetics in German Theatre, Arts and Design
Edited by Birgit Wiens

Sound Effect: The Theatre We Hear
Ross Brown

Immersion and Participation in Punchdrunk's Theatrical Worlds
Carina E. I. Westling

Consuming Scenography: The Shopping Mall as a Theatrical Experience
Nebojša Tabački

Digital Scenography: 30 Years of Experimentation and Innovation in Performance and Interactive Media
Néill O'Dwyer

Sites of Transformation: Applied and Socially Engaged Scenography in Rural Landscapes
Louise Ann Wilson

Contemporary Performance Lighting: Experience, Creativity and Meaning
Edited by Katherine Graham, Scott Palmer and Kelli Zezulka

Extended Reality Performance

Scenographic Practice in Virtual and Augmented Reality Technologies

EDITED BY
NÉILL O'DWYER, JO SCOTT AND GARETH W. YOUNG

methuen | drama
LONDON • NEW YORK • OXFORD • NEW DELHI • SYDNEY

METHUEN DRAMA
Bloomsbury Publishing Plc, 50 Bedford Square, London, WC1B 3DP, UK
Bloomsbury Publishing Inc, 1359 Broadway, New York, NY 10018, USA
Bloomsbury Publishing Ireland, 29 Earlsfort Terrace, Dublin 2, D02 AY28, Ireland

BLOOMSBURY, METHUEN DRAMA and the Methuen Drama logo are trademarks of Bloomsbury Publishing Plc

First published in Great Britain 2026

Reprinted 2026

Cover design by Burge Agency
Cover image: *Bury the Wren*, by Beth Kates and Neil Christiansen, actor: Valerie Campbell, 2019 © Beth Kates

A catalogue record for this book is available from the British Library.

A catalog record for this book is available from the Library of Congress.

ISBN: HB: 978-1-3505-0743-2
ePDF: 978-1-3505-0745-6
eBook: 978-1-3505-0744-9

Series: Performance and Design

Typeset by Integra Software Services Pvt. Ltd.
Printed and bound in Great Britain

For product safety related questions contact productsafety@bloomsbury.com.

To find out more about our authors and books visit www.bloomsbury.com and sign up for our newsletters.

Contents

Illustrations

Colour Plates

Figures

Notes on Contributors

Victoria Bousis is an acclaimed cross-media director, screenwriter and creative technologist specializing in immersive storytelling across mediums, platforms, devices and spaces. She received international acclaim for directing and pioneering a new genre in filmmaking, Cineplay, which uniquely merges mediums to elevate storytelling and audience engagement. Victoria is the founder of UME Studios (UME), an award-winning technology and creative studio known for making 'the ordinary extraordinary' by bridging physical and digital worlds to deliver impact-driven stories across platforms. UME is recognized for its innovative pipelines, creating hyper-realistic digital worlds and customized digital human replicas, integrating interactivity and artificial intelligence to deepen emotional connection. Victoria holds a Master's in Media, Technology and Innovation from Massachusetts Institute of Technology (MIT), and a Juris Doctorate in International Law and Human Rights.

Neil Christensen has built many interactive applications over a twenty-five-year career in digital media. He successfully developed a wide range of award-winning consumer and business applications, entertainment and instructional software, and interactive marketing for global brands. He most notably received the Grand Prix at the Cannes Cyber Lions in 2000 for his work with Nike. Currently pursuing the opportunity to create experiences in virtual and augmented reality, Neil seeks to intertwine natural user interfaces with 3D space, information visualization, animation, hi-resolution video and spatial audio.

Camille Donegan is a creative and tech-savvy professional who seamlessly blends theatre production and technology. As a community builder, she led Attic Studio, a collective of actors, writers and directors, for over seven years, managing large-scale, interdisciplinary projects. Co-founding Eirmersive with James Corbett, they advocate for the immersive industry, ensuring members' needs are addressed. Her fifteen-year IT career includes roles such as .Net developer, operations manager and scrum master. Camille also founded Alive-O Productions, creating immersive, family-friendly theatre shows focused on Irish mythology. As an XR Producer, she develops award-winning AR/VR solutions, notably for CAMHS and FBD. Passionate about AR and VR storytelling, Camille frequently speaks at events.

Kesia Guillery is Research Fellow at the University of Greenwich, where she has supported a range of practice-as-research projects in partnership with ZU-UK both as a writer and co-ordinator. Her research explores interactivity and participation, the intersection between theatre and games, and role-play and fiction as tools towards transformative, socially engaged experience. Research projects worked on in collaboration with ZU-UK include 'RADIO GHOST', exploring serious games methodologies towards promoting ethical consumption, and 'WITHIN TOUCHING DISTANCE', deploying arts-led immersive experience in the field of healthcare simulation. She has written, directed and produced performance for a range of venues and festivals.

Nicholas Johnson is Associate Professor and Head of Drama at Trinity College Dublin, where he co-directs the Trinity Centre for Beckett Studies. With Jonathan Heron (Warwick), he co-founded the Samuel Beckett Laboratory, co-authored *Experimental Beckett* (2020) and co-edited the 'Performance Issue' (23.1, 2014) and 2020 'Pedagogy Issue' (29.1, 2020) of the *Journal of Beckett Studies*. Most recently, he co-edited the *Edinburgh Companion to Modernism in Contemporary Theatre* (2023). He directed the *XR Play Trilogy* (2017–19) and has worked as a dramaturg with Pan Pan Theatre since 2015. He was appointed Arts and Health Lead for the Global Brain Health Institute in 2023.

Beth Kates is an award-winning, lighting, set, projection and mixed-reality designer, VR theatre maker and 'digital dramaturg'. She began her design career, at 14 years old, doing lighting for rock bands in Toronto. According to her mother, she started her career as an *artist* the minute she could hold a crayon, and more seriously when she began studying visual art, at age 7, with artist Edith Kernerman. She is the co-founder/creative director of PixelStageXR, Digital Alchemy Creation Lab and Playground Studios, whose interactive installations include *The ToyBox*.

A leader in new forms of performance creation, the co-creation *Bigger Than Jesus* (2003) marked her initial exploration into melding emerging digital technology and live performance. Over the decades she has collaborated on hundreds of productions with celebrated Canadian directors including Jillian Keiley, Peter Hinton, Paul Thompson, Jackie Maxwell, and Daniel Brooks.

Her best production is her son, Aaron, who is often in the theatre (and in VR) with her.

Jorge Lopes Ramos was born and raised within Borel (one of Rio de Janeiro's largest favelas) to a Polish and Romanian family, and is a multi-award-winning London-based artist, curator and researcher working in the intersection between disability art, technology, games and social impact. Jorge is Co-founder and Executive Director of the not-for-profit theatre/digital arts company

ZU-UK. In a world where mainstream narratives normalize hate and fear, and where contemporary loneliness is a new epidemic, Jorge believes in the need for shared rituals, new narratives and experiences that empower those most vulnerable to have a voice and participate in culture. He advises on a range of institutional and government committees and was invited to present his work at the Prime Minister's Council for Science and Technology as a successful case study of XR and arts applied to healthcare.

Deirdre V. Lyons and **Stephen Butchko** are pioneers in the field of live theatre in virtual reality (VR), a new genre of storytelling that is still in the early stages of development. As two of the co-founders of Ferryman Collective, an award-winning VR theatre company which currently includes Christopher Lane Davis, Whitton Frank and Tanvi Agrawal, they have been integral in all the collectives' productions since the first show in 2020. Theatrical experiences have received international acclaim and have travelled around the world, even translated into multiple languages. This journey has given them the experience of what creating and performing theatre on this emerging platform requires at an accelerated pace.

Kevin Mack is a groundbreaking artist and a pioneer of digital art, virtual reality and visual effects. Mack received the Academy Award for Best Visual Effects for his work *What Dreams May Come* (1998). Mack works at the cutting edge of creative technology and uses procedural modelling, artificial life and artificial intelligence to combine emergent discovery with intentional control. Mack's art is designed to inspire awe, engage the imagination and promote well-being and is informed by research in a wide range of fields, from neuroscience to artificial life. Mack's work has been exhibited at festivals, galleries and museums around the world. Mack's artificial life world, *Anandala* (2021) was an Official Selection of the 78th Venice International Film Festival of La Biennale di Venezia. *Namuanki* (2022) was an Official Selection of the 79th Venice International Film Festival and was nominated for Best Immersive World in the 2022 Raindance Film Festival.

Jo Mangan is a cultural leader and director with vast experience in the arts and creative industries. Jo founded The Performance Corporation, transforming it into a festival and events provider. As the former director/CEO of Carlow Arts Festival, she directed for Irish National Opera and The Abbey Theatre. Jo supports artists through The Performance Corporation's SPACE Programme and other initiatives. She has served on boards of various arts organizations and lobbied for the arts as Chair of Ireland's National Campaign for the Arts. Her expertise includes artistic direction, arts programming, consultancy and coaching, with a passion for boundary-breaking, off-site work.

Persis Jadé Maravala is Artistic Director of multi-award-winning interactive theatre/digital arts company ZU-UK. Ethnically Iranian/Yemeni/Indian and raised in East London, Maravala is committed to reclaiming public spaces to reduce barriers to participation and fairer opportunities for working-class people. Recent work focuses on mediating relationships between strangers through the use of spatial sound and instruction-based performance, and the application of serious games and XR technology within healthcare simulation. Her work is taught at universities across the UK and abroad, and has been commissioned by LIFT Festival, FACT Liverpool, Southbank Centre, Summerhall, British Council, Macau International Festival and the Brazilian Ministry for Culture.

Néill O'Dwyer is a research fellow and the principal investigator of *PIX-ART* (Performative Investigations into Extended and Augmented Reality Technologies) in the Department of Drama at Trinity College Dublin, where he also lectures on performance and technology and contemporary performance research. He is the author of *Digital Scenography: 30 Years of Experimentation and Innovation in Performance and Interactive Media* (2021). Néill specializes in practice-based research in scenography and design-led performance focusing on digital media, computer vision, human-computer interaction, prosthesis, symbiosis, agency, performativity and the impact of technology on artistic processes.

Ben Samuels is Artistic Director of Limbik. He is an award-winning writer, producer and director. His genre-defying work extends from visual storytelling and music theatre to immersive audio and film, and celebrates ensemble, collaboration and internationalism. For Limbik, he writes, directs and produces at the intersection of live performance and immersive digital technology. Recent projects include Edgeland (2025), *Rebel Rabble* (2022) and All the Water in the World (2023). Ben was a MyWorld Ideas Fellow, working with Complicité, researchers and the Bristol Old Vic to explore the digital presentation of *Drive Your Plow over the Bones of the Dead* (2023).

Jo Scott is an artist-researcher and educator, based in central Portugal. Jo's artistic research is conducted through making performances, installations, sound walks and sonic experiences. She is currently exploring human relationships with changing, disturbed and damaged landscapes through the creation of sited sonic experiences. Alongside her artistic research, Jo is also an academic researcher with a broad interest in performance practices making creative uses of digital technologies – a field in which she has published widely. See www.joanneemmascott.com.

Bart Simon is Professor of Sociology and Anthropology and Founding Director of the Milieux Institute for Arts, Culture and Technology at Concordia University in Montreal. He specializes in game studies and digital culture and has co-developed numerous experimental games, including the proximity sensor dance game 'Propinquity' (2012) and the immersive theatre game 'The Other Market' (2023).

Sophy Smith is Professor of Creative Technologies Practice and Director of Games and Creative Technology at the University for the Creative Arts (UCA). As a practice-based researcher, Smith focuses on inter/transdisciplinary collaboration at the intersection of the arts and science/technology, exploring new performance paradigms offered by emerging technologies. Her academic and creative work includes numerous publications for publishers including Routledge, Cambridge University Press and Taylor and Francis, which contribute to the discourse on digital creativity and performance. Sophy's composition work has most notably included her collaborations with Motionhouse for more than twenty years, creating soundtracks to large-scale outdoor work, as well as for international touring shows. Her work continues to shape the future of artistic and technological practices, making a lasting impact on the wider creative community.

Aljosa Smolic is Professor in the Computer Science Department of the Lucerne University of Applied Sciences and Arts in Switzerland and Co-Head of the Immersive Realities Research Lab. Before he was Professor of Creative Technologies at Trinity College Dublin heading the research group V-SENSE, Senior Research Scientist and Group Leader at Disney Research Zurich, and Scientific Project Manager and Group Leader at Fraunhofer HHI. He is also Co-Founder of the company Volograms, which commercializes volumetric video technology. Professor Smolic's expertise is in visual computing (covering image/video processing, computer vision, computer graphics) with focus on immersive XR technologies.

Tom Swift is Content Editor for the President's Office at Dublin City University. With over twenty years of journalism experience in radio, TV and online media, he previously edited news for Newstalk and Today FM at Communicorp Media News. He has produced TV news for TV3 and award-winning radio documentaries for Today FM. Tom also edited Dublin City Council's 'bid book' for European City of Culture 2020 and contributed to their Creative Ireland Strategy. As an award-winning playwright and artistic director of The Performance Corporation, he creates site-specific plays and events. His work includes the operatic version of James Joyce's 'The Dead' and the book *Tom Swift: Selected Plays* (2012).

Joris Weijdom is a researcher and designer of extended-reality (XR) experiences focusing on interdisciplinary creative processes and performativity. He designs site-specific performative mixed-reality installations and functions as a technical dramaturge in other artistic and applied design projects. Working as an associate professor at the HKU University of the Arts Utrecht, he leads the HKU Artistic Extended Reality Lab and teaches several BA and MA courses. His PhD project involves developing the performative prototyping methodology using embodied design techniques in collaborative mixed reality environments to create novel experiences for/through XR in professional and educational settings in collaboration with the University of Twente.

Kerryn Wise is a dance artist, performer and researcher exploring the intersection of dance and digital technologies and is co-lead of Displace Studio, a Mixed Reality Performance Studio. Kerryn is a QuestLab Dance Artist alumni at Studio Wayne McGregor and a member at Near Now, Broadway's Studio for Arts, Design and Innovation. Kerryn has been creating performance work for over twenty years and has shown her work at a range of festivals and venues nationally and internationally. Kerryn is a Senior Lecturer in Performing Arts at De Montfort University, Leicester, and a freelance Creative Producer. kerrynwise.co.uk / displace.org.uk / @StudioDisplace

Yong Suk Yoo is Associate Professor of Directing at Carnegie Mellon University's School of Drama, John Wells Directing Program. A Korean-born, US-based theatre director and educator, he teaches experimental theatre-directing methodologies, including immersive theatre, site-specific theatre, post-dramatic theatre and devising. His work focuses on transnational identities and cultural fluidity, merging ancient imagination with digital media to craft innovative, interactive performances. By challenging traditional narrative structures and integrating Eastern and Western aesthetics, his approach redefines the boundaries of contemporary theatre and fosters new forms of audience engagement.

Gareth W. Young is an interdisciplinary Assistant Professor in the School of Computer Science and Statistics at Trinity College Dublin. In the Graphics and Vision discipline, he researches the intersection of artistic practice, human-computer interaction (HCI) and extended-reality (XR) technology. His academic interests have grown from a lifelong passion for technology-mediated creativity, as applied in multiple disciplines and co-creative media contexts. Haptics, audio and visual stimuli focus much of his research on exploring human experiences of digitally mediated creative practice and the tools applied in conceptualizing and realizing artistic works.

Acknowledgements

This book emerged from ongoing relations between the editors and the Scenography working groups at the International Federation of Theatre Research (IFTR) and Theatre and Performance Research Association (TaPRA). These academic networks continue to provide inspirational and rewarding environments where our work, particularly practiced-based research, is encouraged, nurtured, supported and constructively critiqued.

The editors would first like to thank the series editors, Joslin McKinney, Scott Palmer and Stephen A. Di Benedetto, for their support and feedback throughout the process. We would also like to thank Maria Chatzichristodoulou for bringing us together to work on this project as an editorial team. In addition, a big thank you to Mark Dudgeon, Ella Wilson and all the Methuen Drama team at Bloomsbury for their invaluable support in organizing peer reviews and helping us formulate the manuscript. We also thank the anonymous peer reviewers who offered such detailed, rigorous and careful feedback on the draft manuscripts of the book.

We are very proud of the fact that this book is outstanding in the Design and Production series of Methuen Drama because it has a section with colour images. This privileged inclusion is financed by PIX-ART (Performative Investigations into eXtended and Augmented Reality Technologies), which is in turn funded by Research Ireland, Grant Number 212320 (IRC-21/PATH-A/9446), Award Number 17266. These images are a vital component of our collective effort to communicate a genuine, evocative sense of the vibrant, multidimensional work represented in the collection.

Finally, the editors extend their thanks to all the contributing authors for their dedication to the project and, through their varied and innovative practices, for opening up what XR performance is and does.

Gareth: I would like to express my heartfelt gratitude to Aine, whose support, patience and encouragement make work possible for me. A special thank you to Nigel Madden and Timothy Kittensworth for their companionship during the long writing and editing days – they provided comic relief and a much-needed reminder of life beyond academic manuscripts.

I am incredibly grateful to my fellow professors and researchers in the School of Computer Science and Statistics at Trinity College Dublin. Their ongoing dedication to interdisciplinary collaboration inspires and affirms the transformative possibilities of research that bridges the arts and sciences. With its XR technology and performance exploration, this collection is a testament to the value of boundary-pushing and cross-disciplinary exchange.

Néill: I would especially like to express my deepest gratitude, first and foremost, to my wife and children. Your unwavering love, encouragement and support are, and have always been, my guiding light throughout this book project and life generally. To my wife, your belief in me and your patience during the long hours and challenges these academic projects demand mean more to me than words can convey. To my children, your joy and enthusiasm inspire me every day; everything you do fills me with immense pride and joy. Thank you for being my rock and my reason for striving to be better.

I would also like to extend my heartfelt thanks to the members of the Drama Department and the School of Creative Arts at Trinity College Dublin, including all academics, administrators and technical colleagues. Your mentorship, guidance, support and dedication have been and continue to be invaluable throughout my career. You have challenged me to grow as both an artist and a thinker, and for that, I am profoundly grateful. Thank you for fostering an environment of creativity, exploration and support.

Jo: I offer the biggest thanks to my partner, Scott, for being a consistent and reliable 'cloudbuster' and for drawing me out of my head into the material, growing elements of the world. Thanks to our cat, Mindy, for lap warmth and the unfailing ability to live vibrantly in the present – a lesson to us all! Finally, big thanks to the warm and welcoming communities of Tábua in central Portugal who made our move here during the editing of this book so much jollier and gentler than it might have been. Muito obrigada.

Introduction

Extended reality (XR) technologies, including virtual reality (VR), augmented reality (AR) and mixed reality (MR), are transforming the performing arts. This book explores their methodologies, theoretical frameworks and practical applications, bridging the gap between technology and artistry. By focusing on XR's practical applications in performance, our collection of works offers a comprehensive understanding of what XR performance is and how it works, which will empower both practitioners and researchers in the field.

Defining XR performance

Milgram and Kishino's (1994) 'reality-virtuality (RV) continuum' is often used to characterize the capabilities of visual display technology. It continues to frame our understanding of virtual and augmented reality (Skarbez et al. 2021). The term 'mixed reality' was first introduced here to cover all technologies merging the physical and virtual worlds, ranging from the physical environment through AR and 'augmented virtuality' (AV) (1994) to VR. However, considering the technological leaps over the last twenty-five years, many researchers have embraced the RV continuum while mainly ignoring the taxonomy. XR today describes the range of technologies providing access to the RV continuum, and this interpretation of the continuum is broader than the earlier definition. It encompasses all immersive technologies available – including AR, VR and many other technologies at any point along the RV continuum.

For clarity, this text prefers the term 'XR' to refer to the broad range of digital immersive media technology available today – those 'applications that situate digital information in the world' (Rouse et al. 2015). We offer a 'spectrum of extended reality performance (XRP)' with detailed explanations of where the practices within this collection sit on that spectrum and in relation to definitions of augmented, mixed and virtual reality later in the chapter. In terms of what it is and what it *does*, we consider XRP to be theatre, performance and other interdisciplinary forms that use immersive media technologies to create embodied, spatialized and interactive experiences for audiences (or participants) and often interrogate disciplinary boundaries. The forms of practice here include a soundwalk, live audio theatre, augmented reality performance, a 'VR, AR, Carbon Reality Experience' (see Kates, this volume), participatory theatre, XR performance, immersive environments, VR dance-theatre, a new genre called 'cine-play' combining cinematic storytelling and interactive elements, virtual scenography, as well as live performance and the creation of virtual worlds in social VR. This diverse list exemplifies perfectly that XR performance is extending and re-shaping our understanding of traditional media forms and of performance through its inherent technological capacities to hybridize.

In addition to this, and drawing from the wealth of diverse practice in the collection, we define XR performance as being characterized by practices of *extension*, through four distinct qualities, which are expanded upon later in the introduction. Firstly, XRP opens and extends into **new modalities of intersubjectivity**. Secondly, performance environments and narratives become **'storyworlds' – some*where* to be reached, discovered and explored**. Thirdly, experiences of reality are extended and diversified, with XR performance characterized by the **curation and choreography of types of reality**. Finally, XRP extends and reshapes embodied experience, through its **experimentation with modes of embodiment**. In combination with the hybridizing of disciplinary forms, we see XRP as actively extending and re-shaping understandings of what performance in the twenty-first century can be. In doing this, it is clearly enabled by the huge growth in access (for some) to immersive digital technologies.

XR technologies and the performing arts

XR technologies have been in the techno-cultural pipeline since the 1980s, and, despite an initial (Utopian) over-enthusiastic surge, they suffered a decline in the noughties; however, in the last five to ten years, they have come into their own because the audio-visual quality and stability now afford a suitably immersive experience. Economic forecasts should be taken with a pinch of salt; however, comparing four reports from different sources shows that the global market was worth about USD 25 billion in 2021 and, following the estimation of a CAGR of about 33 per cent, it is predicted to grow to about USD 345.9 billion by 2030 (Precedence Research 2022). With such predictions for growth and as more significant percentages of the masses become more comfortable with working, conversing and playing in virtual and augmented worlds, the performing arts sector must continue to have a strong representation in the field, especially in an industry that intersects so heavily with arts, culture and entertainment. Major influencers of the growth prediction are the adoptions of XR tech by medical/health services for research and simulation and by the business sector for the post-pandemic drive towards remote working.

More generally, XR technologies have recently enjoyed a considerable burgeoning thanks to hardware and software engineering improvements, permitting high-fidelity audio-visual representations. These advances and developments in mobile technologies and wireless communications have opened the way for high-quality immersive and interactive digital content to be experienced through consumer-grade head-mounted displays (HMDs) and smartphones. However, despite the rapid technological progressions and ardent uptake by, for example, the gaming sector, the performing arts sector has been slower to embrace these technologies.

Nevertheless, groups of early innovators have produced high-quality performing arts content using XR technologies and theories appropriate to these new practices. Both are crucial for establishing a vocabulary and grammar for the emerging sector, which this book undertakes with rigour and enthusiasm. It outlines some critical early progressions in the field, providing a developmental framework for performance artists, theorists and stakeholders to practically and theoretically engage in extended reality performances (XRPs).

In recent years, the performing arts have been altered by the development of digital audio-visual technologies, opening a new subgenre of 'digital scenography'. In *Digital Scenography* (O'Dwyer 2021), the theory of the avant-garde was used as a mainspring for conceptualizing the experimental endeavours of artists exploring the intersection of art and computer science in the context of the 'second scenographic turn' – that is, the transformation of scenographic practices in the wake of the digital revolution which took place during the 1990s and early twenty-first century. Equally, since the dawn of the internet (*c.* 1990), through collaborations with computer science and electronic engineering, the performing arts have been central to some essential innovations in human-computer interaction (HCI), (dis)embodiment, telepresence and networked intersubjectivity.

As the performing arts continue to be transformed by technology under the auspices of XR, artists hold the potential to prompt the responsible and creative uptake of the technologies by society (Stiegler 2010). As multinational tech giants develop XR technologies, it is no secret that their business strategies aim to implement these transformative developments to serve their current internet and social media business models that are centred on tracking, data harvesting, surveillance and hyper-targeted marketing/public relations in the interests of safeguarding existing power-wealth strata (Belfiore and Bennett 2007; Carey 2010). This dichotomy (between creative potential and biopower) underpins the toxic and remedial characteristics already starkly present in contemporary digital technologies, and XR technologies can further intensify this condition.

The relation can be considered a top-down versus bottom-up association. The former manifests in content controlled by tech giants and wealthy government institutions, and the latter in the creative articulations of artists, technology enthusiasts, amateurs and non-professionals. This book intends to foreground the latter and critique the former. The difference between the two is a question of access to technologies and resources or, more specifically, *grammar* (language and skills). These factors represent the same obstacle–enabler underpinning the digital scenographic revolution of the post-internet rupture (O'Dwyer 2021, 17). This book provides a platform for the voices of the new avant-garde artists of XR – that is, those enthusiastic discoverers of novel epistemologies that seek to break new ground, open new avenues of exploration and rejuvenate the symbolic-cultural landscape of the twenty-first century. Crucially, their vision is an alternative to the aspirations of big-tech corporations whose 'metaverse'[1] is founded on the shallow, superficial, invasive, addictive and surveillant attention-to-cash business models so successfully rolled out on mobile phone platforms. These artists, each in their unique ways, demonstrate how high-quality, rich, rewarding, engaging cultural content can be created within the scope of XR specificities. This book aims to provide a platform for amplifying and disseminating their voices.

Methodological approaches and critical frameworks

In its foregrounding of practitioners' voices, this volume takes the approach that creative practice can be 'theory generating' (Bolt 2010, 33) – this aligns with methodologies associated with 'practice research' where new insights, understandings and 'knowings' emerge from creative practice's 'doing-thinking' (Nelson 2013). Each chapter within the collection reveals a practitioner reflecting on their creative practice through an 'insider account' of making and sharing XRP. By speaking about and reflecting on their practice, they 'offer us new perspectives which are valuable to practitioners in learning about other processes and compositional strategies' (2013, 89).

Particularly in the emerging field of XRP, the methods, creative choices, adaptations and problem-solving these practitioners share offer vital findings and contributions that support our understanding of what XRP can be and how it is made. In the spirit of exploratory research through practice, the approach is not exclusively to share the successes of those creative processes but also to offer insight into the specific challenges associated with making performance with these relatively new technologies. Throughout, the practitioner's voice is deliberately privileged as we believe vital new 'knowings' (2013) about XRP arise organically through their innovative work. In addition, the contributions reveal how the designing and shaping of audience experience, which sits at the heart of this new mode of performance-making, is also offering fresh, highly creative and sometimes resistant modes of incorporating these commercial technologies.

Many theoretical methodologies are employed, and they vary across the individual chapters as each author takes a different approach to describing, thinking about and reflecting on their work. However, overarching theoretical areas are common to many practice-based researchers/artists. Below is a brief overview of these areas with explanations of why they are essential to this book.

Scenography

The practice of scenography concerns the conceptualization, design, implementation and staging of performance, considering how material and environmental factors intersect with human, textual, choreographic and performative factors. It is a rich field of artistic practice at the heart of theatre, and through considerations of the mise-en-scène, it provides deep critical discourse of performance. Arnold Aronson points out that the word 'scenography' comes from the Greek words 'skene' (σκηνή), meaning 'stage', and 'graphia' (γραφία), meaning 'writing' or 'drawing', and was already in use by Aristotle at the nascent stage of theatre critique within the Western canon (2005, 7).

Scenography now encompasses audio-visual, participatory, immersive and design-led approaches, challenging traditional performance conventions (McKinney and Palmer 2017). 'Expanded scenography' (2017) celebrates performances imagined, pursued and formulated through design processes where the dramaturgical vision is determined by the mise-en-scène and the availability of specific material, technological and environmental conditions, each of which influences how the audience engages with and experiences the work (Brejzek 2011; Lotker and Gough 2013). This expanded view of scenography conceptualizes performance as the spatialization of storytelling, challenging the conventions of (auditorium-based) performance – the rectangular proscenium/cinematic format of framing fiction – and the privileging of text. These are scenographic qualities that can flourish under the specificities of XR technology. Integral to this synergy is the fluid and evolving role of technology and the *efficacy*, or *performativity*, it holds over the various stakeholders of the performing arts (Aronson 2005; Baugh 2013).

Within the discourse of expanded scenography, there is a thread that follows the influence digital technologies have over how performance-makers innovate and invent new ways to engage and reach new audiences. Digital technologies hold an increasing agency over contemporary dramaturgical processes, and scenography – which intersects with many spheres of arts practice and experimental sciences – 'occupies an important position in arbitrating' their reconciliation (O'Dwyer 2015; 2017).

Digital Scenography finds that 'contemporary scenography is largely propelled by and dependent on digital technologies and represents a rich, fertile domain, where unbridled creativity can explore new techniques and challenge the limits of knowledge' (2021). This position is supported by the subsequent publication of Caitlin Vincent's study on the use of digital scenography in Western opera production, in which she 'identifies key correlations between the use of digital scenography in practice and subsequent impacts on creative hierarchies, production design processes, and organisational management' (Vincent 2021). Both books provide a robust platform for advancing digital media scenographic theory into the emerging field of extended reality. This is also developed through Rebekkah Myer's (2020) concept of 'double scenography' in VR performance and Aneta Mancewicz's (2024) perspectives of the transformative use of XR technologies in theatre to 'change … the audience's perception of space, time, their own body, but also other bodies (those of performers and other participants) in unique ways' (p.4).

The recent emergence of these discourses testifies to the pertinence of scenographic theories to contemporary performance discourse and the growth of scholarship in XR theatre and performance. Furthermore, it underscores the importance of the relationship between scenography and digital technologies, which this book develops through its focus on the intersections of scenography, performance-making and new XR technologies.

XR and performance

There is an existing scholarly discourse around virtual technologies and cyborg culture which dates back to the 1990s. However, one of its cultural-linguistic repercussions is that 'the virtual' is often employed in the loosest sense possible, for example, conflating it with quotidian cultural phenomena like internet banking or shopping, or talking to people on video conferencing software, like Skype or Zoom. Furthermore, the discourses were often very speculative and theory-heavy, lacking empirical evidence to support the claims; instead, they tended to be dominated by academics working away from the front line of performance practice and who were informed by spatial theories proposed by macro-analytical lenses like ontology, anthropology or sociology – this is precisely why the art practitioner's, or performance-maker's, voice is so valuable. They offer phenomenological, ethnographic lived experiences and salient articulations of what it means to create, communicate, listen and perform with and experience performance through XR technologies. Additionally, these reflections are historically much more rare.

One early volume to buck this trend was Steve Benford and Gabriella Giannachi's *Performing Mixed Reality* (2011), which emerged from the ongoing practice-driven experiments at The Mixed Reality Lab of the University of Nottingham. They have a successful working relationship with the influential collective Blast Theory, one of the most innovative, successful and forward-thinking performance groups researching the potential of storytelling in the XR field. There is also an evolving dialogue around XR technologies that includes influential hubs in North America where, among other theories, there is a strong recognition of the need to build a new grammar around the concept of '*storyworlding*' (Bailenson 2018) as opposed to *storytelling*, where the former prioritizes the spatialization of narrative over the incumbent linear, temporal format. The Institute for the Exploration of Virtual Realities at the University of Kansas is an institution of note that exemplifies practice-driven exploration, giving prominence to the performance-maker's voice over theoretical speculation (Reaney 1999), a methodological framework that this edited collection seeks to endorse. Equally, Arizona State University (ASU) was a prominent early innovator in digital performance practice as academic research with John D. Mitchell's establishment of the 'Intelligent Stage'. They also hosted the International Dance and Technology Conference (iDAT' 99) (Hansen 1999), which marked something of a watershed moment for ground-breaking contributions, for example, from Troika Ranch (Coniglio 2006, 78–84) and Gibson and Martelli. ASU continues to have a strong presence in the discursive economy of XRP by offering specialized qualifications in their annexed Sidney Poitier New American Film School at the Herberger Institute for Design and the Arts in Los Angeles, with VR legend Nonny de la Peña at the helm.

In more recent scholarship, the *International Journal of Performance Arts and Digital Media* (IJPADM) produced a special issue on 'Performance and VR Practice' (Francksen and Smith, 2018), arguing that the arrival of high-fidelity VR tech finally permits genuine dramaturgical possibilities in VR (Fromell, 2018). Equally, there is now an emerging body of work concentrating specifically on elements of XRP (Francksen and Smith 2018; Jarvis 2019; Baía Reis and Ashmore 2022; Mancewicz 2024). However, there are only a handful of volumes on the subject and there is still much to do in the field.

Despite the growth in scholarship, we argue that *a common vernacular for practitioners to engage in, for theorists to analyse or for schools to teach XRP, is yet to be established.* These are precisely the knowledge gaps that this book aims to address. By providing a collection of reflective practice chapters, it seeks to gather and chart the working processes and conceptional rationales of XRP-makers (from various countries across the globe) to contribute to establishing *a grammar of XRP*. Hence, the 'doing-thinking' (Nelson 2013) methodology is given precedence because the technologies are so new and the experiences are so novel. As such, it is the alchemical and experimental actions of the artist that will generate the grammar.

Not all the chapters explicitly deeply engage aesthetic and philosophical questions concerning technology in performance; the work often does the talking in this regard. Thematically, many works posit deep, interrogative questions metaphorically through their practical entanglements of the human with contemporary subjectivities, represented using cutting-edge materials and technologies. They challenge audiences to reflect deeply on the multifarious external forces that shape individuals' subjectivities and identities within modern technocratic societies.

The cohort of artist-innovators working with XR technologies represented here are not just explorers and experimentalists; they are contributing to the reification and manifestation of a new vernacular that will furnish art-going publics with, on the one hand, the grammar/vocabulary to engage the work and to *think* about it and, on the other hand, an understanding that may help catalyse deeper, interrogative, critical questions concerning the base and superstructures of power that constitute contemporary reality. For this reason, we privilege the voices of those designing and sharing new XR performance experiences. We turn to them for the 'doing-thinking' which opens new affordances, releasing commercially designed technologies from their primary mass-entertainment purposes and deploying them in creating experiences that are, by their nature, interrogative of our contemporary positioning in 'the universe … of virtual and non-virtual worlds' (Chalmers 2022).

Objectives

Early speculations on networked/online existence, fluid identities and the overtaking of the embodied self by its digital double – teased out in cyborg, posthuman and digital-cultural theories (Haraway, 1991; Hayles, 1999; Ascott,

2003; Braidotti, 2013) – are now becoming the new reality of contemporary, quotidian life. The emergence of high-fidelity XR perception technologies partially accelerates this condition. However, as with all philosophical and cultural theories, they were composed of speculative elements that need updating. While many aspects of their speculations are accurate (e.g. social media, the semantic web and the mass distribution of on-demand digital audio-visual content), their theories' elements are inaccurate or redundant due to unexpected, surprising and indeterminate technological evolutions. For example, when Haraway wrote the cyborg manifesto in 1985, did she envisage a world driven by Tik-Tok influencers and reality stars, or by toxic cultural phenomena like trolling or mysoginistic echo-chambers?

Equally, the Covid-19 global pandemic delineated the need for every sector (industrial and cultural) to engage with digital telecommunications technologies to meet/collaborate. The explosion in the value of videoconferencing services, for example, reported by Zoom to have grown from 10M to 300M users in just a few months (Betz 2020; Center 2020), testified to the economic potential of globalized and mediated dialogue. However, the limitation (the lack of a sense of physical presence) of simple video streaming technologies is obvious – especially for dance and theatre, which rely heavily on a sense of embodied presence or, at least, some semblance of it. The quasi-physical qualities of XR technologies have the potential to address this deficit in the perception of presence and embodied interaction. However, there is the problem of a fundamental lack of an established grammar (in terms of practice, reception and behaviour) for human-to-human or human-computer engagements. As such, a significant objective of this book is **to contribute to the establishment of a practical and theoretical grammar** that will help pave the way for future cohorts of creative, performing artists and performance-makers as they continue to migrate their working processes to XR platforms.

As XR technologies continue to develop and become more accessible (in terms of cost for individual artists and collective audiences), there is now an emerging body of medium-specific performative content available to potential audiences. In this regard, a new genre with its medium-specific practical grammar is starting to emerge as professional practitioners become *au fait* with the technology and develop the technical know-how particular to XRP. This inspires the **subjective/thematic grammar** that affords suitably appropriate contemporary content. Furthermore, funding agencies are starting to invest in the genre by financing artists to work with the technology and performing arts institutions to create the right conditions for viewing the work. Therefore, from an audience perspective, there is an asynchronous evolution of an **interpretative grammar**, furnishing an evolved performer-audience contract and accommodating new expectations of what it means to be an audient-spectator (aka an 'immersant') in an XRP, and, subsequently, to *engage with* (and not just watch/listen to) the content.

Performing arts schools worldwide lack the **pedagogical grammar** and infrastructure to teach current and future cohorts of creative artists the skills to express themselves using XR techniques. As the Generation Z demographic cohort grew up knowing nothing but internet access, Generation Alpha students will grow up engaging primarily with the evolved screen technologies of HMDs. They are the ones who will be doing work for XR media, and it is our cultural imperative to prepare them for it. Now is the moment to write the rules, establish the grammar and define engagement and reception modalities (and ethics). If left in the hands of multinational conglomerates, these media will inevitably be employed towards two main scenarios: (1) reinforcing the established, ongoing paradigm of mindless interaction based on the addictive binary 'swiping' of shallow content that aims to capture and hold attention through social affirmation and their toxic culture of insults dressed up as 'comments', instead of producing meaningful subjectivities (TikTok, Tinder, etc.); or (2) transposing traditional, linear, unidirectional media and stories onto the new devices of perception without any effort to innovate or create metaphorical or nuanced medium-specific content (e.g. Oculus's series of embarrassing 360 film recordings of performing musicians, or pornography). The former elucidates the greedy, neoliberal capitalist philosophy that co-opts attention and social insecurities (particularly of teenagers) and monetizes them; the latter perpetuates a lazy, deleterious and (fundamentally) toxic employment of the technology that short-circuits the innovative possibilities and artistic potentialities opened by XR.

This book addresses the need for a comprehensive volume that documents and presents a combination of measured, practice-led methodologies of corporeal artistic experiments with the aesthetic insights of cultural theorists, performance scholars and scenography studies experts. A large body of scholarly literature in performance and scenography analyses live and mediated theatre-based and site-specific digital media performance; however, within this discourse, the voices of performing arts practitioners are often lacking – their insights into how they work, how they see the field evolving and the challenges and opportunities. Their voices are crucial to the project of establishing the grammar of XRP.

Given the trajectory of internet media corporations and the direction in which they drive technological development, XRP presents a territory where new approaches can be explored and new intersubjectivity invented. When technology is developed and before it takes hold on a mass-global scale, there is a window of opportunity when early innovators can have a say in how that technology is employed and wielded; that moment is *now*. Indeed, opportunities for creativity are diminishing already as Facebook (Meta) takes over Oculus and seizes the means of access, driving use cases down one particular avenue. *Now* is the opportunity for individual performing artists and collectives to contribute to establishing a new grammar of XRPs, writing the rules and defining expectations. The chapters in this collection help to nurture a new 'cultural vernacular' (composed of a new grammar and vocabulary) apt to the new world of XR, giving improved articulation to performing artists, improved interpretative capacity to audiences and a robust ethical framework appropriate to future pedagogical contexts, as we outline below.

Main thematic and technical throughlines ('The spectrum of XRP')

This book collects works exploring XR's potential in performance, emphasizing the practitioner's voice and digital scenography's evolution. Creating an XRP is not a simple increment of, for example, putting screens onstage or projecting audio-visuals in a theatre because the rules of engagement, intersubjectivity and interaction are significantly transformed. On the one hand, VR technologies enable the spectator (or user) to forego their present, physical and embodied reality and perceptually (audio-visually) enter an*other* non-physical, disembodied space, for example, in the work of Lyons and Butchko (Chapter 12) or Kevin Mack (Chapter 13). On the other hand, AR technologies superimpose audio-visual content onto sensory perceptions while preserving the sense of being grounded in physical reality, for example, in the work of Jo Scott (Chapter 1) or O'Dwyer et al. (Chapter 4).

We present a broad spectrum of XR experiences that extend digital content consumption between physical and virtual environments, afforded by various methods and approaches to engaging with XR technologies. Considering this continuous spectrum, the book is organized around a conceptual framework we call the *Spectrum of Extended Reality Performance* or the *Spectrum of XRP*, which classifies performances based on their position along a continuum that spans between physical reality and virtual reality. Importantly, this thesis primarily analogizes these modes of reality concerning the audio-visual regime or, more specifically, representation and hardware platforms. As such, the book opens with chapters concerning pieces that strongly emphasize and interact with physical environments. As the book progresses, the chapters become increasingly focused on 'storyworlds' that place less emphasis on the physical world, advancing along the continuum towards pure virtual environments that sometimes even break the rules of physics as we currently know them. The spectrum is subdivided into the child taxonomies of physical environment (PE), augmented reality (AR), mixed reality (MR), virtual reality (VR) and any other technology that blends the physical and digital worlds (see Figure 0.1).

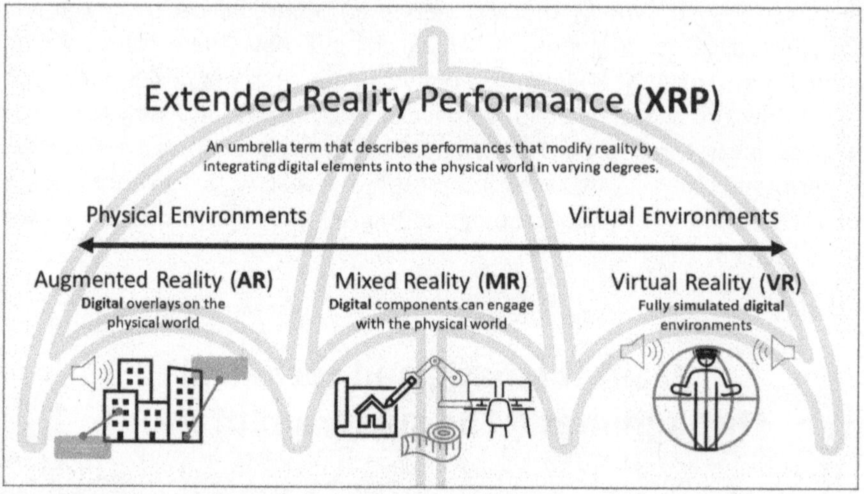

FIGURE 0.1 A visual correlation of technologies to the 'Spectrum of XR Performance', 2025 (© Néill O'Dwyer, Gareth W. Young and Jo Scott)

As such, chapters are grouped into subsections according to the taxonomies that best categorize the presented artworks.

Physical environments to augmented reality

It is hardly surprising that sound design becomes pivotal in the experience of XR projects anchored in physical environments. In this regard, Jo Scott's *Wanders in the (Wild) Smart City* (2022) provides the basis for the opening study of the collection because, in this project, there are no fabricated visual scenographic elements. This chapter delves into a geo-located sound-walk that aims to give voice to the data-rich spaces of the contemporary smart city. It unveils the ephemeral occurrences of networked processing and data exchanges by smart devices and sensors. While akin to AR practices, it challenges the term's visual-centric association, asserting that vocal refrains triggered by location offer a more dynamic and embodied experience. The sound walk converges invisible data processes, physical cities, placed sound and song, creating a momentary intersensorial encounter, revealing the digital 'spirit world' that pervades urban spaces.

Moving along the Spectrum of XRP, Limbik's *Rebel Rabble* uses a similar 'promenade-style' engagement paradigm; however, as well as geo-located sound events, the artists introduce 360-degree spatial audio, physical set elements and situated performers at specified locations. Ben Samuels (artistic director) reflects on the particular challenges of designing an MR performance experience that combines a precisely calibrated 360-audio soundscape (delivered via headphones) with live performance, all produced in the wild, unstable and constantly shifting landscape of Norfolk's Mousehold Heath. The chapter is precious in its articulation of how to design for XRPs that incorporate sited, material elements (such as costume and fabric props) with the natural landscape to define a mode of 'aural XR' that is actively in conversation with the audience's embodied experience of outdoor theatre, achieving an overall 'multiplicity of extended and embodied realities'.

The final work that falls under the 'physical environment' taxonomy of the Spectrum of XRP is that of ZU-UK's *Binaural Dinner Date*. This chapter is particularly significant in considering incorporating XR techniques into a *live*, participatory XR experience. Here, the artists offer a detailed reflection on their methodology of using real-time binaural audio mixing, combined with live human performance and everyday elements, to disrupt familiar preconceptions of dating and intimacy and prompt new reflections. It is a playful and intimate XRP that challenges cultural norms, emphasizing the hybrid nature of technology as a craft that bridges external and inner worlds, which has vast potential when combined with an immersive, participatory theatre-making dramaturgy. Crucially, it engages participants to reimagine familiar experiences under the aegis of a transforming digital culture, termed by ZU-UK as 'hacking the familiar'. As a leading innovator in interactive performance design with a range of digital and XR technologies, the reflections of ZU-UK on this piece are valuable in building the practical aspects of a grammar for XRP.

Augmented reality

The transition to the next chapter marks the beginning of a new section and a leap along the Spectrum of XRP. It shifts to AR, that is, the superimposition of digital visuals onto the perception of audience-participants. AR technology allows people to visually merge virtual/graphical/computer-rendered objects with natural-world objects and scenes using a mobile phone, a tablet or a HMD. Unlike VR, users can still see the physical world around them; it does not close off the outside world by fully immersing the audience in a computerized simulation. AR technology is highly suited to allowing people to interact with stories at site-specific locations. It is ideal for location-based, immersive, participatory and site-specific drama; therefore, the dramaturgical resonances with the preceding audio-based projects are apparent.

These were precisely the goals of O'Dwyer et al. in *Augmented Play* (2019), an AR rendition of Samuel Beckett's *Play*, and the third and final episode of a three-year XR research trilogy. This immersive production merges volumetric video (VV) technology with AR, allowing users to interact closely with characters in a site-specific crypt-like setting, breaking traditional stage barriers. It offers a novel immersive approach to mediated performance while empowering viewers with control over script pacing and plot reveals. While this innovative approach enriches Beckett's classic, it raises pivotal questions about modernizing canonical works at the intersection of technology and art. *Augmented Play* challenges audiences to reconsider perspectives on theatre, technology and the human experience in a concise, thought-provoking manner.

Moving towards mixed reality

Much like AR, MR is an evolving field where elements of both physical and digital worlds are merged, creating an immersive and interactive environment where digital and physical objects coexist. A further characteristic of MR that sets it apart from AR is that it describes a perceptual context where digital content is integrated into physical environments so that users can simultaneously interact with and manipulate physical and virtual objects, blurring the boundaries between the physical and virtual realms (Skarbez et al. 2021). There is a strong argument that this redefinition of MR is just a market-driven manipulation of language towards the reinvention of AR, driven by big tech companies as they attempt to create fresh panic around their latest technological innovations to seize a chunk of the XR market. However, a noteworthy technical difference to AR HMDs, for example, is the use of 'pass-through' camera technology: that is, where the user dons a VR HMD and cannot see the physical word, but they can see an immersive video representation of it that spatially and perceptually correlates to the tangible objects and structures within the physical environment.

Moving along the Spectrum of XRP towards the liminal space between the ambiguously defined fields of AR and MR marks an apt terrain for the positioning of Beth Kates' and Neil Christensen's co-created work, *Bury the Wren* (2019). This interdisciplinary XR artwork, blending theatre design with technological innovation, was showcased at the Alchemy Festival at the University of Calgary (2019) and World Stage Design (2022). It is a hybrid AR, MR and VR project whose tendency to straddle three domains casts further doubt on the distinctive differences between the original RV continuum taxonomies (Milgram and Kishino 1994). The authors examine processes of devising and designing with emergent technology as a collaborator, emphasizing the centrality of design and 'digital dramaturgy' to enable a holistic synergy among storytelling elements – design, performance, text and audience experience – informing one another iteratively. This symbiotic approach facilitated adaptive problem-solving for technological challenges, especially concerning actor performance within the predominantly VR-based audience experience. The authors generously elaborate on innovative practices devised to navigate the challenges of embodied performers acting in immaterial, virtual, immersive scenographies.

This holistic, careful consideration of synergistically and corporeally responding to the specific agencies of digital systems/frameworks is also a salient ethic in Joris Weijdom's chapter 'Embodied Experience in XR Performance-Making: Collaborative Design of XRP Experiences through Performative Prototyping'. Weijdom's is an inquiry infused with academic rigour that seeks to develop a practice-based methodology, which he terms 'performative prototyping'. Charting progress across two projects – *36Q° Blue Hour VR* and *1984: Back to No Future* (GobSquad) – the chapter explores a new embodied design approach to collaborative design practices in XR environments. He does this by integrating the physical body into collaborative design processes from the project's outset, thus establishing XR environments as shared explorative spaces. Weijdom also pushes the virtuality category of 'mixed reality' to an even greater degree by correlating the physical architecture and props in the space (the scenography) to that of the virtual environment, permitting the actors/performers to interact with and manipulate the virtual and physical worlds simultaneously. Thus, these projects underscore the meaningful connection between participants, actors and scenographies in mixed, virtual and physical spaces, contributing to the evolving field of XRP and experience design. The chapter also discusses the need for adaptability, framed by the imposed shift from offline to online VR platforms due to Covid-19 restrictions.

Sophy Smith's chapter describes the practice-based performance experiment as another MR category genus. Part of the 'Audiences of the Future' demonstrator project exploring immersive technologies' impact on live performance, the MR paradigm in this scenario is scaffolded by a participant's sense of affecting change in a virtual environment through their corporeal, biophysical movement. Over six months, a transdisciplinary team combined music, spatial audio, motion capture and game programming to create a prototype centred on a cellist's motion – this was achieved by combining live motion capture data with VR technologies using the Unreal Engine game engine. The prototype linked the cellist's movements with the virtual environment's responsive digital graphics and scenography in real time, intending to create a symbiotic feedback loop that inspired improvisation on the musician's part. Funded by UK Research and Innovation, the research investigated virtual environments for improvisatory composition and interaction. Like Kates' project, there is an inclination to elevate the computer to a co-creative agent. The chapter documents this process by analysing the collaborative efforts and participant experiences. It highlights the innovative potential for future performance practices in this immersive domain.

Mixed reality

The transition from Smith's chapter to Kerryn Wise's represents a further shift along the Spectrum of XRP towards that liminal area where clear delineations between MR and VR become blurred. Wise's work can be thought of as something like the mirror image of AR, where real-world data is captured and imported into the virtual environment to imbue scenographic elements (sets, characters, objects, etc.) with a greater sense of naturalism. In this regard, MR can be employed to describe occurrences of photorealism in VR, which augments the virtual environment. The most valuable technologies for this category are 3D photographic and video capture techniques, such as photogrammetry and volumetric video. Wise harnessed these techniques in her VR dance-theatre production, *Facades* (2021). In this chapter, Wise outlines how harnessing these technologies informed the development of new, unique, creative approaches to devising for XR. The chapter offers critical new insights into scenographing MR experiences, specifically by adopting practices that challenge established VR protocols, creating an experience that 'playfully toys with the audience's sense of space, presence, and agency'. Through analysing the performance design of *Facades*, Wise contributes new understandings of audience perception and embodiment in virtual environments. By drawing on audience feedback, the chapter also builds and contributes to the *interpretive* grammar of XRP design and how audiences experience it.

The documentary XR experience featured in Victoria Bousis' chapter, entitled *Stay Alive My Son* (2023), further develops the concept of MR. While it uses photorealistic scenographic elements and characters, for example, VV and photogrammetry techniques captured in the physical world and remediated for VR, it also introduces hyperrealism, especially by representing the protagonist as a Metahuman whom participants embody. *Stay Alive My Son* recounts a father's quest to preserve the memory of his son who was lost during Cambodia's Khmer Rouge era. The narrative explores grief and healing as players solve puzzles, unveiling hidden memories; successes are metaphorically symbolized in the therapeutic healing of the crumbling scenography of Angkor Wat. In the chapter, Bousis delves into her VR creation, charting creative, conceptual and directorial decisions concerning cutting-edge techniques, evolving storytelling paradigms and their potential for innovative audience experiences. She also discusses the emotional weight, emphasizing the ethical handling of tragic content and highlighting VR's therapeutic potential for trauma survivors. It stresses the role of VR in fostering empathy for the untold horrors experienced by others. The work intricately blends technical design with profound emotional exploration and ethical considerations, showcasing VR's broader social and psychological impact. Therefore, the work contributes to essential aspects of the interpretative grammar of XR concerning public awareness, human rights and social justice around political conflicts and acts of state-sponsored violence.

Virtual reality

In Chapter 10, Camille Donegan, Jo Mangan and Tom Swift (aka The Performance Corporation) present their pioneering work, *Emperor 101*, exploring the intersection of theatre and social VR. While moving assertively along the Spectrum of XRP towards VR (the dominant mode of engagement), it still maintains a strong foothold in physical reality – also speaking to the MR genre – because the audience members are guided (in a promenade style) around a warehouse setting, moving between and inhabiting bespoke designed pods (or cubicles) where the VR scenes and narrative elements are engaged. This ground-breaking production allowed real-time interaction between live performers and VR-engaged audiences. In addition to live actors and avatars embodied by audiences, the virtual scenes present unmediated interactions with remotely present actors as an XR appendage, challenging participants to question the limits of their general perception of reality. Thematic exploration delved into online conspiracy theories and the rise of far-right extremism. Collaborating with RETinIZE's 'Animotive' platform, avatars and worlds were expertly embodied using Unity. The Performance Corporation anticipates expanding this digital theatrical genre, envisioning global accessibility for future productions. Their chapter reflects on technical intricacies, creative challenges and the unique dynamic of live audience interaction in social VR.

Another experiment in live performance-making within virtual reality is *Find WiiLii*, which writer and co-director Mina Hyeon describes as 'a simulation system that allows users to see and touch the memories of others' in her interview with Yong Suk Yoo, in Chapter 11. This piece of XR immersive theatre moves us firmly into the virtual realm, in that actors perform live within virtual reality and audiences can join the performance remotely via their own VR headset. Unlike *Emperor* 101, there are no material elements or physical co-presence within the piece – the performance happens entirely within virtual reality. In this immersive space, Hyeon is particularly interested in exploring 'the act of remembering' through designing 'a virtual reality experience to see and touch others' memories'. In her reflections, she also discusses the modes of storytelling and navigation which are enabled in virtual spaces as well as how this is affected by the positioning of the audience-participant as 'a first-person protagonist, a third-person observer or a second-person helper'.

In our continued movement away from any overlaps with MR and traces of physical presence, Deirdre V. Lyons and Stephen Butchko (Director and Producer of the Ferryman Collective) also offer a series of astute and learned reflections on the practice of producing work rooted in the totally virtual end of the Spectrum of XRP. Having made four shows since 2020, they advocate the new accessibility of a VR-theatre hybrid artform (spurred by the pandemic) and its new affordances, including an emerging (virtual) space for co-present situations of remotely located audiences and actors. They argue that (1) the performing arts' intersection with VR extends beyond existing media, facilitating new hybrid performances, where live actors and audiences virtually convene to experience something entirely new; (2) VR's versatility, enabling alterations of real-world rules and settings, allows for the deepening of performance experiences, blending elements of gaming, cinematic storytelling, and intimate interactions; and (3) immersive theatre shifts focus from traditional stage conventions, decentralizing the audience to a new efficacious and agential role. Lyons and Butchko hold that crafting audience-centred VR experiences can lead to dynamic, emotionally impactful and enriching storytelling forms. They draw on previous productions as examples and personal experiences as producers and performers to illustrate their innovative fusion of traditional theatre and twenty-first-century technology.

In Chapter 13, *Namuanki* (Mack 2022), the subject of Kevin Mack's reflective practice writing, marks the most extreme position along the Spectrum of XRP towards an asymptotic horizon of total VR. A completely born-digital world, *Namuanki* is an ancient aquatic oasis, a resort destination from the distant future and a virtual getaway to an otherworldly reality designed to encourage a transcendent experience of awe, mystery and imagination. The chapter delves into the creation of *Namuanki*, a futuristic virtual world for the cloud-hosted social VR platform VRChat, showcased at various esteemed festivals. The author details procedural modelling techniques and their role in crafting digital scenography. Discussions revolve around emergence and discovery and their impact on worldbuilding, story creation and performative aspects, including the apparition of the author as a mythologist cum tour guide. The author navigates limitations through a hybridized approach while exploring the interplay between mythology, world development and performative elements. This style prompts reflections on redefining storytelling in VR, prioritizing sensory experiences over traditional narrative structures, and generally challenges the limits of storytelling paradigms. The chapter concludes with valuable insights into the potential of generative AI in fostering creative emergence, and though any detailed discussion about the use of AI in current XR performance-making is beyond the scope of this introduction, we also acknowledge its likely significance in future practices.

Mack's position aligns with academic domain experts such as Stephanie Riggs, who indicate that what is needed is 'nothing short of a paradigm shift in how we approach and conceptualize immersive narratives' (2019). Not only do the technologies demand new practical techniques and methods but there is also a need for new themes and theories to conceptualize the shift that is taking place under the profound sociological influence of XR technologies. Below is an explication of some dominant qualities of extension that recur in the numerous projects, linking them together as XR performance, while announcing their individuality and singular methods of engaging audiences.

Key themes and ideas

Through its various contributed chapters, the collection establishes a range of critical themes and ideas that emerge from the reflections of practitioners making XR performances.

Intersubjectivity

Firstly, **new modalities of intersubjectivity** are enabled through these experiences. Performer-audience relations, as crucial modes of intersubjectivity, are particular areas of exploration for XRP makers. This involves playing with remote and proximal performance methods, shifting and interrogating the role and position of the virtual performer, and moving the audience member into and through a range of positionings and ways of activating their presence within the shifting realities of the work. These methods are evident in how Kerryn Wise plays with the 'fractured edges and glitched appearance' of the performer in her VR work, *Facades,* 'prompting the participant to consider how digital representation is created and exposed'. In Beth Kates's account of *Bury the Wren*, the performer's presence is also a site of instability between virtual and physical spaces. Here, the 'ghost-like' character of Annie Donnelly is played by a performer who is physically present in the performance space with the participant but is invisible to them in the VR world. When the participant puts on the headset, Donnelly is transformed by digital AR effects and revealed as 'a living daguerreotype photograph'. In both cases, the 'ghostly' edges of the mediated representation within XR technologies provide fertile sites for playing with the performer's presence and their relationship with the participant.

Curation of types of reality

The **curation and choreography of types of reality** is another central theme that emerges in this collection. In these examples, we see practitioners playing dramaturgically with the positioning of the technologies and the various virtual spaces they create. This often draws attention to intersections of physical and virtual reality, as *Bury the Wren* does, shifting between virtual, augmented and physical realities. Indeed, in this example and other instances (e.g. in the works of Weijdom and O'Dwyer et al.), XRP-makers deliberately construct blended, threaded and shifting reality experiences for their participants. This blending of the Spectrum of XRP can also be seen in the *Emperor 101 experience* (Donegan, Mangan and Swift), which leads the participant through physical sites that double up as proxies for parallel VR worlds and which 'reflect the mind and motivation of the conspiracy theorist', deliberately playing in the liminal spaces between physical and virtual reality but also using the movement between them as a way of shifting the participant into a deliberately 'skewed vision of reality'. Conversely, Kevin Mack's work falls on the end of the XR spectrum closest to pure simulation. He argues that, by building *Namuanki* in VRChat, he was creating a world 'native to virtual reality'; he does not attempt to recreate physical realities in VR spaces but to engender virtual worlds that are 'realities in and of themselves'.

These reflective practice chapters elucidate how XRP practitioners invest in and carefully curate the participants' embodied experiences – how audiences exist in and move through the created 'story worlds'. In this way, we might link the notion of XR performance to what the philosopher David Chalmers calls 'Reality+', a concept that he uses to argue that 'virtual realities are genuine realities' rather than 'second-class' versions of physical reality (Chalmers 2022, xvii–xviii), elaborating the 'multiverse of both physical and virtual realities' (2022, 108), within which we already exist. Rather than seeing an XRP as something constructed from physical and 'artificial' versions of the real, this collection of chapters helps elucidate it as a subjective choreographed journey – engaging various modes of perception – that is brought into being at the intersection of technology and the body, and the networked consciousnesses of participants and actors. This is evident in ZU-UK's *Binaural Dinner Date*, an extended reality experience brought into being through a participatory dramaturgy. Through real-time binaural audio mixing and performance, participants are prompted to 'hack the familiar and taken-for-granted rituals, norms and expectations around dating and intimacy'.

Storyworlding

The notion of '*storyworlding*' (Bailenson 2018; O'Dwyer et al. 2020), as opposed to *storytelling*, is vital to understanding the fundamental shift at the heart of performative experiences under the aegis of XR. The former prioritizes the spatialization of narrative over the (conventional) linear, temporal format. The types of *storyworlding grammars* at play in these examples of XR performance include worlds that emerge and are made manifest through the rejuvenated mobility of audiences within the experience, worlds that prompt a mode of exploration to discover the narrative within XR spaces, worlds where narrative elements surround the audience members, or can be embedded within their bodies giving them new forms of agency and prompting activity and efficacy in the unfolding of the 'storyworld'. The latter is particularly pertinent to Lyons and Butchko's account of the live VR performance piece, *The Severance Theory: Welcome to Respite*. In this work, participants are either cast as Alex, a child experiencing symptoms of dissociative identity disorder or as extra-corporeal aspects of Alex's personality. The latter manifest as invisible avatars who are afforded free movement around the virtual space and the ability to assist Alex in overcoming the symptoms of her disorder. Here, those experiencing the work are concurrently critical agents in its happening and sit at the heart of how it unfolds as performance within VR. In Mina Hyeon's account of *Finding WiiLii*, she also discusses the positioning of the audience-participant as an active participant within the storyworld. Hyeon reflects that situating them as 'second-person facilitator', rather than 'first-person protagonist', balances their immersion in the storyworld with the narrative movement of the piece as a whole.

In yet another positioning of the participant within the storyworlding concept, Kevin Mack's *Namuanki* (Chapter 13) invites visitors to enter an 'ancient aquatic universe from the distant future'. Built within the VRChat platform, the world of Namuanki unfolds through the explorations of the participant guided by Mack, who positions himself in a sort of shamanic mystagogue role that emerged in congruence with the world itself and its representations at various immersive art festivals. As a result, *Namuanki* is 'about spatial presence more than narrative storytelling' (Mack 2023). This opens a reflexive discussion of his thinking around the evolved context of experiencing (non)narratives in VR, which Mack believes demands a radical rethinking (or deconstruction) of storytelling under the aegis of an experiential paradigm that prioritizes a multi-sensory, diverging spatial format over the traditional, logocentric temporal one.

Experimentation with modes of embodiment

The collection explores various modes of embodiment in XR, focusing on the participant's physical and virtual experiences. A striking example is the methodological concept of 'performative prototyping' conceived by Joris Weijdom (Chapter 6). Weijdom argues that despite its engagement with virtual worlds, XR performance is centrally about the physical and embodied experience within those worlds. As such, Weijdom centralizes embodied experience in creating XR work. Analogously, Sophy Smith (Chapter 7) reflects on the kinaesthetic impact of a cellist's physical movement in virtual space by playing their instrument under the surveillance of motion capture technologies. The cellist also experienced the environmental impact of the virtual environment in real time and responded accordingly in a reciprocal feedback loop of creative symbiosis with the computer system. In both instances, processes of prototyping XR work are taking place with actual bodies in digitally extended physical spaces, amplifying a focus on the movement and responses of those bodies in their dual existence across physical and virtual environments.

It is also striking how many of the works are not distributed across multiple virtual and physical spaces, with remote audiences engaged in the making of the work, but are much more intimate, situated experiences, which are 'deeply locative' (Rouse et al. 2015) in their engagement of XR technologies. This is evident in the two examples above, where the physical spatial setups and positionings of bodies are crucial to the explorations, as well as in Jo Scott's geo-located sound walk practices (Chapter 1) where a participant's movement through specific physical city spaces triggers sound in response to the GPS technology on their mobile device. However, many of the chapters are also deeply engaged with the other (dis)embodiment paradigm that these technologies enable: the practice of extending the disembodied self into simulated, virtual space. This includes engaging with the symbolic and almost unlimited possibilities of virtual spaces, such as the fantastic virtual world of *Gumball Dreams* described by Lyons and Butchko (Chapter 12); playing between concrete physical spaces and virtual extensions and mirrors of spaces, as in *Facades* (Chapter 8); or deliberately generating an area where the virtual and physical are woven into a dramaturgical experience, as in *Bury the Wren* (Chapter 5). The last can also be seen in Ben Samuels' evocative description of the meeting of the immediate physical presence of woodland with its mythologized historical past, generated through a combination of 3D audio and physical performance in *Rebel Rabble* (Chapter 2).

The XRP practices here offer practical and conceptual spaces of extension in performance-making. This element links to the conceptualization and creation of performance environments as some*where* to be reached, discovered and explored. It also connects to the exploratory modes of making and creation processes that the contributors describe. Within XRP practices, the embodied experience of the participant or audience member can be actively extended to happen within and through virtual realities. The space of performance is also one of extension through the capacities of the technologies to create navigable 'storyworlds' to explore. Finally, the notion of what performance is, how and where it happens, and the types of intersubjective relations it includes are all re-shaped, shifted and extended through these XR performance works.

Ethics, politics and socioeconomics

The featured authors also reflect on the ethical, political and socioeconomic contexts of their work; every author, in their way, connects their work to overarching metanarratives in ways that offer novel, fresh and theoretical reflections on the societal contexts of their work. For example, in *Stay Alive My Son* (Chapter 9), Bousis explores the ethical handling of tragic, true-life stories, VR's role in fostering empathy and VR's profound social and psychological potential as a therapeutic for trauma reconciliation. Other projects manifest as transdisciplinary research endeavours, like Weijdom (Chapter 6) or Smith (Chapter 7), that seek to push the boundaries of the experiential and discursive economies of the field. By forming alliances with collaborators in diverse scientific areas, the contributors to this book challenge the limits of existing techniques and epistemologies to invent new cultural artefacts that continue to transform the experiential economy of a society becoming increasingly comfortable with *mutable reality*, that is, a reality composed of the evolving spectrum of technologies that make up XR.

Summary

Integrating XR technologies into performance practice heralds a new era of creative exploration and audience engagement. As illustrated throughout this introduction, the fusion of physical and virtual realities offers unprecedented opportunities for innovation while posing unique challenges that require new theoretical and practical approaches. By foregrounding the voices of pioneering practitioners and providing a platform for their insights, this book contributes to establishing a robust grammar for XRP. This evolving landscape enriches experiences of the performing arts and prompts critical reflections on the sociopolitical implications of their intersection with these nascent technologies, ensuring that they remain a dynamic and transformative force in the modern digital age. Ultimately, the book aims to highlight emergent practical, thematic, interpretive and pedagogical grammars and to situate what the contributions offer to the new cultural vernacular. In addition, it provides an important rebalancing of the discourse around XR technologies, privileging the voices of performance designers and highlighting their creative knowledge-making, as a vital way of understanding what new forms of experience these technologies enable.

Note

1 This was a term that was coined on grass-roots forums and was widely in use for several years. In 2022, Facebook decided to appropriate the term and to rebrand their parent company as Meta, probably with the marketing intention of getting people to associate the notion of the metaverse with Facebook, and submit to their limited and controlled vision of access.

1

Geolocated sound and augmented reality: Walking with digital spirits in the smart city

Jo Scott

Nigel Thrift (2014) argues that the information technology, communications, sensors and data embedded in the city's surfaces and objects render it sentient – aware, emerging, able to experience sensations and respond to itself. He describes the data-soaked physical world of the smart city, 'chattering to itself', like a kind of spirit world, which can 'speak' to itself and to us. We might therefore need practices of 'divination' rather than rational techniques to help us locate and understand what is happening.

Place your hands on the bench and listen through your fingers.
Can you feel the chattering?
Can you hear it in the air?

Stand up – turn round slowly once, twice, three times.
Now we're ready to enter the digital spirit-world,
raise some data-spirits and perhaps even exorcise
them … for a little while

Introduction

This chapter reflects on a geolocated sound walk, *Wanders in the (Wild) Smart City* (2022), from which the italicized text above and such texts scattered through this writing are taken. The walk traces a route through the city of Manchester, UK, and gives voice, through song, to the data-soaked spaces and 'new material surfaces' (Thrift 2014, 18) of smart city infrastructures that are present, but not always visible in urban landscapes. In so doing, it reveals the ephemeral happenings of networked processing and data exchanges activated by smart devices and sensors. Such sound walk practices 'situate digital information in the world' (Rouse et al. 2015), through digitally 'attaching' a sound file to a physical environment, which is then triggered by the movement of a participant into that space, through GPS tracking technologies. As such, geolocated sound walks can be categorized as 'augmented reality' practices in that they layer digital content (in this case sound) onto actual spaces, creating an environment where 'digital information appears to become part of the real world, at least in the user's perception' (Schmalstieg and Hollerer 2016).

However, in considering this mode of practice, I contend with some of the implications of the term 'augmented reality' (AR), in particular its primary association with virtual *visual* overlays of physical spaces, as well as the notion that such practices are focused on physical environments that are 'enhanced/*augmented* by adding virtual computer-generated information' (Carmigniani and Furht 2011, 3). In contrast, as I outline below, the locating and activating of vocal refrains through GPS triggering generates a more active, entwined and complex experience of reality, which is *raised* and brought into being through the participant's movement. In this context, theories related to the virtual 'augmentation' of reality – or indeed positioning the practice on a spectrum between reality and virtuality (Milgram and Kishino 1994) – are less useful. In this mode of 'placed' sound walk practice, invisible data processes, physical city spaces, placed sound and song meet in a momentary intersensorial (Klich 2017) experience in 'code/space' (Kitchin and Dodge 2011). The experience happens uniquely in the perception of the individual participant and through their physical movement, activating the presence of the digital 'spirit world' that increasingly shadows and haunts our urban material spaces.

What would you like to hide right now from the cameras and the sensors, from the surveillance capitalists and data gatherers who are so very invested in what you might do next?

Turn to the wall, whisper that private something and leave it there – unsensed, unnoticed, unmobilized, latent, hanging, without function, without a journey, without value.

An incantation to exorcise those wild and wilful digital spirits.

Geolocated sound walks, 'placed sounds' and 'code/space'

Wanders in the (Wild) Smart City is a geolocated sound walk which aims to reveal the often-invisible infrastructure and processes of the 'smart city', particularly in the form of networked technologies and objects embedded in physical spaces, whose purpose is to collect data about air quality, traffic-flow and behaviour of citizens. Vincent Mosco (2019) describes this 'smart' infrastructure 'bring[ing] together the Internet of Things (IoT), cloud computing, big data analytics and advanced telecommunications systems' (59) through 'embedding monitoring and data-gathering technology into roads, sidewalks, buildings, streets and their lighting, as well as throughout homes, schools and workplaces' (60). Mosco points out that 'wherever they are located, these sensors form a network of things that accumulates vast amounts of data and delivers it to cloud computing systems for storage and processing with big data analytics. The result is real-time monitoring of transportation, communication and energy use' (60), and it is this real-time data activity and processing of our movement and behaviour that I wanted to highlight through this practice.

I constructed the walk using the mobile application, Echoes, which is designed for the creation of geolocated sound walks and provides 'digital tools for our community of makers, storytellers and explorers working with locative audio (sound triggered by a listener's physical movement)' (Echoes n.d.). Within Echoes, makers can identify a physical space and then, using an online map, draw a zone or 'Echo' into that space and attach a digital sound file or multiple files to it. A participant engaging with the walk through the application will automatically trigger the sound by walking into the Echo zone through the GPS location tracking embedded in their mobile device. The maker of the walk has a range of options to control how that sound happens for the participant, which can be looped, become louder as they move to the centre of the zone, stop when they leave the area or can be set up to play in full when they enter. These zones or 'echoes' can also be overlapped to create layered sound experiences and synced so that a musical composition can build up as a participant moves from one echo to another.

In this sense, Echoes allows for a type of 'locative media' to be in play which links to what Frauke Behrendt describes as 'Placed Sounds', where 'the distribution of sound in space is pre-curated and users create their own version or remix of the service by choosing their path through the sounds' (2012, 286). Though the type of 'remix' Behrendt describes is certainly possible if the participant chooses to veer from the route, *Wanders in the (Wild) Smart City* is designed as a chronological experience on a defined path through the city. In addition, through the prompts of the audio instructions, participants are often asked to consider, interact with or look for specific physical objects in the urban environment. In this sense, the practice aligns with Rouse et al.'s (2015) notion of an MR^x experience as 'deeply locative' (discussed in further detail below) in that it prompts participants to actively engage with the specifics of where they are. A particularly 'locative' element of the walk is the connection of vocal refrains to individual objects, such as CCTV cameras.

Just in front of you, you will see a black pole, with a streetlamp on top and that's a camera just below.

Get a little closer to hear it sounding into the spaces around you and walk around it, then stop and watch it whirring its way around, looking at the square.

If you return its digital gaze, you might find its attention turn towards you.

In the example above, the participant hears the 'song' of the CCTV camera when they move closer to it. Here and throughout the walk, I am interested in the triggering and activation of 'placed' song – seeming to emanate from an object, material surface or location – by the body of a participant moving into a geofenced 'code/space' (Kitchin and Dodge 2011). Kitchin and Dodge explain:

> Code/space … occurs when software and the spatiality of everyday life become mutually constituted, that is, produced through one another. Here, spatiality is the product of code, and the code exists primarily in order to produce a particular spatiality. In other words, a dyadic relationship exists between code and spatiality.
>
> (16)

Though they generally reflect on the practices of code/space in the management and operation of everyday spaces, such as airport check-in areas and workplaces, the concept maps onto and illuminates the creative practice of geolocated sound walks. The mutual constitution of the space of the walk, as produced through the dyadic and dependent relationship between code and space, offers a productive reading of how a 'new spatiality' is produced by this practice. In a geolocated sound walk, code/space emerges between the coded geofenced zone, the physical space of the city, the digital sound attached to that space and, crucially, the movement of the participant into and through the urban environment. Equally, the idea that our experience of everyday spaces is produced in conversation with computational code is particularly pertinent to these walks, where new spatialities emerge through the specific intersections of 'placed sound', such as the song of the CCTV camera, and movement through the city.

Kitchin and Dodge go on to describe how 'code/space emerges through practice' as 'contingent, relational, and context-dependent' and in 'multifarious and imperfect ways, embodied through the performance and often unpredictable interactions of the people within the space' (18). Again, there are ideas here which resonate with geolocated sound walks. Such practices are inherently contingent, dependent as they are on the specific timed movement of the participant through the geofenced locations to activate the sounds which have been placed there. Such sounds may remain in the physical space of the city, but the spaces themselves can often evolve and even change completely, shifting how the sound is experienced by individuals. Paying attention to the contingent and relational elements of code/space is valuable in understanding how the unpredictable movement of the participant in and through the Echo constitutes new and bespoke iterations of code/space that are specific to that individual.

Finally, due to the embedded nature of the software or 'code' in physical objects and space, Kitchin and Dodge argue that code/space 'often appears to be "automagical" in nature in that it works in ways that are not clear and visible, and it produces complex outcomes that are not easily accounted for by people's everyday experience' (5). I recognize in this creative practice the automagical quality referenced by Kitchin and Dodge in relation to the embedding of software in space. The automagical capacity of geolocated sound walk practice lies exactly in how the sound and audio prompts embedded in the code of the app are designed to 'happen' in close alignment with the physical elements of the space through which the participant moves. This generates a code/space that 'clicks' in the participant's perception, but happens to them without their intervention, as the Echo is triggered by their movement rather than through direct interaction with a device. In this walk, at various points and as explored below, the code/space of the Echoes releases sung notes and words – vocal refrains designed to unleash productive 'imaginaries' – making present normally hidden processes of networked data-exchange in the city. The automagical element of the sounds happening to the participants is also particularly pertinent to the theme of this walk, where the computational processes and data exchanges of the smart city are cast as digital spirits who we chase through the urban environment. Before considering examples of how 'placed song' emerges in the automagical 'code/space' of *Wanders in the (Wild) Smart City*, I address ways of understanding geolocated sound walks in relation to augmented and mixed reality theories, and as 'intersensorial' (Klich 2017) experiences.

Augmented reality and geolocated sound walk practices

As we walk through this next geolocated Echo, tracked by satellites above and directed by algorithmic structures in our pockets, as we follow the path of fibre optic cables beneath the street, forming the physical infrastructure of the ephemeral data of the smart city, let's think about our role in this wild world of data trails and data shadows – the digital spirits chattering to each other, marking your movement, behaviour, where you stop, for how long, what you buy, what you see, who you call. Their irrepressible and wilful energy intersects with and is shaping just about everything we do.

Within the outline of practices that can be offered through their mobile application, the Echoes website describes 'Audio AR' as 'sound that layers and enriches the physical world without sucking you into your screen' (Echoes n.d.), forming a contrast with more familiar forms of augmented reality (AR), which often involve looking *through* a screen to experience the physical world, layered with digital visuals. Rauschnabel et al. (2022) state that 'AR has been defined in a number of ways, but it typically refers to a combination of digital information with the real world that is presented in real-time' (2). This is a more expanded definition of augmented reality than that offered by Carmigniani and Furht (2011) above, where the focus is specifically on 'real-world' environments that are 'enhanced/*augmented*' by the addition of 'virtual, computer-generated information' (3). Indeed, the focus on a combination of different types of information, which is 'presented in real-time', connects to the mechanics of 'placed sound'. In geolocated sound walks, sound *happens* in combination with the 'real world' information that is offered by the physical environment through which the participant is moving, constantly creating new 'code/space' in the process. A slightly different conception of AR is offered by Bolter et al. (2021). They describe augmented and virtual reality as '*reality media*' in that 'They place themselves figuratively or physically between us and our perception of the everyday world, and in this sense, they redefine or construct reality itself' (xix). This is an interesting definition to place in relation to geolocated sound walks, particularly the notion that the inputting of digital information works to 'redefine or reconstruct reality'. It certainly aligns with my sense of these practices, and responses of those who have experienced them, that the 'placed sounds' of the audio prompt a participant to see, experience and interact with urban spaces in new ways. In addition, as a walk designed to 'reveal and highlight' smart city infrastructure, *Wanders in the (Wild) Smart City* opens up the presence and activity of these technologies in the city, through sonic prompts activated in the various code/spaces of the walk, as outlined below.

Look at the people passing you on the street, sounding, leaking, emitting, resonating with data, even those who aren't texting, or calling, or searching or navigating (see Greenfield 2017). It's flowing out of all of us.

That 'sounding' is also a resounding (Thrift 2014), as we reverberate with all the other data points in the smart space of the city, with sensors and attentive computational programmes, learning more about us and mining, quarrying, extracting what is useful from our actions.

However, these definitions do not effectively characterize the active and entwined qualities of the experience created between the sound, its triggering through movement, and the elements of the physical spaces which are activated to create new code/space. Considering such qualities is also outside the scope of the much-cited mixed reality continuum developed by Milgram and Kishino (1994). This outlines 'related technologies that involve the merging of real and virtual worlds somewhere along the "virtuality continuum" which connects completely real environments to completely virtual ones' (in Fisher 2021), including augmented reality, augmented virtuality and virtual reality. As Fisher outlines, in this model 'the ratio of physical reality to virtuality is essential' (2021) and it is the taxonomy according to levels and ratios of virtuality and physical reality which does not effectively apply to the type of experience that is created in a geolocated sound walk. The mutually constituted code/spaces emerging within and between the digital sonic elements, GPS tracking and physical spaces of the city in these practices open up different questions which sit outside those related to the ratio of physical and virtual realities.

As such, I follow Rouse et al. (2015) in their call to 'rethink the technical focus of this definition in order to capture the experiential dimensions of MR and offer a humanistic framework for a growing class of experiences that we label MR^x' (175). They describe MR^x experiences as 'having three primary qualities', which are 'hybrid', 'deeply locative and often site-specific', and 'esthetic, performative and/or social' (178). Such qualities are a helpful starting point for thinking through the particular mode of experience generated in geolocated sound walks. I certainly recognize the 'hybrid' quality, though I would also argue that in this type of practice it is not a stable hybridity that is established and then sustains through the experience. As Kitchin and Dodge suggest, the mix between the elements in play is both 'contingent' and 'relational' and I would go further to describe it as inherently unstable. Within these practices, certain elements rush to the fore and then recede, depending on the nature of the sonic prompt, how it is triggered and how it intersects with the participant's movement through the space in question, generating a 'flickering' experience. For instance, a sonic prompt to reflect, remember or consider might draw the participant into a more internalized and reflective state. In contrast, an instruction to look, touch and interact might open the participant more concertedly to the external physical reality of the space they are moving through. In addition, as I outline below, the particular use of song to embody, give voice to and animate elements of the smart city adds another dimension, specifically in 'raising' and bringing into focus the 'digital spirits' of the smart city.

Returning to Rouse et al.'s qualities of MR^{x} experiences and as referenced above, geolocated sound walks are, by their nature, 'deeply locative' in that the sounds can only be experienced and happen if you walk into a particular space. There is variation in the extent to which such triggered and located sound explicitly connects to the space itself. Some sound walks create compositions, texts and soundscapes which are loosely related to the space where the sound is triggered. Others are reliant on and dramaturgically hinged to physical spaces, in that the sound prompts the participant to look at specific elements and objects, or seek out particular locations, with this material connection forming the core of the experience. *Wanders in the (Wild) Smart City* largely falls into the latter category and could therefore be described not just as locative but also *specific* to the site of its occurrence. There is a causal and dependent relationship between the movement through specific locations and the sound that happens, prompting interaction with their physical elements – it is a 'dyadic' and deeply co-dependent relationship, as Kitchin and Dodge (2011) propose.

As referenced above when discussing the automagical potential of 'code/space', the 'deeply locative' quality of the practice also offers the possibility for moments of 'melded', clicked or aligned experience that can feel magical. This can happen when a participant approaches a particular object and it starts to sound or sing, or when the audio text directs them to an element within a space that is not immediately evident and *reveals* something new to them. For me, this is the element of geolocated sound walk practice, which can elevate it to the 'performative' mode that Rouse et al. reference. In such moments a mode of mixed or melded reality – a new form of flickering, active code/space – is brought into being through the real-time meeting of GPS tracking, digital sound, physical space and individual movement.

As I outline below, this magical mode of flickering reality is also an 'intersensorial' (Klich 2017) experience where vision, hearing, touch and proprioception are brought into discourse. I develop the idea of the intersensorial by reading particularly well aligned and 'clicked' experiences in geolocated sound walk practice as points where the participant momentarily 'holds' the multiplicity of a digital-physical happening. This also brings into being an expanded *feeling* that happens through a tracked body 'clicking' into and activating the next code/space. From the participant's movement, threads of digital sound emerge, reaching out into the physical spaces and shifting how those spaces happen for the participant. This experience is 'held' and happens in the body and the participant's perception. In my experience of such practices, it is momentary in nature, before the elements disperse and re-form into other, less heightened modes of entwinement. The nature of this experience is not accounted for by the types of categorization offered by the mixed reality continuum. However, it certainly leans towards the outline of an 'MR^x experience' proposed by Rouse et al. Below, and following on from the consideration of the 'intersensorial', I outline two moments from *Wanders in the (Wild) Smart City*, where the practice was reaching towards this type of melded experience between its elements. I explore how these moments were developed, made manifest in the walk and experienced by participants.

Headphone theatre and the 'intersensorial'

As the above reveals, geolocated sound walks are of interest to me specifically because they engage with the moving, perceiving body of the participant. In these practices the participant is an activating agent, triggering and bringing into being an audio mix that offers prompts to engage in the real-time surroundings of the city. These types of sound walk practices can align with what is being sensed and perceived, but also use that aural soundscape to shift how the environments of the city are experienced. As Rosie Klich (2017) outlines, this can be understood as an 'intersensorial' effect in that 'the activity of listening implicates various perceptual systems' (374) and, in certain formations, 'can make one not just aware, but wary, of sensory information' (370) that is happening outside the headphone track.

When discussing the potential wariness that can be induced by binaural sound in particular, Klich is referring to theatre pieces that deliberately play with the relationship between what is seen and heard, disrupting and unsettling that relationship for theatrical and dramaturgical effect. In addition, Klich states that the 'headphone theatre productions' she discusses 'present an extreme transformation of space in that they transpose the listener into a sonically rendered virtual reality ... that replaces the real with the metaphoric' (369). In contrast, these sound walks, as discussed above, generate a mixed reality experience. Rather than creating a sonic 'virtual reality', the sound is designed to intersect, align with, shape and actively mix with the 'real' space of the city, creating new mutually constituted code/spaces. However, there is certainly something about the sound the participant hears, which shifts, frames and arguably manipulates how they respond to what they are seeing and experiencing. Indeed, this is very much part of how the sounds I attach to different locations are shaped. In creating the walks, I pay attention not just to the quality of sound or content of the text but also to their temporal positioning, how they meet the participant's moving body and the features of the space that the sound reveals or attempts to re-shape.

In this sense, the geolocated sound walk is an intersensorial experience that is brought into being *through* the movement of the participant and where the sound, as outlined below, is designed to prompt an embodied response, through other senses, to the spaces of the city. This quality is particularly captured in Lynne Kendrick's account of Don Ihde's phenomenological listening, where 'in the overlapping auditory and visual fields, objects are not merely seen and heard but are synthesized in a moment of movement between sensory fields' (Kendrick 2017, 56–7). This characterization uncannily maps onto the mutually constituted code/spaces of a geolocated sound walk, where the particular capacity to 'synthesize' the auditory, visual and physical is mobilized through the participant moving between these 'flickering' and occasionally aligning 'sensory fields'.

Below, I expand on these emergent understandings of geolocated sound walks as mixed reality, intersensorial practices, creating unstable, flickering and occasionally auto-magical experiences in and through code/space. This characterization is developed through a detailed examination of two instances from *Wanders in the (Wild) Smart City* where 'placed songs' are activated and brought into being, 'raising' the digital 'spirits' of the smart technologies that are active in these city spaces.

Exposition/analysis of examples from *Wanders in the (Wild) Smart City*

Manchester City Council recently invested in artificial intelligence or AI technology to manage the flow of different types of traffic, using algorithms trained to adapt quickly to different traffic conditions and different volumes of users at junctions, learning how to manage their intersection more efficiently. Perhaps this is one of the junctions that has been made smart, neatly controlling and optimising who can pass and for how long – part of the invisible, wild spread of machine learning technologies into our city spaces.

In the first example from *Wanders in the (Wild) Smart City*, participants are asked to cross over a junction, where two busy roads meet and which is perhaps controlled and managed by AI technologies. As they cross, they listen to the sounds of the 'sensors', manifesting as a non-verbal song, which is triggered and plays through their headphones when they cross the road[1]. There is no certainty that these artificially intelligent sensors are in operation at this particular junction, though as the text of the walk outlines, we know that they are present in Manchester, due to online reports and press releases. This lack of certainty meets the ephemeral, hidden nature of much sensing and surveillance technology in contemporary urban environments. Here, the processes happening through smart sensors are not accessible to us and are not perceivable in the environment of the city. The geolocated non-verbal song that I created gives voice, presence and a possible physical location to the *activity* of these sensors. As the participant passes over the physical markings of the crossing, they trigger and experience the sensors' song, made present by the movement of their body into this code/space.

Step forward now and cross over Portland Street. As you walk, listen out for the sensors' songs, measuring, calculating, sifting and sorting us into patterns of data. Pass through those hoards of wildly energetic digital spirits busily at work around us and on our behalf, and really try to FEEL their activity and presence.

In this example, the code/space is mapped onto the physical space of the traffic crossing and the machines controlling it, but prompts something else – perhaps a little more 'auto-magical' – in the suggestion that the participant is moving through 'hoards of wildly energetic digital spirits'. There is a reaching and performative quality to this moment. The walk wants to 'raise' these spirits through song and bring them into being, positioning them in this banal space, so that as the participant moves, they can 'FEEL their activity and presence'. This is where the song, as a lilting and playful representation of hidden digital processes, can intersensorially shift the everyday experience of crossing a road, affecting how the participant moves and what they feel is present around them as they walk. They are also prompted to 'hold' the imaginary they have activated in their senses, as they cross. As they reach the other pavement and 'click' into a new code/space in the walk, that moment disperses and disappears. The 'auto-magic' of the data-spirit song is in a sensory discourse with the geo-tracked body crossing the road and flickers out of existence as soon as the body leaves that space and moves into the next Echo.

Circle Square is a privately owned public space – you can be here, but only because you have the permission of the owners. This development of residential flats, offices, retail and leisure spaces is a joint venture between Bruntwood SciTech and Vita Group, all centred around this space, Symphony Park

It's quite a strange and alienating space in the heart of Winter, but it certainly has those smooth clean lines of an idealized smart city space, with its neat sweep of grass and towering steel and glass buildings.

In the second example, four vocal refrains are 'seeded' into a city square, one of Manchester's many privately owned public spaces. The participant is asked to engage in a game-like activity, following clues in the audio to find locations in the square which will trigger the sung refrains, all of which reflect in their lyrics, themes of digital surveillance and control[2]. Unlike the sensors' song, the 'placed song' in this instance is not attempting to make manifest smart city infrastructure. Rather, the activity is framed as a form of gentle resistance to the insistences of the contemporary smart city. It particularly resists the insistence that we occupy this city in narrowly *productive* ways, as workers and consumers. This is an unproductive activity on those terms, and is a deliberately playful engagement with a corporate feeling and arguably unwelcoming space. Each placed song is the 'key' for the participant to access the next one as they move through the square and ultimately, the songs will release them, as the walk states, 'back into the public realm'. As such, the melded code/space becomes a site of searching and discovery, of finding the positioning of the body that will 'release' the digital spirit latent in that part of the square, between the geolocated tracking capacity of the mobile device and the physical markers that are used to guide them in the clues.

To break those lines a little, we are going to engage in some play, gently disrupting the insistent symphony of digital tracking and processing, resisting our inevitable role as consumers in the smart city and the forces of private capital bearing down on us.

There are four vocal refrains seeded in this square, like smart city sensors embedded in the space. See if you can find them. Each sound will give you the clue to the location of the next one. Only when you've found all four can you escape from Symphony Park, back into the public realm!

The square is sung into being, not through imagining the digital processes as spirits surrounding the participant, but rather through the songs emanating *from* physical spaces. They are latent, locked and ready to be released from the bricks, grass, steel and glass by the participant's movement. In this sense, the feeling might be of an 'auto-magical' transfiguration, whereby the code/space that emerges is one where stones, windows and paving slabs sing, and sing of their transfiguration into sensing, intelligent, tracking entities. The songs evoke a 'sentience' in the smart city, which the participant's passing unlocks. In this instance, the 'active' nature of the code/space is held more closely by each individual – they have to seek, reach and find the physical positioning which can unlock that presence and make the code/space we all exist in manifest through song. Ultimately, the participant is asked to use this journey to unlock the singing and escape from the computational spatiality of the smart city, which is designed to track, gather and profit from our movement and behaviour. Though this may be a false promise, the seeding of the songs into this particular corporate space aims to evoke an expanded feeling and intersensorial engagement with what generally cannot be seen or felt; to open up these processes through a moving and feeling response on the part of the participant.

This city is dipped in code
This city is dipped in code
This city is built from zeros and ones
This city is dipped in code

Autonomous
Deciding with us
Deciding for us
Helping us on our way
Watching us as we go
Autonomous

It runs runs runs through me like a stick of rock
It grows grows grows in me like a seed
It's woven, it's woven with my spirit and my soul – my soul
It runs runs runs in me like a stick of rock

You recognise our faces
But you don't know who we are
You care about our bodies but you can't feel them
You track and notice and seed
But we are invisible, you can't see us – we have escaped

Conclusion

As the more detailed discussion of these moments reveals, a number of moving elements meet in geolocated sound walks and combine to constitute their code/spaces. In particular, the participant's movement is an essential element in making that code/space happen, bringing an 'intersensorial' experience into being, comprising an entwined and complex set of relationships. The experience happens between the computational patterns and structures of the smart city, the material qualities of the urban spaces and the activity of the computational GPS tracking to locate the participant's body. This tracking and movement prompt the new melded code/spaces of the walk to come into being, with the sounds knitting together the moving body with the physical spaces they can see and the computational processes they cannot.

Though geolocated sound practices may be characterized as 'Audio AR', the experiences they create are not effectively accounted for through theories which focus on virtual elements 'augmenting' the physical environment or which categorize practices according to a ratio of physical and virtual realities. Such experiences lean more towards Rouse et al.'s (2015) notions of the 'MR^x' in their 'hybrid', 'locative' and 'performative' qualities. In addition, these walks bring their code/spaces into being through movement, activating entwined and flickering states in 'auto-magical' (Kitchin and Dodge 2011) and 'intersensorial' (Klich 2017) ways. This shifts how the participant experiences the 'data soaked' spaces around them. Within *Wanders in the (Wild) Smart City*, the more playful, heightened, open and reaching quality of the sung voice evokes, raises and brings into being ephemeral computational processes. The digital spirits of the smart city are sung into being in the experience of the participant, creating sensory discourses between their movement, the physical spaces through which they move and the streams of data that are emanating from their mobile device and from the sensors embedded in the city.

We are coming to the end of our wander through the wild smart city and though we have chased those energetic and irrepressible digital data spirits through Manchester, I'm not sure we've captured or exorcised them. They always manage to elude us – they are always a step ahead.

But what if that's because they are already in us, already possessing and imbuing us with their wild energy, their will and movement and emergence ...

Notes

1 To hear the song of the traffic sensors, follow this link: https://on.soundcloud.com/eqNmbsQeCotzoyVr7.

2 To hear the four refrains that are seeded into Circle Square, follow this link: https://on.soundcloud.com/hWYWmFAuhJZGzPPe8.

2

Spatial sound and site-specific performance: On the use of 3D audio in Limbik's *Rebel Rabble*

Ben Samuels

Prologue: The whims of nature

It's raining, horizontally. The metallic poles of an outdoor shelter slip in my hands, as my toes grow sodden. Once this shelter is up, we can gather underneath it and assess the situation. Showtime: two hours.

We're on the edge of a large, open field, maybe 400 square metres, ringed by tall birch trees. In the Victorian era, this was once a cricket ground on Norwich's Mousehold Heath, in the East of England, but it has since been left to its own devices. Periodically, the council cut the grass, sometimes with a scythe.

We leave the electronics and the masks in the car. With the rain pirouetting elegantly across the wide, open field, we don't want to risk the silent disco headsets and transmitters, even under our shelter. Likewise, the masks.

The masks are made of hessian, glue, cornstarch, wool and a bit of acrylic paint. They are inspired by Charles Fregér's photos of European folk costumes, as well as Peter Schumann's iconic creations for Bread and Puppet Theatre. Designed and constructed by our friend and colleague, Will Pinchin, the masks are rough, misshapen and look like they were hewn from the woods from which they emerge in performance (see Plate 1).

They also lose all turgidity in the rain. They pancake out and require tender care and reformation, with the aid of a little glue and a gentle song.

So, the masks remain in the car.

I wander up to the top of a hill on the show's walking route, for a better look at the grey clouds that slowly, unrelentingly pass over us. From the top of the hill, it's an unbroken sheet of angry sky.

'It's in for at least the next hour', I report back to our production manager. One of our performers has arrived, and huddles under the rain shelter. By day, Amir is an environmental consultant. 'Have you looked at the radar?' he asks.

Radar? We have looked at the Met Office, the BBC and a host of apps. But radar? Amir points us to an app with radar. Technology, when it works, is a marvellous thing. The radar ticks along through time, showing a green and yellow band moving steadily over Norwich. Then, miraculously, at 2.00 pm – showtime – the angry, green storm disappears.

The production team huddle for a consult. If we are going to cancel, we need to cancel in the next forty-five minutes, because the staff back at the theatre's Box Office are closing for lunch. We look at the radar, at the green band vanishing at 2.00 pm on the dot. We make the call: the show will go on.

Sound, space and imagination

Theatre happens in space and time. This chapter explores how tools from digital space might generate a theatrical moment in time. If it begins with a detailed description of the weather, it's only to draw attention to the fact that most live performance must navigate the unique conditions of its environment – be it the shape of the stage, the number of bars in a lighting grid or the Great British Summer. We chose Mousehold Heath as the location for *Rebel Rabble*, Limbik's outdoor, site-specific, promenade work of live audio theatre, because it was the site of Kett's Rebellion in 1549,[1] a famous uprising over the right to common land. The heath was home to Kett's rebel camp. We wanted to make a piece of theatre that used 3D spatial sound to re-tell that local history, as a framework for exploring what rebellion meant to Norwich's citizens as they emerged from the pandemic in 2022.

With all audience members wearing headphones and listening to a narration of the historical events, *Rebel Rabble* is framed as an audio tour. But this is a ruse. Out of the audience step three characters, who each have their own stories of rebellion, which reflect and refract the unfolding historical tale. As each of these characters appears, their interior monologue overtakes the historical narration in the headphones. When the story from 1549 returns, we see it embodied by a band of rebels who emerge from the woods, wearing those masks and matching hessian sackcloth, carrying sticks. Both the fictional characters and masked rebels are all played by participants from the local community (see Figure 2.1), and as the audience walks from one 'stop' on the trail to the next, they hear verbatim interviews that capture the community participants' own moments of, and reflections on, rebellion.

These three discrete narrative strands continue to interweave as the audience winds their way through the woods: (1) historical, (2) fictional and (3) verbatim. Each strand occupies a different aural space, shaped and supported by an immersive 3D audio soundscape. This creates a formal tension at the heart of *Rebel Rabble* – between its physical location of open heath and dense, sloping woodland, filled with walkers, dogs, children and the occasional muntjac, and the highly detailed, digital soundscape that drives the narrative. While the digital elements are precise, specific and controlled, the environment itself is wild, spontaneous and indeterminate. Over time, we learnt that the urban woodland of Mousehold Heath was a place of constant change. As we developed the piece, trails disappeared, branches fell, sinkholes emerged in the soil and, most noticeably in the summer heatwave, the waterline of the 'vinegar pond' shrank to a puddle. One of the unique challenges in creating the piece was both to write an audio script that resonated within this ever-changing, natural environment, and to create a sound design that supported the audience's journey through it.

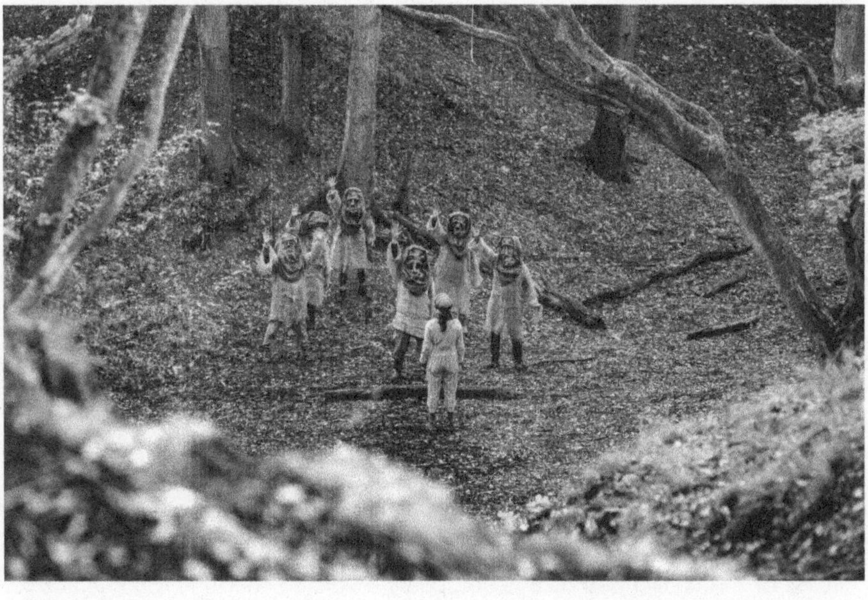

FIGURE 2.1 Sylvia and the rebels, *Rebel Rabble*, 2022 (© Jon Driscoll).

Writing about the Walkman in 1984 and the new capacity it offered to listen to audio via headphones while on the move, Shuwei Hosokawa noted the 'distance it poses between the reality and the real ... It decontextualises the given coherence of the city-text, and at the same time, contextualises every situation which seemingly does not cohere with it' (1984, 171). Rather than de-contextualizing the urban woodland of Mousehold Heath, we wanted to re-contextualize the space, using 3D spatial audio. In creating the audio, we discovered that the sound design also had to capture some of the spontaneity and mercurial nature of the environment. In this chapter, I explore how *Rebel Rabble* used 3D spatial audio, experienced via headphones, to blend a mythologized, historical past with an immediate, physical present, inviting its audience to experience a multiplicity of extended and embodied realities. Spatial audio mixing allowed for a polyphonic collision of past and present, of historical, fictional and verbatim narratives, with each occupying a unique aural space and resonance. Each narrative layer proposed a discrete imaginative space, which existed in constant dialogue with the ever-changing, transient woodland of Mousehold Heath. In *Rebel Rabble*, an interplay between physical and virtual space sat at the heart of the audience experience. Spatial audio allowed for this layering of realities and fictions, creating an aural extended reality that pushed and pulled, dynamically and imaginatively, against the audience's embodied experience of the heath itself, with its distinct textures, smells, atmospheres and semi-wild nature.

Flashback: Initial journeys towards the extension of reality

My interest in working with spatial audio emerged from writing and producing Limbik's *Fatherland* (2018–19), which explored the use of real-time motion capture technology in live performance, using VR and video projection. A motion-captured performer (me) played out a story to audience volunteers in VR. The story revolved around a father suffering from dementia, his son, and their carer, and the son's growing, internet-fuelled speculation that his father's illness was the result of inter-species meddling from the neighbourhood crows. The volunteer assumed the perspective of different characters in the virtual world of the story, while the performer played multiple roles around them (including a dancing crow). For the rest of the audience, we projected the point of views of the VR headset and other 'virtual cameras' onto three large cinema screens which enclosed the central performance space.

One of the challenges of this setup lay in voicing the different characters. Early on, we decided to use pre-recorded voices, rather than the live actor. Initially, in a fantastic theatre hack, these voices played through a Bluetooth speaker strapped to my chest. However, as the piece moved into its touring phase, we started using a motion capture system drawn from consumer-based Vive trackers.[2] This created too much wireless interference for the Bluetooth speaker to function. Instead, we built a speaker array around the performance space, and sent different dialogue cues to different speakers, depending on where the performer was in space relative to the audience volunteer. This is a common approach for placing sounds in theatrical space, and working on it made me curious about how sound exists, and can be manifested, within physical and virtual space. How does sound take form in 3D virtual space, and how might that inform how we use sound in physical, theatrical space?

This is how, two months after *Fatherland*'s premiere, in November 2019, I found myself sitting in a computer lab in Beaconsfield, England, having my mind blown by a softly spoken German sound engineer named Henrik Oppermann. At a weekend 'bootcamp' in 3D audio design at the Storyfutures Academy, Henrik explained the basics of 3D spatial audio – the approach to sound design that we would come to use in *Rebel Rabble*. The basics were simple and elegant: we have two ears, each on either side of our heads, and in between them is a large mass of bone and brain. Because sound travels in waves, a sound will always reach one of our ears before the other one. It is through this very simple fact of anatomy that we can discern sound as coming from the left or right, near and far, above or below.

Three-dimensional spatial sound aims to recreate this sensation. Imagine a sphere around your head. Sounds can be placed anywhere on that sphere. This creates a more 'immersive' listening experience, as if the sound is unfolding in the physical space around you. Rosemary Klich refers to this experience as, 'stepping into another set of ears' (2017, 369–70).

This ability to create a sense of imagined space through sound made me sit up and pay attention. As my work in the performing arts increasingly drew on digital technology, I had been asking myself questions around the relationship between the live and the digital: What is fundamental and non-negotiable in making a piece of theatre? Foremost among my answers was this: the desire to create an act of shared imagination between performers and an audience. What Henrik was getting at that morning in Beaconsfield was that every space has a sound, and sound has space. The potential that I saw in spatial audio was its ability to provoke this moment of shared imagination by providing, through sound, a sense of imagined space.

Lessons in physical and virtual space

As a theatre director, writer and producer, 'space' is a fundamental consideration in my creative methodology. I studied Lecoq-based approaches to making-theatre at LISPA (London International School of Performing Arts). Lecoq's training is famously through the body, but it is also about the space in between bodies, and about those bodies in space. In *The Moving Body (Le Corps poétique)*, Lecoq argues, 'I have always given priority to the external world over inner experience … to observe how beings and objects move, and how they find a reflection in us. We must give priority to the horizontal and the vertical, to whatever exists outside ourselves, however intangible' (2001, 17).

This affinity with 'intangible' space was one of the reasons we found the transition to working in *Fatherland*'s virtual reality relatively seamless. It was easy to imagine the virtual space we would be playing in, even before it existed digitally, because 'making the invisible visible' was such a fundamental part of our practice. Eventually, *Fatherland* would offer its live audience a kind of deconstruction of virtual reality in physical space. It allowed the audience to witness the play between multiple realities, physical and virtual, simultaneously. The theatricality of *Fatherland* lay in demystifying the illusion of the virtual – of laying bare the mechanics behind it, and then inviting the audience to nonetheless invest imaginatively in the world, both onstage and in VR.

Rebel Rabble flipped this dynamic on its head. Mousehold Heath was both the physical stage and natural set for the piece. The reality of the living, organic woods provided the visual, olfactory and proprioceptive experience for the audience. But what they heard in their headphones – the auditory clues placed in a virtual sound sphere – hinted at additional layers of extended reality, inviting the audience to invest in them. These aural 'realities' played both in contrast to, and in congruence with, the physical reality of the woods themselves. The physical space was fully present to the audience – in the smell of the trees, the way dirt gave way beneath their feet and the way they had to negotiate each other's presence along the narrow trails. As I detail below, the virtual layer, the elements which presented the audience an imagined world, existed in sound.

Writing for space and sound

Mousehold Heath is a complex woodland, a maze of trees and hollows, with steep banks rising up to higher ground. In 1549, a ragtag band of local farmers and tradesmen established a rebel camp that numbered in the thousands, led by local farmer Robert Kett and his brother William. They abandoned their farms and small holdings in protest of the 'enclosure of the commons', where larger landlords fenced off common land for their own private use. The camp issued a series of demands to the Duke of Somerset, then Lord Protector, for a more equitable society, and its very existence was a statement – an effort to rebuild their world. The rebels refused the offer of a pardon, defeated the first army government force sent to confront them and seized the city of Norwich (Bindoff 1949, 3–5). It was only a matter of time before a violent confrontation would determine their fate. The Earl of Warwick led a mercenary army against a band of peasants. The outcome was inevitable: 'Their cause was already lost. They had only to go down fighting' (Bindoff 1949, 23). What interested us about the story was not just its connection to the physical location but also its contemporary resonance and relevance. What did it mean to people living in Norwich today? What were their own stories of rebellion? From the outset, *Rebel Rabble* was conceived as a participatory, community-based project. Work on it began in the spring of 2021, with the UK still in lockdown. Through a series of Zoom sessions, we invited an intergenerational group of participants to share their own stories of rebellion and write new ones. Limbik's Co-Director, Sarah Johnson, and I combed through these stories, looking for common themes. Three strong threads emerged: One was the degree to which the Covid-19 pandemic had forced people, at a very existential level, to interrogate their existence. Why were they here? For what purpose? To what end? Secondly, we saw how rising anxiety in younger generations seemed to contribute to a sense of paralysis in the face of mounting crises such as global warming. Finally, in a more personal sphere, we were struck by a series of stories from older women in their sixties and seventies recalling the moment they chose to leave their partners and disrupt their family unit, due to a sense of feeling stifled and unfulfilled.

Each of these strands came to be embodied in a character we planted on the 'guided audio tour' of Kett's Rebellion: Bernard, an older man whose life of relative comfort is upended when his wife is hospitalized with Covid; Hazel, an older woman whose daughters' failure to join her on the tour triggers her memories of when she chose to leave their father; and finally Sylvia, a young history student facing eviction from her shared housing.[3] Working with our dramaturg, Juan Ayala, we explored the thematic resonances between the contemporary and historical narratives: privatization and public ownership, personal freedom, the interconnectedness of life on earth.

The writing challenge for the piece was presented by the space itself, as well as the mode of delivery. What kind of language – what quality of language – felt most organic and responsive to both the intimacy of a pair of headphones and the tangled beauty of the woods? To investigate this, we recorded short extracts of our text and listened to it on location. We quickly discovered that the woods themselves required language that reflected the environment: loamy, meandering, spacious. The resulting text emerged in verse, leaning into the poetic.

The Guide:
Between the home,
And the wild,
There was the common.
From the Greek, 'ko' 'moin',
Held in Common.[4]

We wrote each individual voice separately, as a series of monologues, which we then started to weave together.

Bernard:
And I was, I will confess, angry.
This thing was already here. Already out there. Already amongst us, invisible, waiting to take everything away.
And it's possible that in that moment,
When the paramedics returned
in their ridiculous plastic bin bags,
it's possible that when they left our house,
with its wooden floors, and high windows, and sparkling-white fence,
It's possible that when they left our house
I wondered what the point of any of it was.[5]

The process of structuring the material also evolved in response to the space. We walked the woods daily, looking for natural 'stages' and evocative, atmospheric locations.

Sylvia:
Obviously, I'm in denial,
or in the middle of some weird coping mechanism,
because look –
I made a shelter,
from my raincoat and some sticks.
like we used to when I was little.
That's me sorted then:
I'll hunt squirrels and eat mushrooms.
There's a mushroom right there …
It will probably kill you, slowly.
What was the thing about mushrooms we learned in school … ?
I can't remember …

We tried to match these places to moments in the characters' stories and the historical narrative.

Hazel:
Love is not always kind.
Sometimes it is fierce.
'Go on girls ... go to the woods,
lose yourselves ... get properly lost,
we'll all get lost.
You'll find your way out.
I'll be waiting.'
I turned my back on the door,
On the house that used to be my home,
And *I* walked away.
I walked away.
It was all a long time ago:
I am real now. I'm real.

We were looking for physical spaces that best served the dramatic possibilities implicit in specific moments. We also had to keep in mind the audience's own journey through the woods, mapping a trail that allowed for multiple types of access, and offered a dramatic arc of its own.

Capturing the sound of space

The fundamental approach of testing material on-site converged with the process of building the 3D spatial audio soundscape for the project. I made binaural recordings of Mousehold Heath to create an audio foundation that captured the sound of the physical space, and the changes of environment that the audience moved through. The sound of an open field is not just different to the sound of being enclosed beneath a canopy of trees – the feeling of that sound is different. In audio-speak, each space has different 'reflections' – the aural resonance of a space that results from sound waves bouncing off the physical elements that comprise it. We feel environments as 'wide open' or 'sheltered' not just because of how they look but also because of how they sound. As Lynne Kendrick writes in her book *Theatre Aurality*, 'Sounds ... become the co-ordinates by which we understand space' (2017, 63).

I recorded a 'wild track' from each of the different locations we used in the woods, from the same physical orientation as the audience. When the audience stands on the edge of a large field, they are hearing in the audio a 3D capture of that exact location. The sounds they hear reflects the space they see. The aim here was to create a baseline elision of sound and space – an illusion of the aural reality 'matching' the physical reality. The recording captures a sense of height and distance that feels precise and 'real'. But of course, it is not real. It is a layer of aural extended reality, which the piece builds upon, as it adds historical, fictional and mythological layers into the soundscape.

In these recordings, there was an emphasis on capturing the sound of the moment. I wanted aural artefacts from the different locations always present, in the background. The more atmospheric sounds of birds twittering were complemented by a dog barking in the distance, its owner calling, kids laughing, an aeroplane flying overhead and the ever-present, distant rumble of local traffic. While the conventional wisdom in audio is to clean these sounds out of the soundscape, I wanted to keep them in, as a reference point for the audience. These sound artefacts from the present day helped to create a shared extended reality for the audience through sound. They all heard the same airplane fly overhead. Even if there was no plane in the sky, their collective imaginations placed one there.

Additionally, the use of present-day artefacts contributed to the elision of past into present at the heart of the piece. At one stage, as the narrative approaches the Rebels' 'point of no return', the audience walk down a narrow trail, which eventually opens out onto a dry glade, with a beautiful oak tree towering in its centre, wrapped in red fabric (see Plate 2). A sound montage accompanies this journey through the woods. It collides elements from the physical present and imagined past – birds in the trees, an aeroplane flying overhead and a distant motorbike combine with the clanging of metal, a crowd, horse hooves galloping and more surreal elements that provide more texture than clarity: the jangling of keys and chattering of teeth. All these elements are also spatialized: as the audience walks, sounds fly past on different sides of them. The auditory world of the space – real and imagined, like the rebels themselves – is now fully in motion.

As *Rebel Rabble* progresses, and the story of the rebellion moves from hope to devastation, the sound of the space itself becomes more ominous. The twittering of a robin gives way to the cawing of crows. The presence and pressure of wind in the trees intensifies. The footsteps become a march, popping and cracking. Other sounds, inorganic to the environment, grow increasingly present. This includes music and additional sound effects and soundscape. A heartbeat, spatialized to feel as if it is in the audience's own chest, increases in tempo to underscore the rising panic felt initially by Sylvia, but ultimately by all three characters. As Sylvia's panic mounts, a tinnitus sound revolves around the audience's head. Later, Sylvia will encounter the voice of Robert Kett himself, who by this time in the historical tour has been hung, drawn and quartered. Kett's voice floats high above Sylvia in the treetops, providing comfort.

Kett:
In the end there is a return to silence …
Listen: do you hear that?
One sound dies away while another waits to be born.[6]

Polyphonic realities

Spatial mixing and the calculated use of different sizes of reverb reflections also served to differentiate the narrative 'realities' at play. While the voices of the three characters were recorded by actors in their own homes, an audio spatializer plugin then placed those voices in relative proximity to the actors' physical position relative to the audience. A spatializer allows an audio editor to take a sound source and move it around an imagined head, in 360 degrees. In my experience, spatializers are most effective when the sound source is placed in motion. Without an initial point of reference, my ears tend to fall back on their dominant mode of stereo hearing – that is, in a pair of headphones, they hear a sound as coming from the left or right. However, once that sound starts to move, relative to its starting position, the magic of spatial audio kicks in.

Of course, this is an imperfect science. With the audience spread out in space, a character, inevitably, exists in a slightly different relationship to each individual. We used the spatializer to continually establish the character's voice relative to the audience as a whole. It kept that voice alive, active and in some degree of motion. We also added a touch of reverb to the characters, to increase the sense of their text being an internal thought. These elements all contribute towards the audience's collective investment in the imaginative world of the piece. We ask them to connect the voice they hear to the person they see and project the emotional journey of the text and soundscape unfolding in their ears onto the figure they see walking in the woods. To facilitate this, the actors' work was defined by a subtle, minimalistic performance style in a precisely tracked physical score: eat a crisp on this line, put away your glasses here. Because the inner life of the character is voiced, the external work of the actor becomes highly cinematic. They don't need to play much external emotion, as their inner world is alive in the audience's ears.

The disembodied voice of the Guide, meanwhile, generally sat slightly above the audience, with a little less reverb than the characters, while the verbatim interviews were not spatialized at all, but rather were presented 'dry' and 'mono', to underscore their 'real world' quality.

Conclusion: On listening

Lynn Kendrick refers to aurality as the 'many states of hearing and listening, resounding and voicing, sonance and resonance, moving and feeling' (2017, 1). This sensory process, she writes, 'brings all those qualities of auricular engagement – of feeling, movement, immersion and multiplicity – to the forefront of our relation with the world' (2017, 7). Since our work on *Fatherland*, one of the key elements of our approach to working with technology has been that a digital mechanic carries its own metaphor. Through centring the experience on sound, *Rebel Rabble* invited its audience to listen – not just to the complex soundscape we had constructed but also to the world as it exists in the present moment. In perhaps the show's most evocative moment, with the peasant army losing their battle against the King's mercenaries, we ask the audience to stand at the edge of Mousehold Heath's 'Vinegar Pond', named after the alkalinity of the water (see Plate 3). Clanging swords, horse whinnies and battle cries whirl around until a 'high-pass filter' thins out the sound, making it more febrile, ghostly:

GUIDE
A group of rebels retreated to this very spot.
Here, their backs to the water, they fought on.
Local dog walkers say that if you listen closely,
you can still hear the echoes of their last stand.
Please remove your headphones and listen …
You will know when to put them on again.

The audience remove their headphones and listen to whatever sound is unfolding around the pond at that moment. There are the real cries of birds, children playing nearby, a dog splashing through the water, a conversation in the far distance, gusts of wind, raindrops, the crunching of feet as the rebels join the audience, carrying their masks in their hands, the faces of the actors revealed for the first time. Together, they listen with the audience. It is a moment of suspension, stopping, stillness, of active listening: a moment to engage in the present, the here (or hear) and now. The act of shared imagination, driven by the audio, shifts in this moment to an act of shared presence and present-ness.

Rebel Rabble ends by asking what from the past lives on in this present moment, even in the face of failure. The piece draws inspiration from the mycelium networks, running across the forest floor, the fungus trails that provide the communication networks for the trees themselves. Fungi feed off the decaying life around them. So too *Rebel Rabble*'s final message is of hope for a decaying world. The last word of the piece belongs to one of our participants, the Norwich-based artist Helen Wells:

> We all do our bit, and then you're gone and somebody else will do their bit. So it's sort of that longer perspective on all this. We will play a part … then it continues without you … you've done your bit and someone else picks it up and carries on. I mean, I find that a supportive way to think. You're just here for a bit, and you play your part, and then you're gone. It's kind of like – that's just sort of just sort of ordinary, isn't it?

Drawing from different strands of our company's earlier work in physical theatre and with new technologies, *Rebel Rabble* represented a new form of creative practice for Limbik, combining physical and digital elements in an outdoor, site-specific performance. The use of 3D spatial audio created an intimate layer of extended reality for the live physical audience. Yet rather than isolate each audience member into their own world in the performance, the soundscape served as a common reference point. The headphones also seemed to contribute to an increased level of proprioceptive awareness among the audience. As Norwich Theatre's Head of Creative Development Jez Pike put it:

> The experience of being a *Rebel Rabble* audience member left me with an increased sense of wellbeing that lasted for a few days afterwards. Because we were moving as a group through woodland whilst wearing headphones, we needed to be more in tune with the other members in the audience, so we didn't bump into each other or block their view. Without demanding too much, the show asked us quietly to be generous.[7]

Listening, in *Rebel Rabble*, becomes an action. We listen to the past, to the present, to artefacts from our modern civilization and to the sounds of nature. Equally, we are attuned to the other bodies around us. According to Kendrick, 'Binaural recording has the effect of creating something of an audience paradox: the hearing experience is individual yet is undertaken collectively … The listener is simultaneously isolated and accompanied in experience' (2017, 54–5).

It is a kind of irony that asking an audience to tune in to a highly detailed, digitally constructed soundtrack in an expansive natural environment serves to further embody the act of listening. I believe that this impact arose from constructing the audio with the landscape itself. By being attentive to that landscape and shaping the layers of extended audio reality in response, we were able to facilitate this experience of embodied listening.

Notes

1 Kett's Rebellion (1549) is an integral part of Norfolk's history. Traces of the rebellion can be found everywhere from the names of local streets, schools and ales, to CJ Sansom's novel *Tombland* (2018).

2 HTC Vive is a virtual reality headset that uses 'lighthouses' – a kind of camera – to define a 'volume' of virtual space. The company also provide 'trackers', which are objects whose movement can be seen and followed in virtual reality. Any virtual object can be assigned to these trackers, rendering it visible in VR. This includes the human body.

3 Bernard was played by Jamie Zubairi, Hazel by Claire Lacey, Sylvia by Sarah Johnson, and The Guide by Nicole Sawyerr.

4 This passage was directly inspired by Gary Snyder's essay, 'The Place, the Region and the Commons' (Snyder 2020, 33).

5 All text from the show taken from the rehearsal draft script of *Rebel Rabble*, by Ben Samuels and Sarah Johnson.

6 *Rebel Rabble* exists as a digital archive, with the full audio soundtrack, accompanied by photography and video, at https://www.rebel-rabble.com/.

7 As provided to the author in written feedback.

3

Liveness, audio mixing and participatory theatre: Hacking the familiar in *Binaural Dinner Date*

Kesia Guillery, Jorge Lopes Ramos, Persis Jadé Maravala and Bart Simon

#BeTheDate

Binaural Dinner Date (2017–) was developed by ZU-UK over five years of iterative design, using bespoke technology and live performance to mediate encounters between strangers in public spaces. By 2025, the production had totalled over 300 performances in leading festivals across the UK, Macao, Brazil, Greece and Colombia reaching over 4,500 participants at public restaurants and cafés. The experience begins with the purchase of a ticket for some, or an invitation to participate at very short notice for others. You might purchase a ticket in advance – usually through a festival website – or be approached in a restaurant asking whether you would like to experience the next session that day. Either way, you may be slightly confused by the ambiguous identity of the event you are to attend (described as 'part interactive performance, part dating agency') (ZU-UK 2022). Thus, prepared for something hybrid, ludic and intimate, you arrive – or find yourself – at the main event in a makeshift or fully working restaurant. Sometimes the restaurant has appeared in the middle of a field (*Binaural Dinner Date* 2018) and sometimes in the middle of a shopping centre (*Binaural Dinner Date* 2017) – sometimes it has even popped

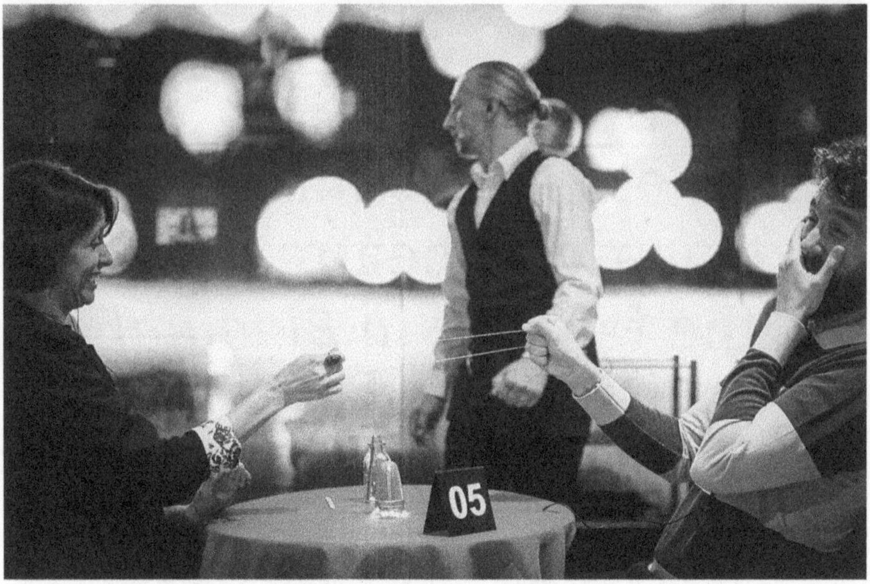

FIGURE 3.1 Participants in *Binaural Dinner Date*. W performed by James Turpin, Oi Futuro, Rio de Janeiro, 2022 (© Renato Mangolin).

up as a smaller section of actual restaurants (*Binaural Dinner Date* 2017–20), a restaurant-within-a-restaurant, without a visual separation between those dining and the audience members.

As you sit down, you are allocated a partner – your 'date' – according to preferences you supply in advance or briefly discuss at entry and are seated across from them by an assiduously polite matchmaker-cum-maître d'. You are introduced to your table-waiter, referred to as 'W' – a taciturn, preoccupied server,[1] who will flit between the tables throughout the experience – and you are made aware of a set of small earphones and a microphone embedded in your table. You put the earphones in and realize that you can hear not only yourself, your partner and the general background noise in real time but also a variety of extra sounds. A soothing, sultry and gently ironic voice introduces itself and begins to give you instructions, sometimes accompanied by music and sound effects. The date then unfolds, and through a series of games, questions, stories and twists, you start to connect with the person sitting opposite you.

The slogan accompanying the interactive performance of *Binaural Dinner Date* – on social media, on little badges handed out at some performances, in the subheadings of reviews – gave participants a perplexing instruction: #BeTheDate. What appears to echo the melodramatic, appropriative language of the immersive and virtual entertainment industries – 'Tell no one' (*Tell*

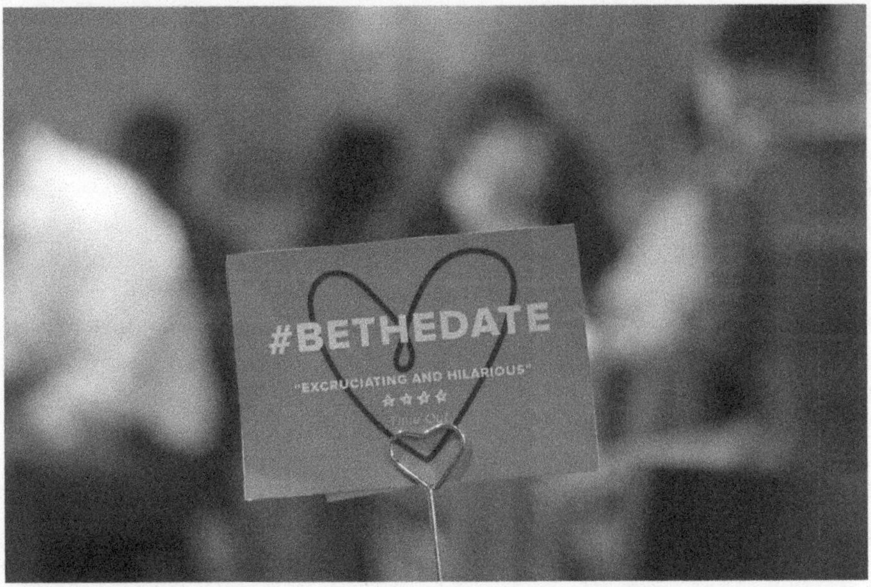

FIGURE 3.2 '#BeTheDate': The *Binaural Dinner Date* tagline, Rich Mix, London, 2019 (© Ludovic des Cognets).

No One 2016), 'every decision is your own' (*The Grim* 2020), 'it isn't Alice's adventure, it's yours' (*Alice's Adventures Underground* 2015–20) – is, on closer inspection, asking people to do something more complex. They are not told to become a part of someone else's story, or to commandeer it themselves. They are instead invited to *be* the event: the whole complex set of expectations, norms, televisually constructed fantasies and memories that constitute the 'secular ritual' (Dunne-Howrie et al. 2020) of dating. In asking participants to 'be the date', *Binaural Dinner Date* invites them to hack into this web of coded interactions and inhabit these behavioural systems (pervading our consciousnesses more and more as technologically mediated experience) as bodies.

Binaural Dinner Date as extended reality performance

In this chapter we provide an analysis of core elements in the design of *Binaural Dinner Date* as an extended reality performance that leverages digital audio operation technologies in a performative encounter to unsettle culturally salient ideas about intimacy, dating and playfulness. The performativity nurtured by the experience combines elements of Barba's 'extra-daily' parameters (Barba 1995), separating performative action from the everyday, and Goffman's contrasting conception of performativity as the presentation of self through the lenses of various social roles (Goffman 1956). The elevation of these performances of self to an 'extra-daily' realm, we argue, is what allows participants in a playful XR performance such as *Binaural Dinner Date* to access a heightened consciousness of their many, performed selves.

Prevailing definitions (Chesher 1994; Egliston & Carter 2022; Jones 2022) and uses of augmented and virtual reality technologies tend to emphasize a break with the user's reality and offer alternative realities and perspectives that can dazzle, shock or entertain. However, even as these very commercial technologies threaten to become more immersive and distracting, they can be put to more artistic uses in reflecting on the users' reality rather than escaping from it.

Audio applications and games that respond to data input from a present reality abound. If *Zombies, Run!* (Six to Start 2012) can be cast as a gamified audio-based XR version of the basic Couch to 5K app (FITNESS22 LTD n.d.), perhaps *Binaural Dinner Date* is in some ways a gamified audio-based version of Tinder. *Zombies, Run!* is a 2012 mobile fitness audio game that has players running to evade the zombie apocalypse while tracking and responding to distance, time, pace and calories burnt; *Binaural Dinner Date* tracks conversation, connection, eye contact – and it responds. The obvious difference between *Binaural Dinner Date* and an online XR audio app is that the technological framework enabling its responsiveness includes a team of live performers, fabricating audio content as they go, observing, intuiting and communicating with each other to create a seamless whole. At face value, it would make more sense to categorize the experience as a quirky theatre piece or immersive artwork: ZU-UK are known primarily as an arts group, operating on the boundaries of theatre and digital art, immersive adventure entertainment and live art intervention. *Binaural Dinner Date* shares much with some examples of audio-led work in this sphere: Rotozaza's *Etiquette* (2007–23), for example, is also an experience for two people seated at a table in a café, guided throughout by instructions listened to via headphones; Rimini Protokoll, a German collective creating interventions, performance installations and audio plays, are also pioneers of audio-instructional performances in public space, orchestrating small- and large-scale interactions between audience-members through carefully worded and timed audio tracks. *Binaural Dinner Date*, however, is a truly XR performance in that the designed material of the artwork itself bends to and incorporates the input of the participants as well as that of the surrounding environment. In this sense, it is more akin to Ben Bengler's *Polymetros* (Bengler and Bryan-Kinns 2013), an interactive music system combining a software application with a multi-user hardware interface and external audio equipment, designed with the intention of facilitating a collaborative musical creative process for a non-initiate audience. Participants are provided with a framework and with content they are able to manipulate into unique new configurations. *Binaural Dinner Date* is, in the same vein, a hybrid platform designed to responsively facilitate playful, social and performative creativity in a collaboration between two. What *Polymetros* wants to do to the music-making experience, *Binaural Dinner Date* does to the rituals of both theatre and dating. The principal design difference from such a collaborative XR system as *Polymetros* is the way 'pockets of agency' (Guillery, Lopes Ramos and Maravala 2022) are embedded into the framework, within which participants are able to improvise their own genuinely new content.

Crucially, what constitutes the extended reality experience of *Binaural Dinner Date*, depends not only on digital technology but on a participatory theatre-making dramaturgy: the way participants are oriented to engage with familiar experiences differently, becoming aware of their self-reflexive interior relationship to shared norms. ZU-UK refer to this dramaturgical strategy in their practice as 'hacking the familiar' (TEDx Talks 2022). Digital technology – in this case, real-time edited binaural soundtracks delivered through headphones – supports the experience without being its most essential medium. The support of these technologies (headphones, microphones, wires, restaurant setting and props, binaural sound editing system and so on) and skilled facilitators (actors, technicians, directors and scriptwriters working in real time as the experience unfolds) scaffolds the mediated experience. The experience is more meaningfully understood as residing in participants themselves, rather than in the scaffold that enables it, in what is essentially a social, not a technological, interaction. What the material wiring of the piece (from mics and Ableton software to menus and shot glasses) does is to frame and reframe participants' familiarity with the norms and expectations around dating and intimacy.

The goal is to effect a subtle but palpable slippage in participants' perception of the experience as simultaneously real (being on a date with someone) and performed (pretending to be on a date with someone). In what follows, we draw on literature from work on pervasive games and game studies (Montola, Stenros and Waern 2009) and theatre (Barba 1995) to examine core elements in the design of *Binaural Dinner Date* to articulate how this hacking of the familiar is accomplished. The first section of analysis explores the interpretive frames 'hacked' by *Binaural Dinner Date* and the second section examines how audio technology builds, then warps, these frames.

Hacking the familiar

Binaural Dinner Date repurposes the recognizable: recognizable technologies like earphones and digital audio-content; recognizable settings and rituals such as restaurants and dating; recognizable tropes like the melancholic waiter, the jilted lover or the 'voice in your head'; and recognizable sensations like discomfort, curiosity or competition. All of these are reinhabited during the experience in such ways that the things participants say, do and think, the ways they say, do and think them, and the temporary co-created identity they form with their 'date', become sites of aesthetic value. The raw, familiar, material is adjusted and combined, remixed and reframed, and appreciated through a metaphorical lens.

The very first moments in which participants find themselves opposite their date establish a tension between a somewhat fictionalized but somehow real setting, thus allowing them to enact role-played and/or real versions of themselves. They are handed a menu and invited to 'get better acquainted with their date'. This restaurant date, they tell themselves, is real. They are sat opposite a genuine stranger, feeling the real sensations of awkwardness, apprehension and curiosity that they would feel on any other date – they do not know what they will say to their date, when they will wish they could hide, nor how close they will or will not have come to each other by the end of the next seventy-five minutes. The Matchmaker-Maître D has addressed them not as audience members but directly as each other's dates. By seating them and handing them menus, she has followed and activated the familiar conventions of restaurant behaviour. To use the terminology of Montola (Montola, Stenros and Waern 2009), adapted from Peirce (1991a,b), to describe the semiotics of pervasive games, here is the possibility of an 'indexical' relationship between the context of the date and the context of the performance: a touch of hands may carry real romantic significance, an extended moment of eye contact may genuinely mean your partner is assessing your compatibility as lovers (see Plate 4).

The idea of contractual boundary-lines, or frames, elevating the experience to something 'extra-daily' (Barba 1995), is nevertheless core to ZU-UK's practice. *Binaural Dinner Date* persistently establishes boundary-lines in order to expand them and achieve a fluid plurality of interpretive frames. Technology – both the digital scaffolding and carefully wrought participatory structures built through writing, performance, game mechanics and live response – functions as a shape-shifting machine that rearranges our usual temporal and spatial perspectives to expose the anatomy of social interactions. The co-existence of frames – familiar and unfamiliar, performative, extra-daily – begins to construct a juxtaposition of private and shared worlds, enhancing awareness of what is always, in fact, the case: the possibility that their interpretation of an interaction might differ from that of their interlocutor's (a mainstay anxiety of any dating process).

The familiarity of the interaction – and, therefore, participants' assurance in their own and their date's interpretations of it – is teasingly subverted at an early point. What participants find on the menu they are given are not food items but different types of questions and topics that will be discussed during the date. Here the indexical segues into something more metaphorical. They realize that some of the familiar elements they are encountering may in fact be hacked and repurposed to stand for something they are not. Such hints at metaphorical relationships between the crude meaning of actions and their meta-meanings act as invitations to an extra-daily interpretive frame. As participants make orders of 'Love at first sight' or 'Dream Job', they implicitly agree to participate in a restaurant-date within which some things carry meanings more than or different to their thinnest descriptions.

Exaggeration of stylistic clichés pertaining to the tackily romantic restaurant context (extravagant frilly fonts in the menu, the immaculate costume, slicked-back hair and obsequious movements of the waiters, flowing red tablecloths, etc.) indicates entry into a dramatic realm. Participants understand that certain cultural tropes are being evoked and, therefore, commented upon – hacked. Since the inception of *Binaural Dinner Date* in 2014, these tropes have entered the public consciousness with avidity via TV programmes like *First Dates*. The real-time operation and editing of the audio track supports this subliminal impression of existing within a TV game- or reality-show and of being on display. At points you hear your own utterances replayed, though you did not know they had been recorded, and live-operated sound effects mark your answers in one competitive couples' game as correct or incorrect, though you cannot tell who is operating or how they are hearing your responses. These sleights of hand are enabled by the complex audio-system detailed in the second section of this paper. Heightened, warped or extra-daily frames start to pervade and inflect the familiar frames of being on a date, at a restaurant, making small-talk with a stranger, without supplanting their presence.

Scaffolding the date

When socially contextualized as it is, as an art experience, the invitation to *#BeTheDate* becomes, also, an interrogation of the social roles of artist, consumer-participant and artwork. Most important here are the twin roles of the waiter, W, and the disembodied voice speaking through the binaural headphones that each participant wears ('Chef'). These elements provide the cues, contexts and frames for the slippage in the practice of dating enacted by the participants. By working like a seamless cyborgian extension of these present human facilitators, the immersive technology prompts reflexivity on, and interrogation of, the real, rather than displacing participants into a sealed virtual reality. *Binaural Dinner Date* makes a paradigmatic case for the role of AR technology itself being that of hacking, rather than 'augmenting', the real.

Chef

The voice of Chef, fed sporadically through the earphones throughout, ensures the couples are continuously in communication with the fictionalized voice of the artist-as-God, while persistently undercutting itself and goading the participants to insurrection. This is technically accomplished through a bespoke audio operating system designed to facilitate the experience, developed by Ross Flight and Persis Jadé Maravala. Forty-two output channels and eleven input channels are all manipulated via one Ableton Live workstation. The majority of the output channels feed out to thirty-six stereo signal earbuds, bringing individually timed and edited combinations of prerecorded and live audio to the eighteen participants (forming nine couples). The remaining output channels feed to the performer playing W and the performer playing the instructional voice in the earphones (unnamed in performance but referred to as Chef by the production team), as well as the sound operator. Chef, hidden from view, and the Operator are able to 'listen in' to nine of the input channels, which consist of condenser microphones embedded in the middle of each couple's table, allowing them to monitor the progress of each couple throughout the experience, incorporate elements of couples' conversations into subsequent tailored sections delivered live by Chef and tailor sound-effects and timing of their delivery to the actual input of the couples, as described above. A customized iPad monitoring application (MIRA app) creates a visual representation of the restaurant tables mapped onto the microphone inputs and permits Chef and the sound operator to select which channel to listen into at any given time. W's output channel, finally, feeds to a headset that he wears, controlled by the sound operator, that taps into the various table microphones according to where his attention needs to be directed. He also receives a precisely timed 'guide track', alerting him to the time intervals at which he needs to initiate dramaturgical switches. He and Chef wear headset microphones – the last two input channels – meaning their live speech can be relayed to any of the participants' earphones when this becomes part of their individualized audio-worlds. This elaborate system seamlessly merges live with prerecorded content and generates a soundscape with a flexible range of interpretive frames – perhaps foremost amongst them is the frame constructed by the guiding, all-too-knowing voice of Chef.

Chef is both present and not-present. To the participant she presents, to all intents and purposes, as a prerecorded disembodied voice, but references to the here and now alert them bit by bit to the fact that she is speaking live into a microphone but hidden from view. Chef sits outside and above – the God presence, the all-seeing, the voice in the head, the one that anchors you and tells you what to do, the one with the instructions, the suggestions, the tips and the knowledge. Perhaps most fundamentally, it is Chef who prompts (in most cases) unspoken critical responses and reflections in the participants, through tongue-in-cheek questions and her own observations.

Faced with this oppressive-permissive split-personality, participants perhaps also begin to understand their own position as a 'prosumer'. As a 'prosumer' (an economic subject) 'involved in the design and staging of ... co-created offerings' (Gilmore and Pine 2013, 34), participants are in charge of both producing and consuming the content of the piece: at times Chef drops them into the abyss of freestyle conversation, only to mirror their statements back to them at a later point, reframed as poignantly lyrical. This mirroring is enabled by the multi-channel audio set-up, which lets Chef navigate and listen to nine separate conversations and makes it possible for her live-written summaries and recordings of what she hears to be fed back to them. This eavesdropping and live-writing process is concluded in a period of roughly eighteen minutes and begins from the moment the first couple is seated. Her real-time creative choices are highly pressurized in terms of hitting the right tone and maintaining ethics of kindness: it is important that Chef (played by the scriptwriter herself) gathers a spectrum of confessions to reveal that are roughly even in gravity – that are raw and teasing, exposing vulnerability, but gentle. They must be sufficiently ambiguous that individuals can maintain anonymity if they choose (though most volunteer identification, laughing and shouting when their own statements are referenced), but recognizable enough that they can clearly recognize their own conversations in what is relayed. Chef must make crucial decisions on the fly on when to switch her listening from one conversation to another and the custom-designed live-mixing software enables the flexibility necessary to achieve this. Participants' identities and interactions become the sites of aesthetic value, in that their conversations and their perceptions of themselves and each other become the sometimes beautiful, often tragic and always reflexive material of the artwork. The triad of artist-artwork-participant (or intention-sign-interpretation) is disrupted, even as the artist-as-God figure (Chef) asserts her power.

Though mischievous and sometimes sinister, this power just about holds to a standard of benevolence. Chef probes insecurities (wondering, with the participants, what they could possibly do to make their date 'love them a little bit more') and is brutal at points (asking participants to observe their date and wonder whether they might be 'a bit of a cunt'), devastatingly cynical (persistently drawing attention to the question 'What is the worst that could happen?') and even violent ('Do your hands seem capable of snapping a puppy's neck?', she asks, with vivid accompanying sound effect). She always, however, draws her reflections back to a core of deep, forgiving humanity. Following her brief as a (decidedly Catholic) God-figure, she exposes her subjects to evil, doubt and suffering, only to absolve them with her boundless forgiveness. When she repeats participants' statements back to them, she exposes them – holding a magnifying-glass to the naked self, its banality, its self-involvedness, its 'fucked-up-ness' – but she simultaneously absolves them, prefacing each statement with 'It's okay that ... '. 'To be really human', she tells them, 'is probably to be unavoidably sentimental and naïve and gushy and generally pathetic'. Participants are both belittled and exulted.

This complex absent presence of Chef creates space in which the total power of the artist-as-God is disrupted, while their responsibilities are upheld. The triad that establishes itself between two partners and Chef, by positioning the God-figure as sensorially but internally, privately present, while externally absent, confers a vital charge on the connection between the partners. They are united and divided by the artist-God's voice in their heads. At moments they look over at each other with suspicion, wondering whether their date is hearing the same content as them or something else, and at moments the voice estranges them from each other – asking them to look at their partner and wonder 'what's the weirdest thing about them that you just don't know yet?' and whether they might be 'capable of locking you in a room and making you eat from a dog-bowl'. At other times, the very fact that this voice is privately present yet externally absent encourages confabulation, collaboration, connection. Participants attempt to combat the discomfort of listening to a private soundtrack whilst seated staring at another person by making little facial signals or side-comments to share their inner world with their date. They often feel compelled to assert their identity as separate from the artwork (which is asking them to do embarrassing things, like hold hands and draw love-hearts), by conveying their own critical distance from it, thus establishing a community of ironic complicity with their date.

ZU-UK's general policy is to avoid requiring participants to learn skills that are not familiar to them – all they need to do to engage with the audio-system is insert an inconspicuous pair of earphones. The technology's only other visual presence is the (not so inconspicuous) Rode NT1 condenser microphone in the middle of the table. It dominates the tiny universe set up to contain the couple. A microphone can be seen as a symbol of power and social capital – it stands, in media culture, for the person who has been given voice over others. 'Passing the mic' has become a generic idiom, meaning to hand over or relinquish influence. The microphone is thus a tool of elevation (marking the date, once more, as extra-daily), a way of tapping into people's egos (they become the star) and a way of empowering. It is also a tool for kindling intimacy because it is, crucially, a shared microphone. Its figure-of-8 configuration means that largely only the two partners' speech and movements are picked up and surrounding noise is cut out. Both become the stars of their own show, but share one input-identity, within the operating system and in the visual presence of the microphone.

Technologically, spatially and metaphorically, they are required to merge. By pitching the complicity of each couple *against* the authority of the God-figure that divides and unites them, *Binaural Dinner Date* is also able to comment upon the status of the artwork in an increasingly digitized world, in which concepts of 'liveness' and 'presence' are re-evaluated. The authors have elsewhere theorized liveness in the digital age, post-Phelan and post-Auslander, as a kind of 'mutual attentiveness'. '[L]iveness', we have proposed, 'is the active attention we have for each other in the case of any media/performance where we could choose to direct our attention elsewhere' (Allen et al. 2022). The voice of Chef hacks the familiar trope of the all-seeing digital eye (e.g. a dating app that knows all your details) and humanizes it by exposing its fallibility and capacity for activating this kind of liveness. We might assume that the digital mediation of human interaction – e.g. Hinge or Tinder – depersonalizes and distorts. However, the Chef's digital persona suggests an alternative possibility, according to which the digital scaffold itself not only facilitates but participates in heightened 'mutual attentiveness'. What we assume has been a recording jolts us into the present by commenting on the unmistakable liveness of surroundings (e.g. a plastic bag that flutters by the window, caught in the wind) and revealing that it has been listening to our conversations in real time by repeating our statements. We become aware that there is a real person somewhere attached to this voice, meticulously compiling our information, and are further reminded of liveness as we see Chef's physically present assistant, W, occasionally falter and stutter when presented with unpredictable participant-input. Hayles (1999, 49) writes of cybernetics and the age of information that 'the emphasis on information technologies foregrounds pattern/randomness and pushes presence/absence into the background', meaning that 'the implications extend beyond narrative into many cultural arenas … one of the most serious of these implications is the *systematic devaluation of materiality and embodiment*' (48). In the moments at which the couples commit small acts of rebellion against the not-quite-omnipotent God-figure that instructs them, they revalue their own material co-presence. W's (and their own) failures, inherently live, problematize the drive towards reproducible perfectibility engendered by the digitization of art and interaction and, similarly, revalue the fallibility of bodies. We are reminded of the physicality and humanity of digital media themselves: we recall that mechanical voices (i.e. that of Chef) are always sensorially present extensions of and creations of humans.

Writing also of the devaluation of presence in an age of digital reproduction, Connor (1989, 151) states that 'it is possible to see how the proliferation of reproductions actually intensifies the desire for origin, even if that origin is increasingly sensed as an erotic lack rather than a tangible and satisfying presence'. Correspondingly, the 'magic-trick' of Chef's disembodied omniscience creates a latent desire to have the mechanics of the trick revealed, which amounts to a desire to encounter the real body behind the voice. The implicit promise, as in a conventional magic-trick, is ultimately denied. This maintains both (a) the 'marvel' factor of obscuring the mechanics of a performance and (b) the ambivalence of omniscient technology. Once again, the triad of artist–artwork–participant is disrupted: the artist-magician holds a certain power as manufacturer of illusion but subverts her own monopoly on the production of aesthetic value by conferring a more prominent value on the insurrectional interactions of the couples and their shared desire to encounter or expose the vanished body. It is their shared glances of amazement and whispered side-comments, when they realize that Chef's live body has been listening to their conversations, that constitute the piece's experiential core (see Plate 5).

By casting Chef as a digital (mechanical) voice, disembodied and omniscient but highly intimate and reactive to live input, *Binaural Dinner Date* gently satirizes our collective fear of the machine 'taking over', only to hand participants back their agency and integrity by the end of the performance. They are told to take out their earphones, then left to say goodbye to their date – suddenly fully responsible for their relationship with the other and their interpretation of the experience.

The waiter (W)

The character of W serves as a bridge between this eerily efficient machine and the deeply human volatility of the participant-interactions. He is the confluence at which it becomes clear that there is no hard-and-fast boundary between the wires and hardware, and the felt and flesh-bound – there is a continuum. Interspersed between the games and conversations with their date, participants glean snatches of what almost amounts to a story: they learn that W is waiting in vain (a 'waiter that waits') for his lover to return, culminating in a section towards the end of the experience in which they watch W approach a passer-by and invite them on a very short date.

If Chef forms and then breaks the expected parameters of the piece's temporality – masquerading as prerecorded, then revealing herself as a live co-present human – W forms and then breaks the expected parameters of the piece's spatial and social aspects. Together, both manipulating and manipulated by the digital scaffold, they engineer and uphold the frame-shifts that constitute *Binaural Dinner Date*'s tangential relationship to reality. W is a mechanism within the machine facilitating the date experience – a flesh-and-blood extension of the God-like digitized voice in our headphones. The continuum from digital operating system through to live performer bodies extends, through W, into our own bodies, reflections and emotions. Participants witness W (and, crucially, the performer playing W) emerging from the spatial and social safety of the performative restaurant community thus far established: he exits the visually demarcated space of the restaurant and approaches bystanders to ask them on a short date with him. If he is successful, he then sits at a table with his date – who is unaware of any of the interpretive frames and parameters carefully constructed for the participants, who watch through a window – and conducts a short exchange with them. He thus also becomes the agent through which the continuum from the temptingly safe confines of a performance-world, through to the facts of our presence in an urban society of strangers, is exposed. At the performative end of this continuum, we can indulge, temporarily, in the illusion that our playful actions can be shrugged off because they are pretend; at the other end, we become painfully unsafe in our awareness that we are interacting with and surrounded by real strangers, and are always very much ourselves, always very much impacted by and impacting on our social environments. Participants see W put himself in the position of vulnerability that they are enduring themselves: an unpredictable encounter with a stranger and the possibility of rejection, discomfort and failure. By overstepping the spatial and social bounds of the frames established, he also shares with participants a tacit acknowledgement of the illusory status of these frames: just as participants sit precariously between the performance of an extra-daily identity and the revelation of their 'true' selves, W is exposed, in this moment, as a denizen of reality. Initially unaware of his performative status, the bystanders he approaches apprehend him as a 'weirdo', a threat or a prankster. He is made as unsafe as participants are in their encounter with their date.

This second key triad – that of each participant couple with W – therefore also serves to warp the firm fences that so often mark the separation of artist, artwork and consumer. The triad of the couple/Chef, established through a series of live-patchworked audio vignettes and instructions, confers aesthetic value on the participants' material 'prosumer' presence by subverting Chef's omnipotent digital authority. The triad of the couple/W, established through the virtuosically choreographed interplay of physical action and audio commentary, jeopardizes the stability of the artwork by blurring its spatial and social boundaries. The interplay of triadic relationships enabled through live audio manipulation expands this disturbance of hard boundaries between private and shared meaning-making to shifting reassessments of assumed boundaries between life and play, art and society, real and pretend.

Conclusion

So much of so-called interactive and participatory media is not participatory at all. The initiation, movement and conclusion of the experience depend heavily on underlying technological systems and the interface. In this sense, much VR, AR, XR and immersive media is done to users, imposed on them, to their delight or chagrin. The example of *Binaural Dinner Date* presents a different line of digital media analysis and design by looking carefully at the knitting together of participants' expectations and actions, material props and technology and skilled human facilitation in order to co-produce experiences that reflect on and challenge familiar modalities of everyday life.

The carefully constructed assemblage invites thoughtful, active and reflexive engagement of participants with an eye to flexible and live human-facilitated care rather than deference to any machine algorithm or system imperative. There can be no *Binaural Dinner Date* app in this case, but the effected experience is no less encompassing than the most advanced pervasive media systems (idealized often as the Star Trek Holodeck). Our analysis of *Binaural Dinner Date* calls attention to ways in which the participatory theatre-making approach of ZU-UK might inform digitally mediated experience design, opening the door to more compelling experiences for audiences.

Note

1 In performances from 2016 to 2019 the role of W was performed by a male actor. The character will be referred to with he/him pronouns for the purposes of this chapter, but since 2020, both male and female actors have represented W in newer versions of the performance.

4

Augmented reality performance: A site-specific volumetric video experience of Samuel Beckett's *Play*

Néill O'Dwyer, Gareth Young, Nicholas Johnson and Aljosa Smolic

Introduction

This chapter presents *Augmented Play* (Johnson 2019), the third and final part of a three-year practice-based research project entitled the *XR Play Trilogy*. This augmented reality project sought to reinterpret Samuel Beckett's *Play* (Beckett 1963), a pivotal mid-career drama, for various formats of digital media culture. The trilogy includes (1) a webcast, *Intermedial Play* (Johnson 2017a), (2) a virtual reality (VR) application, *Virtual Play* (Johnson 2017b), and (3) an augmented reality (AR) version, *Augmented Play*.

Play is a one-act play that features three speakers in urns, their heads the only visible part, whose speech is 'provoked' by a roving spotlight. It was written in English but performed first in German, at the Ulmer Theater in Ulm-Donau, W. Germany (1963). The play is known for its unique structure, which includes the stage direction 'repeat play' at the end, and its exploration of themes such as memory, identity and human connection. Extensive intermedial experimentation has been conducted with the play since its first decade of life, including adaptation to radio, film and new media (Johnson 2022).

Intermedial Play was a collaboration between Néill O'Dwyer (producer) and Nicholas Johnson (director), associate professor in Trinity College's Department of Drama and co-director of the Trinity Centre for Beckett Studies. The performance was screened live using a robotic pan-tilt-zoom (PTZ) camera, normally used in the context of surveillance, in combination with Wirecast and YouTube webcasting technologies (Johnson, O'Dwyer and Bates 2021). The PTZ, in this rendering of the piece, became the 'unique inquisitor' that prompts the actors, its 'victims' (Beckett 2006, 318), into speech. In 2017, it was broadcast from the Dance Studio in the Samuel Beckett Centre, Trinity College Dublin (TCD), with a live audience observing from a remote location in Trinity's east campus. This experiment inspired the creative team to extend the questions of virtuality and liveness, catalysing the next phase of both *Virtual Play* and *Augmented Play*.

Virtual Play was a more radical reinterpretation of *Play*, designed to engage a twenty-first-century audience increasingly accessing content via VR technologies. It was produced in collaboration with V-SENSE (a Science Foundation Ireland [SFI] project funded to research advanced visual computing), whose lab developed the core 3D volumetric video (VV) technology enabling this novel type of creative production. O'Dwyer was employed to champion and curate creative possibilities for the visual computing software innovations under development, the most advanced being VV, and *Play* was selected to be the inaugural creative arts project at V-SENSE.

The VR experience of *Virtual Play* attempted to push the limits of possibility in consumable video and film by eliciting the new power of digital interactive technologies to respond to Beckett's deep engagement with the stage technologies of his day. A central goal of the project was to address ongoing concerns in the creative–cultural sector regarding how to address the question of narrative progression in an interactive, immersive environment. 'Immersants' (cf. Introduction, 10) were invited to don a head-mounted display (HMD), embody the role of the inquisitorial light and explore the narrative by confronting virtual reconstructions of Beckett's characters. The virtual spotlight was aligned with the immersant's gaze, so that they could activate the characters into speaking simply by looking at them. The artwork acknowledged the new condition of active audiences and recognized new opportunities for narrative by affording audiences a central role in its unfurling. The creative team hypothesized that by placing the immersant (audience) at the centre of the storytelling process, they would be more thoroughly assimilated to the virtual world and empowered to explore, discover and decode the story, instead of passively watching and listening (O'Dwyer et al. 2017). The gaming sector has harnessed interactive storytelling techniques using procedural graphics and animation, implying the freedom of the user and providing continuous change. The traditional aesthetics of film, video and the performing arts have not fully resolved how capture techniques might achieve a similar open-ended, 'unfurling' effect in older media. As such, this project attempted to investigate new narrative possibilities for interactive, immersive environments, using VV capture of live actors to generate a dynamic VR system.

Augmented Play had much in common with the earlier VR version, because it used the same VV assets, modes of audience interaction and narrative development. However, the viewing paradigm was different. AR is a technology that allows people/audiences to visually merge virtual/graphical/computer-rendered objects with physical world objects and scenes using a mobile phone, tablet or HMD. Unlike VR, it permits the user to see the world around them; it does not close off the outside world by fully immersing the audience in a computerized world. Therefore, AR technology is highly suitable for allowing people to interact with stories in an architectural context. It is ideal for location-based, immersive, role-play and site-specific drama. In the case of *Augmented Play*, the content was originally built for the Microsoft HoloLens AR HMD, but had improved display on Magic Leap. The team also explored the effect of the AR experience on handheld phone and tablet devices.

This chapter takes the form of a reflective practice essay on the *XR Play Trilogy*'s third and final part. It provides an account of the methodological and technical working processes. And finally, it reports on feedback provided by subject matter experts (SMEs), offering a reflective discussion of the significance of the work and the benefits and shortcomings of working with these technologies in performance contexts. The *Augmented Play* project intersected with three main specialized knowledge areas: XR, the performing arts (especially theatre) and VV. What follows below is a brief survey of these fields, encompassing existing projects.

Background and related work

Extended reality (XR) is an umbrella term that encompasses a spectrum of technologies, including virtual reality (VR), augmented reality (AR) and mixed reality (MR) (cf. Introduction, 11–12). XR refers to the blending of real and virtual environments to create immersive experiences that can be interactive and multi-sensory. It encompasses various devices, such as HMDs, glasses or mobile phones, to simulate or enhance the user's perception of reality by combining elements from the physical and digital worlds. XR has applications across diverse fields, including gaming, entertainment, education, training, healthcare and more.

XR technologies have revolutionized theatre by enhancing performances and engaging audiences. Virtual sets create immersive environments, transporting performers and audiences to different locations or fantastical worlds. AR overlays digital elements onto live performances, enhancing storytelling and creating interactive experiences. MR performances merge physical and virtual elements, allowing live actors to interact with virtual characters or objects in real time. These technologies also enable audience participation through interactive VR installations or AR applications that personalize narratives or allow audience members to affect the storyline. XR is also valuable for training and rehearsals, providing tools for exploring staging options and visual effects without physical constraints. XR technologies push the boundaries of traditional performances, creating captivating experiences that blur the line between physical and virtual worlds. Within XR performances (despite the disputed boundary between AR and MR), AR performances are relatively rare compared to VR, likely due to the complexity of developing apps and the limited computing power of AR glasses. Some notable examples of performance-based implementations that employ AR are detailed below.

The use of visual computing technology within theatre is often a clear signal that a piece could be classified as AR. Adrien Mondot and Claire Bardainne's installation *Mirages & Miracles* (2017) used choreography and graphical representations to animate and augment visual art objects via a tablet. Analogously, Gilles Jobin's iOS augmented reality dance piece, *Dance Trail*, enabled 'users to bring virtual dancers into the real world through their smartphone or tablet' (2020). *The Tempest* (2017) by the Royal Shakespeare Company harnessed AR and holography to create illusions, without placing individual devices with audience members. Advancing the Pepper's ghost technique by projection-mapping virtual characters like Ariel (created using motion capture technologies) onto innovative materials, the RSC designed interactions between physical and virtual elements and live, embodied actors, blending the physical and digital realms. Idris Elba and Kwame Kwei-Armah's *Tree* (2019) incorporated procedural graphics projected onto curved screens, surrounding the audience, allowing actors to interact with virtual props and characters, creating a sense of immersion for the audience while maintaining a strong anchor in physical world. More recently, Glitch Studios collaborated with three Norwegian theatres – Nordland Teater, Teater Vestland and Teatret Vårt – to fuse 'Far Throw AR' technologies with live theatre to enable 'digital characters to seamlessly interact with live actors, covering the entire stage volume and the vast space between the stage and the audience' (Glitch Studios 2024). They supplied everybody in the audience with a Viewforia MR HMD, broadcasting graphical overlays simultaneously to create a synchronized AR theatre experience.

Given that AR sits on the spectrum of XRP (cf. Introduction, 11–12), several relevant examples arise that could be considered borderline cases. Even without HMDs for audience engagement, some contemporary theatre crosses into AR territory when technology deepens immersivity across multiple media channels. In *The Encounter* (2016) by Complicité, for example, the audience wore headphones while watching performers to experience a binaural soundscape of the Amazon rainforest. While the heavy computing power is on the audio in this instance, the experience of binaural sound relies on the presence of visual cues. AR is also important for paratextual and peripheral elements of framing performance. For *UNeditions* (2014) by Unlimited Theatre, the company offered immersive, digital script reading experiences with spatial sound, light and bonus material. Users could access additional digital content on their smartphones, such as interactive visuals, videos and supplementary information. In some performances of *The Lion King* (1997) by Disney Theatrical Productions, AR technology created interactive experiences for the audience. Through specialized AR apps, audience members could bring printed programs or certain scenes to life, revealing hidden animations and immersive content.

To provide content for AR and as a performative capture technique, VV is maturing and finding its way to performance practice. VV technology captures a three-dimensional representation of real-world objects or people, recording external appearance, spatial depth and movement to create a dynamic 3D model. Using an array of cameras or depth sensors from multiple angles, VV allows viewers to move around and interact with the captured content, offering a more immersive experience than traditional 2D video. This technology is often utilized in XR applications, enabling lifelike representations within virtual environments. With AR/VR devices, the resulting VV can be viewed from any angle, allowing audiences or actors to explore content from different perspectives. VV creates photorealistic characters, enabling viewers to enter an interactive, immersive experience, engage with content more naturally and feel present within the same space as the subject.

VV has only recently started to enter the theatre world, and its adoption is still limited. However, it offers intriguing possibilities for capturing live performances in three-dimensional space. VV technology enables theatre productions to explore new forms of documentation, preservation and presentation, offering audiences unique perspectives and a sense of presence. *Museum of Austerity* (Wares 2021) was a moving performance-cum-installation that documented true life stories of the disenfranchisement and marginalization of disabled people during the UK's austerity period (post-2008). Visitors explored the stories as performed VV installations in a holographic gallery using Hololens 2, closely resembling the audience paradigm used in *Augmented Play*. Such performances highlight the potential of merging live performances with recorded elements in immersive experiences. As VV technology advances, we will likely see more innovative and frequent uses in theatre productions.

The *XR Play Trilogy*

Play is a one-act play written by Samuel Beckett, one of the most influential playwrights of the twentieth century. Developed by Beckett in English and German from 1962 to 1963, it is widely considered to be a radically avant-garde text for its time, as well as a pivot point in Beckett's decades-long career. Due to several unusual features of the play – its highly restricted aesthetic of three heads in three urns, illuminated by a single spotlight that prompts their speech; its circular structure, ending with the stage direction 'Repeat play'; and its history of intermedial experimentation – it sparked the interest of the creative team as an ideal test space for VR and AR. The three characters, known as 'W1', 'W2' and 'M', engage in a relentless, circular dialogue, each character recounting their version of a past love triangle involving themselves and the other two characters. The conversation is fragmented, repetitive and overlapping, highlighting the characters' struggle to make sense of their shared experiences. It is also prompted by the movement of the undefined external force of the light, raising deep questions about the relation between the speakers and the technology of the theatre itself. The drama arises not from the unfolding of actions within the plot, which is notably banal, but rather from the real situation of the actors and the conditions of the system. This offers a framing of the play as a game in which variation, uncertainty and agency on the part of both actors and audiences are possible, hinting at an alignment between the performance and VR/AR aesthetics.

As such, *Play* was selected as the main focus of the 'Creative Experiments' remit by the V-SENSE research group at TCD (2016–22). The concept was to remaster it for the emergent genre of XR performance and to reinvigorate audience interest in twentieth-century literature using twenty-first-century technology, thereby generating 'new experiences, modelling the problematics of how cultural knowledge is transmitted from one generation to the next' (O'Dwyer and Johnson 2019, 4).

The project website[1] is the online hub for the *XR Play Trilogy*, which focused on exploring and developing XR technologies in theatrical contexts to merge the worlds of theatre and technology by utilizing innovative technologies such as VV. The project consisted of three distinct versions of *Play*, each employing different XR techniques and approaches to extend the theatrical experience. Several research papers, videos, images and other multimedia content documenting the project's progress and outcomes have been previously published, sharing the findings and results of the research project and contributing to the broader discourse on the intersection of technology and performing arts. Some publications explicate the technologies and techniques used (O'Dwyer et al. 2017) or empirical research methodologies employed to assess successes and shortcomings (O'Dwyer et al. 2020). Others offer insights into the creative process behind the project (Johnson and O'Dwyer 2018), pedagogical and perceptual findings emerging from the research (O'Dwyer, Johnson, Bates, et al. 2018, 1–10; O'Dwyer, Johnson, Pagés, et al. 2018), or the aesthetic vision driving the exploration of XR in theatre (O'Dwyer and Johnson 2019). Overall, the project provided a rich terrain for investigating the potential of transforming and reimagining modern theatre under the aegis of XR technologies and remains a robust resource for those interested in the field.

Methodology: Production pipeline

Although the production pipeline is described in previously published research papers (O'Dwyer et al. 2017), it is necessary to include a brief overview of the process for the coherence of this chapter. Furthermore, after creating the VV assets, the AR experience's conceptualization and fabrication substantially differed from the VR version. Below is a description of both processes, including the artistic and technical rationales.

There are two main types of VV techniques: online and offline. Online VV involves streaming and interactive playback of 3D video content over networks. It uses cameras and depth sensors to capture objects or actors, with as few capture devices as possible.[2] These data are compressed and transmitted via Ethernet to audiences,[3] who can access and interact with the content in real time. Utilizing real-time processing and streaming, online VV enables users to engage with immersive 3D experiences, like VR or AR, without needing local processing or heavy data storage on their devices. The resulting visual output is usually low resolution and glitchy, a trade-off for liveness.

Offline VV involves capturing and rendering content without real-time streaming or internet connectivity. It records a subject or scene from multiple angles using cameras and sometimes depth-sensing devices. These data are processed offline using innovative software algorithms, powerful computers, dedicated rendering systems or cloud servers to reconstruct the 3D representation (Pagés et al. 2018). Once processed, the resulting VV can be stored and played back locally on compatible devices or platforms; however, the footage cannot be edited because, firstly, there is currently no such software, and secondly, within the AR/VR viewing paradigm,

> editing is not used to create situational *continuity* from a sequence of different shots, nor is it used to generate *discontinuity*, for example through montage. VR instead attempts to create a verisimilitude, that is, the simulation of an encounter with the characters, whereby the digital objects appear to have volume and mass.
>
> (Johnson and O'Dwyer 2018, 8)

Offline VV is useful when real-time streaming is not feasible or when precise control over the rendering process is desired. The output is usually higher fidelity and resolution than online VV, resulting in larger file sizes.

The technique used for this project was the offline process, which was under development in V-SENSE at the time. The pipeline involved setting up an array of HD digital SLR cameras in a 180-degree arc, with actors positioned in a similarly curved green screen environment. Each actor was recorded individually, as required by the VV system and the characters' experience in *Play*. Although not necessary, actors were recorded kneeling in the urns to induce genuine physical discomfort, generating a vocal quality and pressured scenario analogous to Beckett's specifications (Beckett 2006, 319). Since user action determined the start/stop points of each text segment, the interlocking, rapid-fire dialogue was restructured into single monologues, performed continuously without interruption. This approach aligned the technically robust way to transmit the story into VR with the preferred method of rehearsing and enacting Beckett's system (Johnson 2022, 202–5). The textual jumps and interruptions, caused in theatre by the roving spotlight, were achieved here by pausing/unpausing the VV audio-visual in the application in relation to the immersant's gaze. Other recording options, such as using hand signals to stay the actor's speech, proved too fragmented during playback and required several hundred short video clips instead of one per character.

After capturing the footage, significant postproduction was required. The actors were segmented (chroma-keyed) using postproduction software, and all videos were colour balanced to ensure consistency during the texture mapping and volumetric reconstruction process. The videos were trimmed to the same length and exported as a series of jpegs. These images were fed into the bespoke VV software developed by V-SENSE. At the time, this cutting-edge software was executed through the command line interface; there was no out-of-the-box VV software package with a graphical user interface (GUI) accessible to creative artists.

The volumetric video pipeline developed by V-SENSE relied on two main computer-vision volume estimation techniques: (1) a 'multi-source,

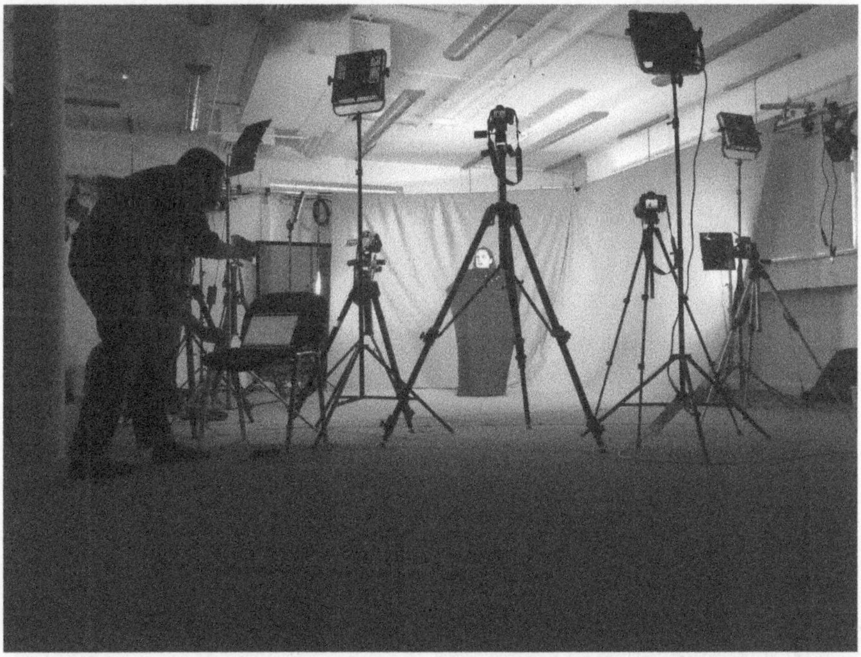

FIGURE 4.1 *XR Play Trilogy*, 2019. Director (Nicholas Johnson) in the foreground with W1 actor (Maeve O'Mahony) positioned in the urn against the curved green screen, with the cameras in the foreground also positioned in an arc, 2019 (© Néill O'Dwyer).

shape-from-silhouette (MS-SfS) approach', using silhouettes, 3D skeleton estimation and colour consistency to generate a 3D volume, and (2) multi-view stereo (MVS) to create a dense 3D point cloud (Pagés et al. 2018). These data were merged using a fusion technique to form photorealistic 3D models for each video frame. The process was computationally expensive, taking several days to process on a desktop computer, requiring a skilled operator to fine-tune parameters and correct errors, often restarting from scratch. It took over a month to process 3 VVs, each approximately 3.5 minutes long. Notwithstanding the labour intensity, 3 dynamic 3D representations of live-action human performances were produced,[4] viewable in 6 degrees of freedom (6DoF).[5] These versatile 3D VV assets could be watched on VR, AR glasses, smartphones and tablets, forming the backbone of the first Beckett in VR project and one of the first VV VR reproductions of a complete dramatic script. However, in VV production, it is not enough to film the actors; the virtual scene must also be designed, and the entire project (including dynamic video assets and static scene assets) must be built in a game engine.

AR scenography

Unlike the preceding VR version, it was not necessary to design and build a scene for this AR version, as the characters were strategically placed around the physical architectural space. Visualization and interaction were achieved through AR glasses or a handheld AR device. The physical architectural features – walls, floors, columns, arches, brickwork – remain visible, reminding the audience of their context. Therefore, the venue choice is paramount to supporting the story and the mise-en-scène. Showing this type of work in a black-box theatre or white-cube art gallery makes no sense, as the architecture may lack contextual coherence with the thematics. We hosted the exhibition in the stone/brick vaulted basement of an eighteenth-century warehouse in Dublin's historic docklands (see Plate 8).[6] This choice amplified the sense of being in an underworld, crypt-like structure, maintaining thematic consistency with Beckett's purgatorial vision.

The only virtual prop consistent across the VR and AR versions was the stone urn, designed and built in 3DStudio Max. One urn was fabricated and replicated for each character in both versions. The VV assets (the characters' heads) were the same as those used in VR. The interaction (or gameplay) mechanic was also the same: when the immersant looks at a character, they speak; when they look away, the character stops speaking. The goal is for the audience to decode the narrative through an inquisitive gaze, shifting between characters, divulging the text and grasping more of the world and its affective texture the longer they engage.

The scenographic feature distinctly different from the VR version was the integration of the physical building and its materials into the scene. AR glasses allowed the audience to see the physical room and perceive the characters as co-present, affording them new mobility. Spectators could walk around the building and up to the characters, choosing their perspective (see Plate 6). This mobile, exploratory audience experience has much in common with immersive theatre productions, such as *These Rooms* (2016) by ANÚ Productions and Cois Céim, *Burnt City* (2022) by Punchdrunk or *Room Service* (2003) by Gob Squad. In these productions, performers inhabit entire buildings, and the audience moves between rooms for close-up, intimate experiences. This engagement was not possible in *Virtual Play*, where immersants cannot see the physical room or furniture, risking injury if they wandered.[7] Consequently, the VR scenography positioned characters in an arc around the central immersant. In the AR (Magic Leap) version, the room could be mapped through the hardware, allowing the scenographer to place characters anywhere, such as corners or alcoves (see Plate 7).

Reception and response

Augmented Play premiered to a select audience of academic and industry subject matter experts (SMEs) at the CHQ building in September 2019. Feedback was gathered from these experts on the evening and again at private screenings in January 2020. A detailed account of the feedback (in relation to XR generally) was published in 2020 (O'Dwyer et al.). Below is a selection of prevailing themes from the feedback discussion, along with our responses and reflections. We have structured this concluding section as a dialogue, with the feedback received in italics and the responses following.

> *While some SMEs identified themselves as relatively traditional in terms of Beckett, the cohort generally displayed an openness to AR technology. They acknowledged that technology brought fresh perspectives to the work, and the AR audience paradigm held significant potential, especially its inherent capacity to captivate audiences.*

The novelty factor has a huge impact on audience captivation. Given that AR glasses are so new, donning them for the first time can be an intense experience. The horizon-expanding potential for arts and culture is immediately apparent, with the expectation that XR performances will gain prominence and viewership. However, emerging art forms must speak to the specificities of new media. This will be pivotal in the success of *Augmented Play*; its circular narrative and active audience paradigm were fundamental to its success, a factor where many new XR performance-experiences fail. Establishing a new *grammar of XR* is essential for nurturing more intriguing artistic endeavours as standalone art forms (O'Dwyer et al. 2020).

A second, more subliminal reason for this observation is the attention-grabbing nature of the screen in general. Screens have long been acknowledged for their ability to capture attention; hence their application in learning environments (Mayor 1997, 1–19). A major finding of our research was the improved comprehension of a notoriously fast-paced text when viewed in VR compared to live theatre. This has sparked further research into applications of the technology in drama education contexts.

> *Although there was a general acknowledgment of theatre's inherent relationship with technology, SMEs expressed caution regarding excessive reliance on it, which could potentially jeopardize theatre's tradition of 'situated action' in which the audience and actor–characters share the same physical space (Salter 2010, xxxiv).*

We would be wary of reducing the argument to a binary polemic similar to that teased out by Phelan and Auslander regarding screens, video and liveness. The adoption of VV to portray characters in AR and VR could be described as potentially disruptive to the ontology of theatre. Just as video enabled the real-time (mediated) duplication of an actor during a live performance (Causey 1999), this AR technology blurs the boundary between live and mediated experiences. This is particularly notable when considering theatre's reliance on the idea of being present in the 'here and now'.

In opposition to VR, AR retains a sense of being present in physical reality because immersants continue to see their physical environments. This also permits a shared experience. While this work operated with one viewer at a time wearing the AR glasses, advances in networked technology could offer viewing paradigms for multiple AR users to simultaneously partake in live-streamed, shared experiences. This holds the promise of enhancing audience intimacy and connection not just with the performers, but also with other audience members, increasing the appeal of extended reality performances. This is known as a feedback loop of emotional contagion, 'whereby we "catch" the emotions of others through a process of low-level, non-conscious, involuntary mimicry' (Smith 2014, 37). It is a crucial social phenomenon that makes communal watching a pleasurable experience, which may otherwise be eroded by the potentially more solitary technologies of VR.

It is arguable that the demands for (inter)activity afforded by AR tech further enhance the sense of presence and immersion for the audience, advancing the sense of immediacy beyond theatre that relies purely on embodied presence. Consequently, the temporal and spatial dynamics of the stage can undergo substantial upheaval in the context of AR.

Several experts problematized XR's accessibility, for example, in terms of expenses associated with it, its operational complexity, content availability and its compatibility with existing storytelling and narrative forms.

The cost of AR technology, including hardware and content development, remains a significant barrier, limiting access for both creators and audiences and restricting the widespread adoption of AR in theatrical productions. For sectoral success there is a growing need for industry partnerships, similar to *The Tempest* (2017).

AR technology can be complex to operate, requiring specialized knowledge. This complexity poses challenges for theatre companies lacking the technical expertise to seamlessly integrate AR for non-expert audiences. The operational simplicity of *Augmented Play* (aligning the narrative trigger with the gaze) was a major driver in its success.

Given the newness of the genre, the availability of content for the intersection of theatre and AR is limited. Whereas adapting a book into a movie made sense in the past, transitioning linear narratives (which often dominate popular media) to the spatialized format of XR is not straightforward. There is a need for exploring new narrative forms to address these paradigmatic shifts, rather than simply porting old story formats into new media. *Play* is unique because of its circular and gamified narrative mechanics, but most existing performance productions are not organically suitable for adaptation to XR platforms.

Education, particularly equipping third-level film, music and performance students with the grammar to engage these technologies, can play a pivotal role in addressing the challenges of content availability and the integration of AR with traditional storytelling and narrative forms. PIX-ART, an Irish Research Council-funded project established to extend the work of V-SENSE and the *XR Play Trilogy*, aims to mitigate accessibility and inclusivity challenges associated with XR by: (1) incorporating XR into the curriculum, (2) establishing an XR lab facilitating collaborative projects, (3) forming partnerships with XR technology companies and (4) encouraging research and development through interdisciplinary and collaborative approaches.

By embedding XR technology and its applications into performing art education, institutions can produce a new generation of theatre practitioners adept at creating AR content and integrating it with traditional storytelling forms. This approach addresses current challenges and paves the way for the evolution of theatrical performances.

The AR glasses also provoked unease among the cohort due to current biopolitical apprehensions around surveillance and information manipulation.

If worn constantly, AR glasses could interfere with perception and manipulate political ideologies even more than mobile phones. The 'pervasive surveillance and powerful algorithmic control procedures' (O'Dwyer 2021, 159) already embedded in mobile computing can deeply invade personal privacy, profiling users' behaviours and manipulating consciousnesses. This intrusion aligns with biopolitical fears, as these technologies possess the power to monitor, influence and potentially determine 'individual and collective destinies, foreclosing the possibility of qualitative embodied individuation and curtailing freedom' (159). This underscores the ethical imperative for transparency and regulation in deploying AR technologies to prevent misuse and ensure that they enhance rather than compromise the autonomy and privacy of users.

This raises questions about power dynamics and who controls the means of access. Technology and creative industries can create exclusionary dynamics, as financial, algorithmic and political power are unequally distributed among engineers, billionaires, states and users. Companies that act transnationally pursue 'a liberal capitalist paradigm and its advocation of proprietorship, commodification, consumerism, and marketing' (132), restricting accessibility and affecting sociopolitical dynamics and individual freedoms.

From an educational and research standpoint, the entire spectrum of XR technologies presents captivating platforms for engaging with both contemporary and classic materials. It was not seen as a misapplication of technology, but rather a means to delve deeper into the playwright's original intentions. Participants also expressed the belief that if Beckett were alive today, he would readily embrace new technology, as he had always been a proponent of exploring technological capabilities. Presently, AR technology allows us to view drama through a new lens, encouraging different modes of analysis and interpretation without necessitating wholesale changes.

Notes

1 https://v-sense.scss.tcd.ie/research/mr-play-trilogy/.

2 It can be achieved with one depth camera, e.g., the Azure Kinect. Even with one camera the data sets are huge; so, adding more cameras quickly makes the dataset unwieldly for transmitting in real time.

3 We are currently unaware of any fully fledged performance projects that transmit live VV data over the internet; hence, we employ the term 'ethernet' here.

4 This particular performance only concerned recording the actor's faces/heads; it was unnecessary to capture their full bodies.

5 6DoF refers to the ability for an immersant to experience full freedom of movement VR; they can look around in all directions, and they can move their entire body horizontally and vertically. Conversely, in 360 cinema (3DoF) users can only look around from a 'baked in' viewpoint correlating to the camera's position.

6 Other more thematically appropriate venues were explored, including the historic crypt of Dublin's Christchurch. This would have been a better setting/context; however, the cost was prohibitive.

7 There are some innovations in the mixed reality genre involving the co-relation of virtual set elements with furniture and structural members in the physical space (c.f. Weijdom, Chapter 6). However, even when virtual and physical set elements are aligned, it is still quite disconcerting for the audience members to move around, and really a guide is required for each participant.

5

Combining augmented, mixed and virtual reality: Reflecting on hybrid XR performance practices in *Bury the Wren*

Beth Kates, with contributions from Neil Christensen

Co-created by the author, theatre designer and creative technologist Beth Kates, and artist Neil Christensen, *Bury the Wren – a VR, AR, Carbon Reality Experience* – is a result of our shared curiosity about the collaborative and creative possibilities in the combination of emergent technologies with live performance, and the different ways that the augmentation and immersion offered by these new technologies can be applied to alter or blur our understanding of reality.

Our collaboration resulted in an intimate, live performance that blends virtual reality (VR), mixed reality (MR), and what I have coined 'carbon reality' (CR).[1] I use CR to differentiate between the digital realities and our carbon-based physical world. While 'physical reality' could potentially be used interchangeably, engaging with carbon – the main element in organic compounds and therefore essential to life on Earth – for me, more accurately, roots the reality that exists outside of the digitally created virtual realities.

Using CR, I ground the difference in an element that has directly contributed to our quantitative understanding of the physical world, hoping that it will aid us in how we think about and describe these reality-blurring technologies. CR holds both a poetic and a specific communication that I find helpful when speaking about these various forms of reality.

Investigating the retelling of Canadian stories and themes of female erasure, *Bury the Wren* focuses on the true-life tale of the Donnelly family, Irish immigrants to a newly formed Canada, who were massacred in Ontario in 1880 by a mob of vigilantes from the community.[2] The text of *Bury the Wren* was created with performers Valerie Planche and Valerie Campbell. The original production was performed by Campbell and operated by myself, Neil Christensen, Adam Kostiuk and Amber Billingsley, and premiered in Calgary, Canada, in March 2019. Through the largely untold female perspective of this historical event, we exhume the voice of Annie Donnelly, who, with her husband Robert, survived the massacre and lived out her days among the murderers – who were never brought to justice.

Entangled hypermedium

Theatre, as Freda Chapple and Chiel Kattenbelt assert, is a 'hypermedium' that holds the 'capacity to incorporate all media' (2006), making theatre an ideal art form to engage with the affective affordances of emerging technologies. AR and VR provide unique modes of human connection that telematically transcend physical space and time, allowing humans to collaborate and experience performance artworks in new ways. Uninhibited by real-world physics, these real-time tools liberate us from the physical boundaries of the corporeal body, traditional storytelling and world-building. With them, we are offered new methods to explore different worldviews and expand approaches to theatrical design, collaboration and performance, bringing us closer to the *Wagnerian gesamtkunstwerk* in new ways. The qualitative results of the study associated with *Bury the Wren* (detailed later in this chapter) also support my belief that technology opens doors to affective human connection versus the opposite.

In my theatrical practice, I engage with digital and emerging media to explore time, space, history and the unseen intangible inner worlds of the characters and the story being told. MR practice historically plays with modifying perception and, as Liesbeth Groot Nibbelink and Sigrid Merx observe, 'even explicitly deconstructs perceptual expectations', while setting up the conditions for 'digitally influenced perceptions and embodied presence' that can often manifest 'as a disturbance of the senses and results in a blurring of realities' (Nibbelink and Merx 2011, 218–9). They contend: 'Theatre makers often deploy digital media in the live performance in order to disturb clear-cut perceptual distinctions between fictional and real, physical and virtual.'

In creating *Bury the Wren,* we intentionally blur the boundaries of reality to ignite new ways of perceiving the world. By combining real objects, physical interaction and virtual elements, we aimed to communicate with our audiences in unexpected ways that would engage their modes of perception and create rich spaces between the various realities – encouraging engagement with the story and promoting deeper listening and reflection on perception itself.

Central to this exploration was curiosity about how far we could challenge our audiences' understanding of reality with this technology and what that might expand in the storytelling. Embedded within this approach was also a dedication to the care of our audience, which created a delicate implementation of the technologies alongside carbon-real objects. The effects of the CR interactions are revealed in many participants' responses. One participant commented: 'Holding an object I can't see asks me to ... REALLY "feel" ... explore the dimensions of the bone, and of the candlestick.' The participant goes on to say that the experience of holding the CR object is 'more than theatre because of its intimacy; it's not quite reality because it's theatre' (Participant 008, 2019).

Cultivating the digital fields: A summary of inspiring work and the current state-of-the-art

Many theatre and performance artists deeply integrate digital and emerging technologies into their creative storytelling practices, which has influenced me as an MR theatre artist. Of that milieu, the often-spectacular mixed reality productions of renowned artists like Robert Lepage/ExMachina, Laurie Anderson, The Builders Association and Josef Svoboda/Laterna Magika inspired and informed the creation of *Bury the Wren.* Of particular note is the hybrid VR performance *Violette* (2018) by Quebec company 'joe jack et john', the first work I experienced in person that integrated VR, CR scenography and a live performer. The VR and CR states, and the dissonance between them, were dramaturgically integrated with a story of abuse. This resulted in a visceral experience that reverberates with me to this day.

The one-on-one intimacy and delicate technology treatment crafted into *Bury the Wren* were also profoundly inspired by Theatre Replacement's (mostly analogue) *BIOBOXES: Artifacting Human Experience*. In this 2007 one-on-one immersive performance, the audience members entered into one of several small boxes. These boxes contained the performer, miniature scenography and different forms of simple technology (iPods, bike lights, etc.). Each new box immersed the audience in a new world – a kind of 'analogue VR'.

While *Bury the Wren* was being created, Jordan Tannahill's *Draw Me Close* was too. A hybrid work that embraces integrating emerging technologies and live performance, *Draw Me Close* was a co-production of the National Film Board of Canada and The National Theatre (London UK) Immersive Storytelling Studio. An 'immersive illustrated memoir' (Dickson, 'Love, Virtually' 13), the live one-on-one production 'blurs the worlds of live performance, VR and animation to create a vivid memoir about the relationship between a mother and her son' (Draw Me Close). By immersing the single audience member in carbon-real scenography and a VR headset, the performance allows the audience to experience life as a playwright and protagonist 'Jordan' inside an animated world, accompanied by a live actor portraying 'mother'. It has been hailed as a 'groundbreaking marriage of reality and VR' (Strange, 'Intimate Stories').

Another significant work is Sngmoo Lee's beautiful and moving *Scarecrow VRC*, which premiered at the Sundance Film Festival in 2020 as a hybrid live/VR experience and was 'pandemic-proofed' into a live, VR-only experience in 2021. Lee and his team created a performance work that cares for the audience who gently engage in this virtual space empathetically, creatively, interactively. The avatars the audience embodies are emotive, and our interaction points are filled with beauty. We are engaged as helpers and makers in a wordless performance filled with love. Indeed, this experience marks the first time I felt *love* in a VR performance.

With each VR performance project comes a new set of creation approaches built on experience, yet must grapple with rapidly changing technology. VR practices can often shift mid-production, requiring all makers to stay alert to changes in platforms and operating systems. A public platform like VRChat can change radically *overnight*. Witnessed in many of these productions are new ways of directing attention in the virtual space, which is experienced differently than space in our physical world. Equally, VR performances each engage with different ways of caring for audiences. Some leave significant room for improvisation, while others exploit the 'wow' factor of the technology. Some centre the performer or prioritize gamification as audience interaction, while others focus on gentle storytelling. The vast array of approaches indicates that VR theatre and performance is a hypermedium within a hypermedium.

The technology

The VR/AR component of *Bury the Wren* consists of an HTC Vive Pro Wireless VR head-mounted device (HMD) and a Vive Tracker, which we modified with a handmade physical object we call 'The Apple' to give the tracker weight and an ergonomic shape. To track the virtual objects and the HMD, we used the marker-based optical tracking system SteamVR, which requires at least two 'lighthouses', each emitting imperceptible sweeping lasers, in the performance area. The virtual objects and world are operated directly from the Unity game engine, which provides a streamlined way to compile the 3D elements and create a production-ready theatrical control board for all the virtual components of the performance. Initial development consisted of approaching the project's complexity in a structured and logical manner, targeting unknown features in isolation and building out multiple proofs of concept to uncover the limitations and intricacies of the underlying technology.

The AR component was accessed through the Vive Pro's embedded passthrough cameras. The cameras provided the ability to switch from the virtual world to a view of the carbon world without removing the HMD. This switching allowed us to meet Annie, the main character, live but mediated. The camera's lenses provided a wider, more distanced view of the carbon world. This slightly strange point of view was enhanced by visual effects applied to the image. Though brief, this interaction in AR created an important bridge and distortion between realities.

Immersants and ghosts: The project

In lieu of 'audience', I use the term 'immersant', drawn from the writing of VR trailblazer Char Davies (1998), who writes at length about the qualities of immersion. She states that her 'concerns with the body in immersive virtual space are not with its objective representation, ... but rather how the immersant's mind and body are subjectively felt, how the immersant senses his or her own interior body as a centre-of-being within immersive space' (p. 65–74).

Bury the Wren begins as the immersant is greeted outside the performance space by a guide who takes their photo and leads them into a black box theatre and a 10′ × 20′ space created by four dark-grey fabric panels. The immersant is fitted with a wireless HTC Vive Pro HMD and enters total blackness in VR. A fiddle playing Niel Gow's *Lament for the Death of His Second Wife* (1809) echoes through the theatre's speakers. A female performer enters the space, reciting W.B. Yeats' *A Dream of Death* (1903). A red book embossed with gold appears in VR, spinning at eye level. Slowly, a room, also appearing to be 10′ × 20′ and made out of mud (floors, ceiling and walls), emerges from the blackness.

The immersant cannot see themselves or the performer. They are both virtually absent – intentionally so – to allow the immersant to (ironically) maintain their connection to their physical body and to emphasize the character's ghost-like quality while preserving her agency. She will reveal herself to the immersant when she is ready. As the performer finishes the poem and closes the CR book she holds with a muted thud, the virtual book simultaneously falls with a virtual thud.

Revealing herself, Donnelly says: 'I am Annie Donnelly. Welcome to my grave.' Her next act is to hand the VR Tracker (an object spatially located by the VR system) to the immersant (see Plate 10). The tracker is transformed, in VR, into a series of virtual objects, including a picture frame, teapot, candelabra, footstool and clock. Each object was created by scanning the original carbon reality objects in 3D using photogrammetry – they are the portals into Annie's story, and the immersant can interact with the 3D objects in real time. The VR operator switches from object to object on cue throughout the performance. It is through these 'hybrid artefacts' (Benford and Giannachi 2011, 65–74) that Annie shares her most treasured possessions, which lead the immersant through her life, from the great love that begins the story, all the way through the massacre and her survival, into old age with Robert. To preserve a gentle, non-gamified storytelling mode, the immersant does not have to complete any tasks, and the extent of interaction with the objects is minimal (see Plate 9).

Once the performance begins, a technician silently brings the following props into the room:[3] A small antique table laden with a teapot, picture frame, clock, candelabra and apple; a chair with a heavy white silk wedding dress, a male thigh bone and a purple velvet scarf on it; a small stool; a muslin bag filled with human male bones. Some objects are the CR versions of the virtual objects, while several of these objects are engaged by the performer and immersant while remaining unseen in VR.

In our mythology, the interactive objects in *Bury the Wren* are the intimate belongings that Annie has chosen to entomb with herself and Robert in their shared grave. Acknowledging the anachronism of using the VR technology of 2019 to tell the story of a woman who died in 1919, we chose to select objects that were evocative of the epoch of the Donnellys (1860 to 1919) but were not beholden to that time. Our mythology embraced the imaginary rupture between time and space in her grave, allowing Annie to access *any* item from *any era* of history. Her grave is her treasure chest of objects that are both comforting and necessarily distressing. The weight of the massacre is particularly embodied in the candelabra and footstool (see Plate 11).

In the small performance space, the actor follows a choreography designed to direct the immersant's attention while engaging with the feeling of human presence through proximity. The performer also creates Foley-like sound effects and a visceral breeze generated by a dress whipping past the immersant. Towards the end of the performance, the actor removes the VR Tracker from the immersant's hand and replaces it with something long and smooth that they cannot see. It is a human femur. From the text:

> Do you think bones can be at peace? Moving them … Sometimes I wonder if I did the right thing bringing him here. I hope so. I hope there are enough molecules in his bones still, that his soul can feel me … I can feel him.
>
> *(She takes the bone and places it down on the wedding dress) (pause)* I have something special I want you to see.

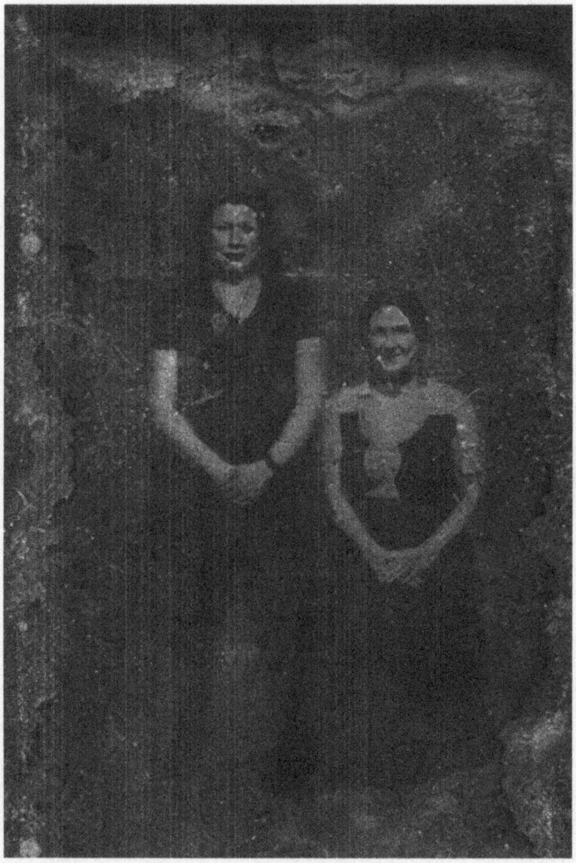

FIGURE 5.1 Beth Kates pictured with Annie Donnelly (Valerie Campbell) in a prototype image of the 'memento of a moment that never happened', 2021 (Image created by Beth Kates and Neil Christensen).

At this point, the VR switches to mixed reality (MR) within the same headset and a version of the performer and performance space are seen by the immersant in the headset. We applied digital effects to the low-resolution black-and-white image so that Annie appears to be a living daguerreotype photograph. On exiting, each immersant is given an envelope with their name. Inside is a daguerreotype-looking photo of them and Annie, a memento we created while showing them a moment that never existed (see Figure 5.1).

Virtually devising: The process design of *Bury the Wren*

For over thirty years, using digital projection technology in improvisation within the devising process has been a distinctive component of my theatrical creation practice. However, due to technical challenges during the devising process of *Bury the Wren*, it was necessary to leave the VR systems in the lab where development could continue more easily. The technological development and CR scenographic design of *Bury the Wren* were established when we began the theatrical devising process. This development stage included limiting ourselves to a fifteen-minute performance time due to concerns about how long the immersant could tolerate VR without experiencing motion sickness or discomfort from the headset's weight.[4]

In a design-led devising method of creation that included historical research, conversation and improvisation, Planche and I focused on using the CR objects. Events like Annie and Robert's courtship and marriage, Robert's imprisonment, the massacre and their survival became our story anchors. We developed connections between those anchors and the objects, which helped us create a guide-map through the story we were developing.

While I worked with Planche on crafting the performance, Christensen continued the development of the technology. However, as a primary collaborator, he also needed to be part of the devising process. His observations helped guide text development, and he was able to contribute valuable information about how technological discoveries from the lab might impact storytelling. His knowledge of the rehearsal progress then facilitated conversations about the performance in our shared technological work in the lab.

Rehearsal/creation with Planche also occurred in the computer lab, where we placed her in VR, and I performed the text. Though the VR and AR components were rudimentary, Planche could engage with them and develop an understanding of the immersant's experience, which supported the continued devising of the performance from an audience experience perspective. This involvement of *all* team members in *all* aspects of creation is, we believe, a major contributor to the successful integration of the technology, story and performance in *Bury the Wren*.

Without the technology in rehearsal, as the director, I had to imagine what it would be like to be in a headset, which was achieved by standing in the middle of the performance space with my eyes closed, simulating the visual occlusion of the headset. Through close observation of Annie's presence in these improvisations, changes were made to the text, blocking[5] and object interactions to optimize all the sensory tools and more deeply integrate them within the storytelling. Over twelve hours working with Planche, we generated the script's first draft, blocking and interactivity.

From the outset of creating *Bury the Wren*, we consciously decided that neither the immersant nor the actor be represented by an avatar in any way. In the final stage of creation, we rehearsed briefly with the completed technology and performer, Valerie Campbell. Here, our attention was drawn to the potency of avatars' absence, which, among many things, allowed the immersant to re-align their point of view to relate to the character the storyteller is evoking. Through my observations, we gained a deeper understanding of how to alter attention by shifting the proximity of the invisible performer. In one rehearsal, we discovered that when Annie stood in front of the participant and spoke about her courtship and Robert's 'blue eyes', it created such a visceral impact that I felt like *I* was Robert standing at the wedding altar with Annie. The lack of an avatar or dynamic gamification in *Bury the Wren* allows the participant to disappear into the story in a very present way. We were both virtually absent from the virtual world and physically present in the carbon world.

We documented forty immersant experiences across various ages, professions and experiences of theatre, VR and gaming.[6] One observed: 'I didn't lose connection with my body in this experience, unlike when I play video games or surf the internet. I was aware of my body and my breath the whole time' (Immersant 017). Immersant 008 stated: 'I was participating, but not participating. I was alone, but not alone. I was the audience AND the performance.' A first-time user of VR was the only one to experience a sense of disembodiment, noting that not being able to see their hands was 'a little strange' (Immersant 032).

Reality dissonance in *Bury the Wren* was reflected in various ways by the immersants – one declaring that the experience was '*So* realistic – I wanted to reach out and touch the objects with the other hand' (Immersant 015). Another described their feeling of being transported and how they were 'surprised by how much I felt I was somewhere else' (Immersant 013). Yet another immersant was struck by 'the breaking down of space and sensation, seeing a thing in one place, not being able to feel it, and then hearing it somewhere else. Which one is real? Is EITHER?' (Immersant 008).

These responses confirm that the intention of altering or blurring the edges of reality positively manifested for an overwhelming number of immersants. Our hope had been for this blurring to allow the immersants' attention to turn to their perception of reality and also to be liberated from our shared CR to allow them to enter new places of listening, emotion and understanding. Responses indicate that this is what occurred, which encourages us to continue this kind of creative exploration of the possibilities held within the integration of VR and live performance.

Modifying the ephemeral

In August 2022, *Bury the Wren* was remounted at World Stage Design with four different intergenerational performers recreating the role of Annie: Valerie Planche, Kristen Padayas, Maggie Kwong and Doriane Irakoze. Prioritizing the actors' processes, I crafted the four rehearsal days to allow the four actors to perform for each other. They each had multiple opportunities to be the immersant, to be Annie, and to observe neutrally. Through observation of the physical and technological demands on the performer, we found new ways to engage with props, space and the immersant. This process also gave each actor an embodied experience of being the immersant and a critical understanding of their experience in the headset (which is invisible to them during their interactions with the immersant).

Final act

The dramaturgies that arise from emerging technologies will change as technologies change. In time, audience members will become more accustomed to VR, just as the technology will be able to provide ever more complex visuals and interactivity. It is exciting to know that traditional methods of devising and designing are useful within a process that engages with cutting-edge technologies. At the heart of *Bury the Wren* was the quest for telling a compelling story that created a human-centric experience amid all the technology. By crafting a simple and gentle engagement *with* the technology, we could prioritize and facilitate human exchange *through* the technology. The creation of *Bury the Wren* is our artistic gesture to help Annie's spirit settle. It embodies Annie's reclamation of self and is a love letter to Robert. Annie exhuming Robert and having his bones interred with her in the steel casket was her final act of love, a final act to find some peace for them both. *Bury the Wren* is our act of love for her.

Acknowledgements

Many trailblazers have been noted in this chapter, but I want to single out Kiira Benzing for her tireless pursuit of art in this space and relentless support of me and my work, and Bruce Barton, Christian Jacob, Justin Maxwell and Jacquey Taucar for their guidance and wisdom. *Bury the Wren* resides in the lineage of Donnelly plays but is a direct 'descendant' of *The Last Donnelly Standing* (2016) – a co-creation by Gil Garratt, Beth Kates and Paul Thompson. So we gratefully acknowledge Gil and Paul and the generous gifts of time and collaboration that led to this work and many of the words written here. Beth and Neil both express their deep love and gratitude for the support and care of their families – Ben and Aaron Chaisson, Sarah, Olivia and Ava Christensen. Most importantly, we honour the souls of the Donnelly family, who never saw justice.

Notes

1 Beth Kates, *Incandescent Edges of Reality* can be viewed at https://prism.ucalgary.ca/items/302ed073-6cde-4006-aebb-295117923db5.

2 In honour of the members of the Donnelly family who were murdered on 4 February 1880 in Lucan Ontario. I write their names here: the elderly parents Johanna and James, sons John and Thomas, and cousin Bridget.

3 A video walkthrough of the room can be seen at https://vimeo.com/446913087/db84ee51bf.

4 Interestingly, the weight of the headset was the most common negative feedback we received in our study. Advancement in hardware will continue to make this less of an issue.

5 Blocking is terminology from traditional theatre that refers to the movement of actors around the performance space at prescribed moments to help convey plot, characters intention and direct attention of the audience.

6 A fully anonymized breakdown of participants can be found online in the *Pre-Performance Survey Report* tab alongside my thesis at https://prism.ucalgary.ca/items/302ed073-6cde-4006-aebb-295117923db5.

6

Embodied experience in XR performance-making: Collaborative design of XRP experiences through performative prototyping

Joris Weijdom

XR as embodied and spatial experience

Today the *Metaverse* concept has returned to the mainstream, rekindling interest to 'spatialize' the internet (Parisi 2021) and efforts to design new virtual environments for social and work-related activities. A survey by the *Institute for Immersive Learning* (2020) shows that more than ninety platforms are designed to facilitate professional collaboration in real-time 3D virtual environments. However, these platforms mostly ignore the central role the physical body has in the experience, even though research shows that the body responds to mediated sensory input in immersive VR as being real, even when we cognitively know it is not (Slater 2018). This suggests that the physical body and environment, combining the physical and virtual, should be considered when designing XRP experiences. But how can this be done, what kind of design environment do you need, and what are the consequences for the design process and its outcomes?

This chapter focuses on the embodied collaborative design processes in and for extended reality (XR) experiences. It unpacks core requirements for designing XR experiences and performances incorporating the physical body in the collaborative process and how to configure XR environments as a shared explorative design space. This *praxis* – that is, theory and practice 'imbricated within each other' (Nelson 2013, 62) – is based on two case-study practice-based, research projects in which I have been involved in multiple roles. These are *36Q° Blue Hour VR* (Cegys and Weijdom 2020) for the Prague Quadrennial 2019 and *1984: Back to No Future* (2021) by Gob Squad. These two case studies show that the meaning-making process *emerges* from these XR environments through collective embodied design improvisations.

This chapter illustrates and discusses how these XR environments can and should be designed as collaborative mixed-reality environments (CMREs) and how these hybrid spaces facilitate multiple embodied inner and outer experience perspectives. It builds on the concept of *performative prototyping* (Weijdom 2022), an embodied design method for XR experiences and performances resulting from my professional artistic practices, like the two case studies, and from higher-art education projects. Finally, a techno-dramaturgical vocabulary is essential to design XR experiences with this method. As such, by describing and discussing the knowledge gained through the two projects, this chapter intends to contribute to the potentially new field of XR experience and performance design.

Researching XR design praxis: Introducing two case studies

My XR design praxis first explored a new embodied approach in designing the performative site-responsive mixed-reality experience *36Q° Blue Hour VR* for the Prague Quadrennial 2019. Here, the physical body was central to the design process and its final experiential aesthetic result (Cegys and Weijdom 2020). The project used the existing Malá ice hockey Sports Hall architecture in Prague as a starting point. However, this XR experience needed to be designed, developed and prototyped in the Netherlands, as the final venue in Prague was only available in the last few weeks before opening. This project initiated the development of *Collaborative Mixed-Reality Environment* (CMRE) configurations and the *performative prototyping* method, enabling art professionals and students' embodied artistic explorations of this novel XR performance space.

At the onset of the *1984: Back to No Future* project, hereafter referred to as *1984*, the Gob Squad collective utilized these offline CMRE configurations in their studio spaces to explore this potentially new 'hybrid stage' during early conceptualization. These explorations concentrated on two week-long events, starting in Berlin and continuing in Leipzig. However, due to Covid-

19-related restrictions, later development and rehearsals partly shifted to an existing online social VR platform, adapted for a mixed-reality and embodied design approach.

While these projects are part of my XR design praxis, they are also the subject of my current PhD research following a *Research Through Design* (RtD) methodology, typified by Dalsgaard as an 'inquiry into the design process itself', whereby the researcher's involvement is a 'key catalyst for knowledge generation' (2010, 201). As such, my praxis researches *through* the XR design process and interrelated XR technology development. This aligns with Frayling's earlier discussion of research *into*, *through* and *for* art and design, whereby 'development work' incorporates 'customizing a piece of technology to do something no one had considered before, and communicating the results' (1994, 5). Finally, this chapter foregrounds the process of design rather than *art*-making, incorporating the development of technology and interfaces as an inseparable part of the artistic creative process and the aesthetic appreciation of its intermediate and final outcomes.

XR design environments, processes and perspectives

While XR is not yet a well-defined academic term and is predominantly informed by industry (Rauschnabel et al. 2022), this chapter follows the popular understanding of XR as encompassing immersive virtual reality (VR) and the classic understanding of mixed reality (MR) by Milgram and Kishino (1994). As such, VR is used in this chapter to refer to the actual head-mounted display (HMD), giving an immersive view of the virtual environment worn by an experiencer and MR for the simultaneous experience of physical and virtual bodies, objects and environments. However, as Skarbez et al. point out, virtual content 'is always ultimately situated in the real world', so 'virtual reality should fall within the category of mixed reality' (2021, 7). Consequently, the term 'XR', as an encompassing extension of MR, is a questionable improvement. Nevertheless, this chapter does not aim to unpack this discussion; instead, it embraces the idle 'explanation' that the 'X' in XR points to the unknown technological developments and artistic experiences that this field might offer in the future.

The potentially new field of XR experience and performance design is inextricably linked to technological development, interface design and usability for (performing) artists. Therefore, concepts and know-how from human-computer interaction (HCI) are used to discuss the two case studies. Consequently, some examples from the case studies might come across as arbitrary technical details or bad interface design, irrelevant to the artistic process. However, this chapter argues that artists should develop a trained and embodied understanding of these technologies, allowing for a co-creative dialogue with XR technology. Having the artistic potential emerge from the collaborative embodied design process, including ongoing technological development, avoids forcing pre-conceived ideas and biases onto the technology or having the design and limitations of the used technologies determine the creative process and its outcomes.

In the following sections, the case studies are unpacked and discussed in three parts, focusing on the design environment, collaborative embodied process and interdisciplinary vocabulary needed, each concluding with a summary of key points.

Collaborative mixed-reality environments

As XR experiences are inherently embodied, they connect to a physical space where the body and the technology facilitating the experience are situated. This implies that spaces for creating the XR experience should also be designed as MR environments. Along these lines, collaborative mixed-reality environments (CMREs) enable collective design processes in a full-scale mix of real and virtual three-dimensional space. They empower the live generation and adaptation of ideas and concepts through full-body interaction with spatial manifestations of real-time computer-generated content in relation to the physical environment. This technologically enhanced physical environment is often seen as a 'background' for the designed experience of the virtual environment, especially in immersive VR applications (Vindenes and Wasson 2021). However, designing and implementing a CMRE is not about preparing a set of 'neutral' technological instruments. Instead, it becomes apparent that the technology and the designer-developer that prepares its configuration have a certain 'directedness' (Verbeek 2008).

Designing and implementing CMRE configurations

The CMRE setup for designing *36Q° Blue Hour VR* had one person inside VR negotiating the MR environment, another operating the virtual environment from the outside and a third person surveying the overall process (Cegys and Weijdom 2020). Learning from this first basic configuration, a more complex CMRE was created for the *1984* project. This setup enabled two VR experiencers in the same virtual world, captured by a mobile live-operated MR camera showing its output on a large back wall projection for the rest of the team to see. Additionally, the two first-person VR perspectives were shown on an adjacent projection on a side wall (see Figure 6.1). Due to time and budget constraints, the chosen virtual objects, user avatars and environments consisted of existing downloaded assets from open-source repositories informed by a preliminary Zoom meeting with Gob Squad.

The technical decisions associated with constructing the setup in Berlin significantly impacted the creative process and its outcomes. For example, operator table placement and wire length of the headsets determined the physical locomotion range of the VR users in the 'performance space' and to what extent they could perform together or alone. Also, the final setup in Berlin had a concrete pillar in the performance space, which needed to be represented in VR to ensure that the VR users would not physically bump into it. Consequently, during the improvisation sessions, this MR 'pillar' was used regularly and became an anchor point for the VR performers to validate their relation to the physical space.

Learning from this experience, we extended the VR headsets' cable length for the second Leipzig event. Furthermore, to address the artistic limitations of prechosen ready-made digital 3D assets, we developed a virtual 'improvisation prop table', so Gob Squad members could pick virtual objects from an extensive database for improvisation. Interestingly, this possibility became a crucial asset in the final performance, whereby one performer in VR built an amateurish nuclear bomb shelter with ordinary things. To summarize, the performance space, physical range of the VR users, digital aesthetics of the virtual world, audience positioning and resulting lines of sight were an outcome of the CMRE technical build-up process. This technical placement and digital aesthetics substantially influenced Gob Squad's experience, dramaturgical considerations and following creative steps.

CMRE Studio setups versus social VR @ home

While both projects consisted of international teams, the embodied improvisation sessions in the CMRE configurations predominantly occurred in physical studios. However, the Corona pandemic forced us to use an online multi-user Collaborative Virtual Environment (CVE) at the last stage of Gob Squad's production. The social VR platform *NEOS VR* (Solirax 2018) was chosen specifically for its real-time capability to create and adjust the virtual environment, objects and avatars while in VR. This online CVE was prepared with the same assets, environments and virtual prop table we had designed for the Berlin and Leipzig events in an offline 3D engine, Unity 3D. This co-located form of collaboration enabled Gob Squad to rehearse the scenes involving VR in their studio in Berlin, while I could assist remotely from my workroom in the Netherlands. Nevertheless, I noticed feeling more detached from the physical interactions, losing connection with the team and the creative process. Also, the technician of Gob Squad felt less confident about implementing the VR technology in the final performance, which unfortunately resulted in them recording their scenes in VR that would then be played back during the performances.

Summary: Collaborative Mixed Reality Environments

Firstly, XR technology is designed and applied with assumptions and limitations, impacting what can be done with it creatively. As such, the technological development of CMREs and implementation in studio spaces are not separate from the artistic process. Therefore, involving the whole team in techno-artistic decision-making is preferable, acknowledging the technical team members as creative co-creators.

Secondly, balance predetermined 3D assets versus choosing them 'on the fly'. The prepared virtual avatars, objects and environments immediately impacted the aesthetic appreciation of the XR experience. The need to add or adapt certain assets became apparent during the improvisations. While making them from scratch takes too much time, using ready-made 3D assets from the internet is a valid strategy. However, a workflow needs to be designed to offer these assets dynamically so performers are free to improvise, like the 'improvisation prop table' for Gob Squad in Leipzig.

Thirdly, the physical environment should be incorporated into the design process. Neglecting to incorporate the physical environment early in the design process results in missed experiential opportunities in the final mixed-reality installation or performance. When working in co-located setups, make sure sufficient technical know-how is represented in all physical locations.

Collaborative creative processes in CMREs

Now that we have discussed some considerations and requirements for XR design environments, this second section focuses on the collaborative embodied design process using XR tools and CMREs.

Collaborative *emergence* through embodied improvisations

Both projects used embodied improvisation techniques to explore the artistic potential of XR, where many new ideas *emerged* from the collective creative process. Both the *36Q° Blue Hour VR* team and the Gob Squad collective worked with a devised theatre methodology, whereby the resulting performance 'emerges from the interactions of the group' (Sawyer 2000b, 182). It is essential to incorporate all design disciplines in these collectively devised theatre processes (Maclaurin 2000). This is why in both projects, the technical disciplines participated actively in the embodied improvisation sessions, often as a *mediated performer*, or *puppeteer*, live controlling MR environment (Cegys and Weijdom 2020; Weijdom 2022). Also, the other team members needed to learn to incorporate the technological tools and environment to develop artistic ideas through embodied improvisations. This embodied understanding of the technology was essential for the non-technical team members to make relevant suggestions for the XR tools and CMRE adaptations.

Multi-stable affordances of XR tools and CMRE environments

When designing CMREs, one could consider 'good design' as 'intuitive' (Victor Kaptelinin 2014), whereby, as in Gibson's 1970s concept of *affordances*, the shape of an object 'naturally' shows what you can do with it. However, many critics have pointed out that an object's use depends on its situational circumstances. Post-phenomenology explains that 'the same technology can have several different *stabilities* in terms of how it is used and experienced' (Vindenes and Wasson 2021, 5). Also, the users' 'sedimented or unestablished relationship with VR technology, or their attitudes toward technology in general, will impact their virtually mediated experience' (2021). Not all affordances in a virtual environment are relatable to physical world experiences, like flying through walls or picking up objects at a distance with lasers-like strings. As such, it is questionable whether a user would recognize these affordances through prior knowledge from lived experience in the physical world.

The Gob Squad CMRE configurations offered tracked physical objects represented in different forms in the virtual environment at the exact same physical location. Additionally, various virtual 3D environments could be selected as staged places where the physical-virtual performers were situated. However, it took the Gob Squad members significant time to understand this

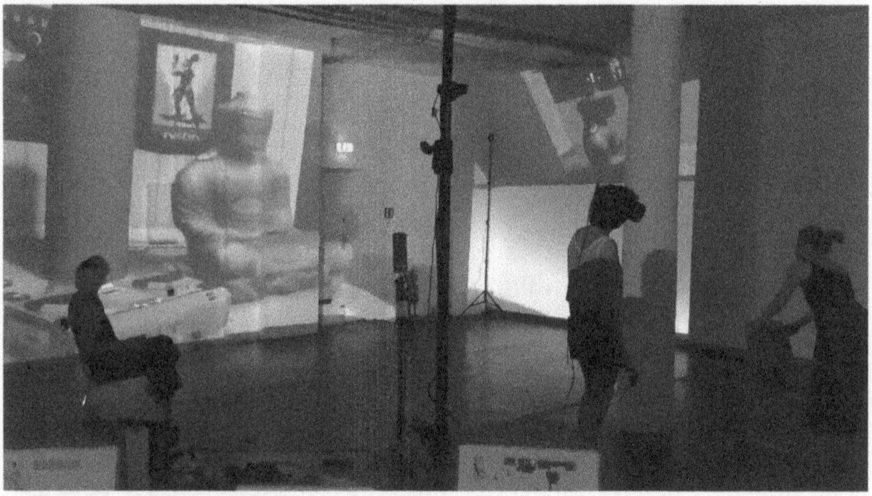

FIGURE 6.1 *1984: Back to No Future* - Video-still of the Gob Squad Berlin set-up, moving the virtual Buddha statue by moving a physical tracked chair. The concrete pillar is visible in the middle of the 'performance space', 2020 (© J. Weijdom).

complex multi-perspective MR space. For example, a Gob Squad member co-performing without a VR headset got confused when moving a virtual Buddha statue, forgetting that its position was accurately connected to a simple chair standing nearby in the physical performance space (see Figure 6.1).

Puppeteering controls and mediated performance

In HCI, controlling certain variables of a system in real time in response to a user to develop and test a system is called 'Wizard of Oz' (or WoZ) (Dahlbäck et al. 1993), which as a technique can also be applied to embodied design improvisations in XR (Sirkin and Ju 2015). In both case studies, a physical control board, or *Midi-controller*, allowed for changing aspects of the virtual environment in real time, like virtual lights' intensities and the type of virtual representation of the tracked physical objects. Here, the operator could manipulate the virtual environment, shown on a computer screen or back-wall projection, in response to the performers in the MR environment. In this relationship, the operator becomes a *mediated performer* of the virtual environment and could thus be called a *puppeteer*. Or, as Kaplin explains, 'while actors animate a sign vehicle from the inside out, using their own feelings, bodies, and voices, puppet performers must learn to inhabit the sign vehicle from the outside in' (1999, 29).

While the Midi-controller was used extensively in the *36Q° Blue Hour VR* embodied improvisation sessions, preparing and using such a setup in Gob Squads' sessions proved challenging. It became apparent in Berlin that operating changes inside the virtual environment from the outside was confusing. After some team frustration with poorly timed changes, the Gob Squad member operating the Midi-controller expressed the need to learn how these controls work by 'freely playing' with them first. Also, in Berlin the Midi-controller itself did not indicate which knobs or sliders would control what, which led to a (somewhat amateurish) labelling of all the controls in Leipzig.

From instruction to exploration to improvisation to rehearsal

In creative collaborations, improvisation is generally understood as 'a creative act composed without prior thought' (Gerber 2007, 1069), although this 'act' is not random or unstructured; instead, it requires 'understanding the underlying patterns' (Zenk et al. 2022, p. 6), for example in recognizing in which phase of the creative collaboration you are in. Improvisation can be used as an idea-generation method (Gerber 2009) or as an outcome (Sawyer 2000a). As with controlling XR technology, improvisation techniques must be trained (Zenk et al. 2022). Unlike the members of *36Q° Blue Hour VR*, the Gob Squad team are highly skilled improvisation professionals for devising theatre. However, they had no experience using XR technologies, meaning they could not immediately start with artistic group improvisations.

First, the multi-perspective CMRE setup was introduced to one member during a step-by-step *instruction phase* while the rest of the team observed. Then more collaborators were invited to join in VR, or operate the MR camera and tracked objects as non-VR co-performers. Those who became more comfortable with the setup shifted to an *exploration phase*, trying out more complex interactions within the MR environment and with each other. While this phase offered dramaturgically interesting moments, they were primarily motivated and affected by technological possibilities and limitations. Only when team members partially 'embodied the technology', not needing to think about the controls for basic interactions, did an artistic *improvisation phase* start. This, however, was a slow process due to team members' various speeds of adaptation and the constant switching of roles and positions in their collaboration. In all these phases, Gob Squad members continuously shared their embodied experiences within the team, alternating between voicing corporal-perceptual sensations, artistic speculation and dramaturgical reflection.

After exploring the artistic potential of XR technology in Berlin, the need for the artistic development of the *1984* project became urgent. During three days in Leipzig, various 'scenes' were developed through structured improvisations in a CMRE, with prepared materials, settings, tasks and roles. In the end, some time was left for a free improvisation session with two Gob Squad members in VR, while a sound designer mixed a live version of Lionel Richie's 'Hello', and a video designer mixed multiple virtual camera perspectives. This resulted in a spontaneous and exciting hybrid experience that combined a live performance and a surreal 1980s video clip on the back wall projection, which became a critical scene in the final performance. This successful improvisation happened due to a combination of factors, including the lack of pressure to create something meaningful, the involvement of other disciplines and an embodied understanding of the VR controls. Additionally, the experience became extra interesting due to a spontaneous technical calibration 'error', resulting in the performers moving away from each other physically while connecting in VR. This made the combined physical and virtual space dramaturgically meaningful in their almost literal divergent representations (see Plate 12).

After these sessions, the final performance was constructed over several weeks shifting from structured improvisation to *rehearsals*. However, in Gob Squad work, final scenes are not fixed in a traditional text-based script but rather structurally organized, setting 'rules and an order in which sequence things are coming', allowing for variations in the performance. Here, the *rehearsal phase* is about continuously re-hearing the semi-structured performance moment rather than practicing a fully scripted scene (Peters 2009, 5). In contrast to Gob Squad's process, the *36Q° Blue Hour VR* project explored, through embodied improvisations, the interaction design and dramaturgy of the individual's experience inside VR rather than predominantly considering the outside perspective.

Summary: Collaborative creative processes in CMREs

Firstly, knowledge of interaction design principles studied in human-computer interaction (HCI) is required to implement and adapt the interfaces for negotiating XR tools and environments. From the HCI perspective of *usability*, the affordances of the tools and environment should be as simple as possible and with minimal options and variations. However, XR tools and environments should also be understood as intricate musical instruments that take time to learn to enable expert and complex creative embodied expressions.

Secondly, learning and embodying new and complex XR technology takes time. For the XR technology (both tools and MR environment) to become part of the performers' body, several distinct phases of skill acquisition must be learned and internalized. Consequently, significant time in the creative process should be allocated to playful explorations of the tools provided before artistic improvisation becomes possible.

Thirdly, the generating, adapting and testing of new ideas happen in distinct phases through interdisciplinary collaborative embodied improvisations. In these improvisations, concepts *emerge* from the collective creative process, including designing, applying and adjusting the technology involved. Therefore, considerable time should be taken for *instruction* and *exploration* phases before *improvisations* and *rehearsals* become possible. Furthermore, improvisations should alternate between free sessions to allow new ideas to emerge through 'serendipity' (Amacker 2019) and prepared 'structured' sessions of rules, roles and sequences, allowing the development of those ideas.

Performative prototyping methodology

Unlike the performing arts, designing with the body is relatively new to HCI since its 'somatic turn' (Loke and Schiphorst 2018). Recently, outward movement-based design methodologies like *bodystorming* (Márquez Segura et al. 2016) are developed in conjunction with inward sensing strategies (Núñez-Pacheco 2018), inspired by Schusterman's *somaesthetics* (1999) and translated for HCI to *soma design* (Höök 2018).

An embodied design methodology in and for XR experiences entitled *performative prototyping* is developed through the discussed and other case studies and artistic projects in higher-art education (Weijdom 2022). This methodology 'employs several embodied design techniques, summarized as *bodystorming*, combined with *WoZ* strategies, with a puppeteering approach'. Furthermore, it 'incorporates an embodied phenomenological- and somaesthetic inside-out perspective with a dramaturgical outside-in perspective to identify and interpret the meaning of the MR experience, whereby one's body both performs its responses to, and becomes performative in, the MR environment' (2022, 9).

As such, the performative prototyping method enables full-body engagement within the creative collaboration to verify and adapt XR experience design decisions. However, this is not a simple task considering the many experiential perspectives involved in this process.

Inside-out somaesthetic and outside-in dramaturgical points-of-view

Like XR experiences, environmental, location-based and immersive theatre traditions have a long history of placing the audience/spectators as an experiencer *inside* the performance space, enabling physically *being-in* the performance itself. Designing XR experiences using the body in a CMRE involves the *first-person* perspective of the experiencer *inside* the virtual environment while simultaneously being situated *outside* in a physical environment. Therefore, this *inside-out* perspective combines an *inward* focus on the body's *internal* sensations with an *outward* focus on how the body re-acts *externally* to the MR environment. These sensations and reactions must be communicated and interpreted by the designer-as-experiencer into first-person *somaesthetic*, or soma design, considerations. At the same time, this experiencer is watched by others not using VR, seeing the experiencer from the *outside* performing in the MR space, using an *outside-in* focus. They must observe and analyse how its performance is staged from a third-person *dramaturgical* perspective. A design team can actively take up these positions, or embodied perspectives (see Plate 13), while designing (Cegys and Weijdom 2020).

Both projects used these somaesthetic and dramaturgical points-of-view. As mentioned, the Gob Squad members communicated continuously from inside-out and outside-in perspectives. However, while impressed with the first-person experience, they became doubtful about the dramaturgical validity of observing performers in VR from an outside perspective, especially if audience members had no prior experience with XR.

Role-shifting in interdisciplinary teams

So far, four perspectives, or design roles, have been articulated. First, the *designer-as-experiencer* experiences the virtual environment from a first-person perspective by using a VR headset. Second, the *designer-as-performer* negotiates the MR environment with their co-performers/experiencers without a VR headset. Third, the *designer-as-puppeteer* manipulates elements in the virtual environment, either from the outside or within the performance space. Finally, the *designer-as-audience/spectator* observes the experience from the outside of the performance space through a dramaturgical lens. As it is hard to maintain awareness of all perspectives simultaneously, it is essential to switch these positions regularly so that discussion and evaluation of design considerations originate from a shared multi-perspective embodied experience.

In both projects, group members had different disciplinary know-how, whereby the team members shifted through all positions to ensure that everybody would have a first-person embodied understanding of each perspective. Especially with Gob Squad, roles and positions would shift with each improvisation session, including the technician, dramaturg and production coordinator. Furthermore, from the beginning, embodied sensations, design considerations, artistic suggestions and dramaturgical observations were constantly verbalized and shared in the group during the sessions.

Vocabulary for XR experience design: A techno-dramaturgy

As Rouse et al. formulate, a technological understanding of XR experiences moves 'from vision to perception, from space to place, and from technology to capability' (2015, 178). However, XR experiences are mediated by high-end technologies that are inevitably physically and experientially present in the aesthetic experience. A *post-dramatic* approach (Lehmann 2006) embraces technology as a recognizable part of the meaning-making experience. Working with the dramaturgies of *36Q° Blue Hour VR* and *1984* shows that the mediation of an experiencer's perception and multiplication of experiential realities, as well as the physical limitations of the used XR technologies, provide implicit dramaturgical potential. The impactful experiential dichotomy of being in two or more places simultaneously forms a fundamental starting point for an XR dramaturgy.

A dramaturgy that embraces technology could be typified as a 'techno-dramaturgy'. King refers to this term as 'the interplay between traditional dramaturgies and the innate, often concealed dramaturgies of technical systems themselves, whether software, hardware or mechanical' (2018, 326). Whereby even technical 'errors' can result in meaningful situations, as the spontaneous 'Hello' scene by Gob Squad illustrates. However, this techno-dramaturgy focuses on the aesthetic evaluation of an *outside-in* third-person audience/spectator perspective looking at a staged performance partly mediated by technology. This chapter suggests expanding this approach with an *inside-out* first-person perspective, taking as a starting point the experiencer's multimodal perception of simultaneously being in multiple places. While the *36Q° Blue Hour VR* project focused primarily on the design of this first-person experience, it also had to consider the outside spectators. Reversely, Gob Squad's *1984* project focused primarily on this outside-in perspective, while rightfully questioning its validity if the audience/spectators had never experienced VR. As such, while a certain perspective could dominate the artistic concept, both perspectives should always be considered in their interrelatedness.

Learning from the case studies, an interdisciplinary vocabulary should facilitate both first-person experiential qualifications, consequential design and technological development considerations, as well as analysis of the third-person aesthetic appreciation of the intermediary and final outcomes. Here, concepts and vocabulary from somaesthetic, interaction design and technodramaturgical practices are needed, allowing for the constant reconfiguration of the technologies involved. This means that an ongoing and non-hierarchical dialogue between artistic and technological disciplines must be maintained.

Summary: Performative prototyping methodology

Firstly, XR experience design incorporates different roles and experiential perspectives that should be switched within the team regularly. The case studies show that experiencing all perspectives is essential when discussing and evaluating from a personal and shared embodied experience. Another approach to ensuring that everybody is experiencing all perspectives is by voicing the embodied experience, observations, questions, findings, insights and suggestions continuously.

Secondly, role- and perspective-taking should be trained in the performative prototyping method. The complex multiple-perspective practice of embodied design improvisations in CMREs needs to be practiced, as well as improvisation skills (Zenk et al. 2022). Particularly skills relating to *somaesthetic reflection* and *kinaesthetic empathy* in design practice (Svanæs and Barkhuus 2020).

Thirdly, XR experience design needs an interdisciplinary vocabulary that embraces technology as part of the techno-dramaturgy. Here the aesthetic and dramaturgical appreciation combines first-person outside-in and third-person inside-out perspectives. Also, it should facilitate the collaborative design process, including soma- and interaction-design observations and considerations.

Conclusion

This chapter describes and discusses two case studies from my praxis in XR experience- and performance design, placing the physical body central to the design process and the appreciation of its aesthetic outcomes. It uses a so-called *performative prototyping* methodology combining embodied design improvisation and WoZ puppeteering techniques in collaborative mixed-reality environments, or CMREs. Also, it implements a phenomenological- and somaesthetic inside-out perspective with a dramaturgical outside-in perspective to identify and interpret the meaning of the XR experience.

It recognizes different roles, which various team members should shift during the design process. Finally, considering the relative newness of this interdisciplinary field, a devised methodology is suggested, whereby artistic ideas and technological development emerge from the embodied improvisation sessions in iterative design cycles.

While the case studies are partly situated in a post-dramatic performance praxis, concepts from the field of HCI are an essential part of the design process due to the highly technical nature of XR. Consequently, the technological disciplines should participate in the embodied improvisations to understand the artistic considerations from direct experience, while the non-technical disciplines need to get an embodied understanding of the 'directedness' and impact of the technologies involved on the artistic process and outcomes. As XR is still an emerging field, so are the current technological developments. Therefore, artists should develop an ongoing interest in these technological developments anticipating possible creative innovations and have the capability to discuss CMRE configurations incorporating new technologies as co-creators in an XR experience's artistic development.

Finally, a vocabulary is needed to facilitate this interdisciplinary collaborative design process and evaluate its aesthetic intermediate and final outcomes. This vocabulary uses concepts from theatre and performance, HCI and the philosophy of human technology relations. It suggests the development of an expanded post-dramatic *XR technodramaturgy* that incorporates both a third-person audience/spectator and a first-person experiencer perspective. However, this is the first step, as XR can mediate and alter our perception, knowledge from neurology and psychology also becomes increasingly relevant in XR design considerations. As such, this XR technodramaturgical vocabulary facilitates a genuine interdisciplinary dialogue in developing this new field while ensuring that artists will be at its forefront. In this context, I hope this chapter contributes to this emerging field by unpacking core requirements for collaborative explorations and development of XR experiences and performances, empowering artists to show its potential by creating meaningful experiences in the near future.

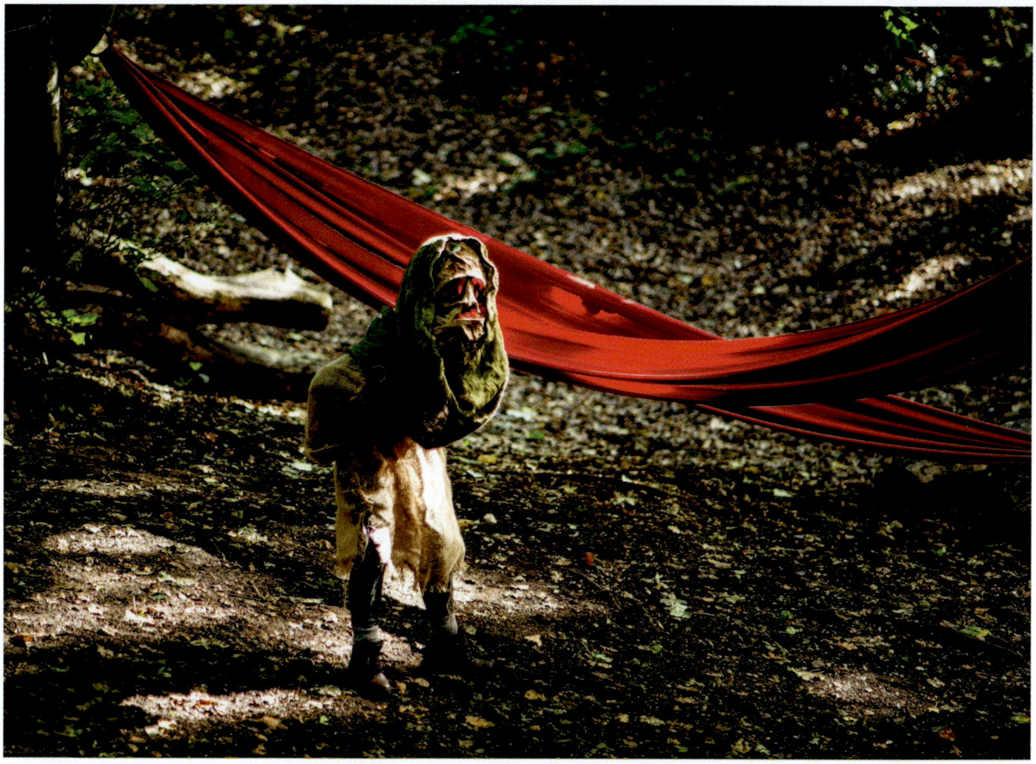

PLATE 1 A masked rebel in Limbik's *Rebel Rabble*, 2022 (© John Driscoll).

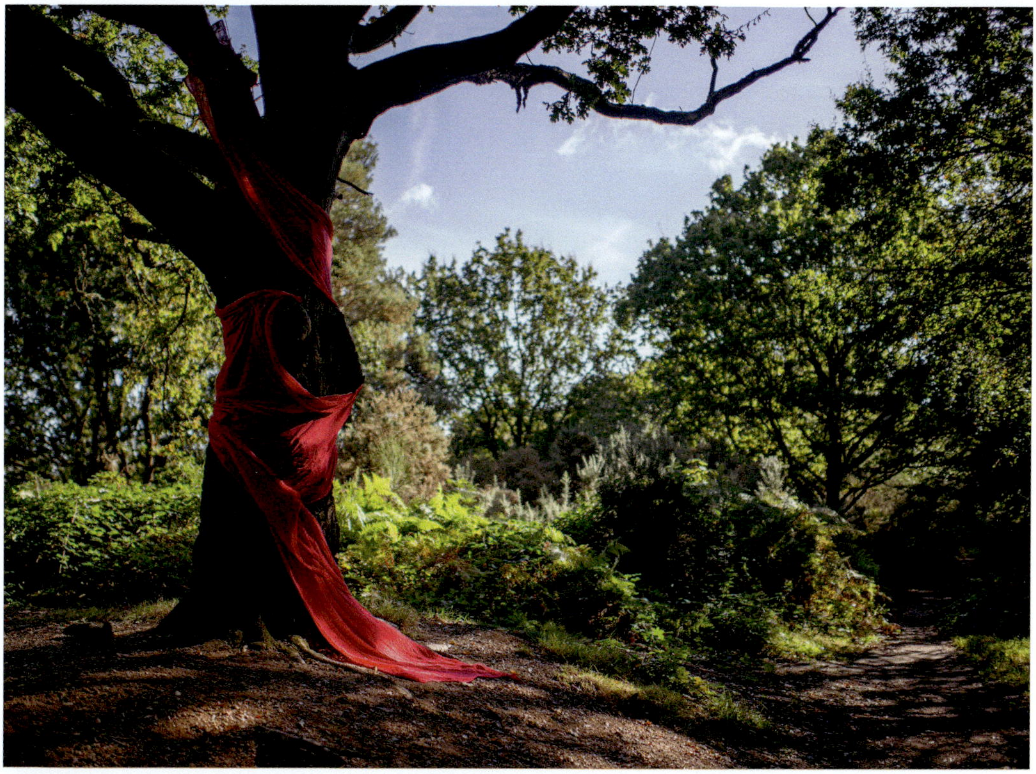

PLATE 2 The Oak Tree, *Rebel Rabble*, 2022 (© David Monteith Hodge).

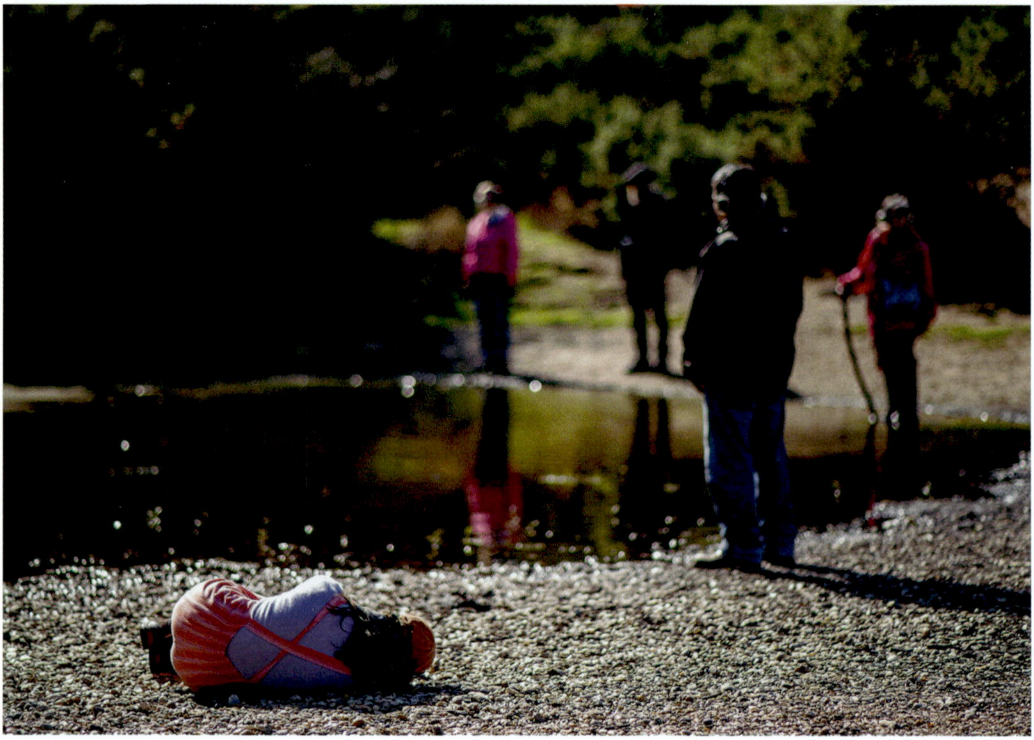

PLATE 3 The Vinegar Pond, *Rebel Rabble*, 2022 (© Jon Driscoll).

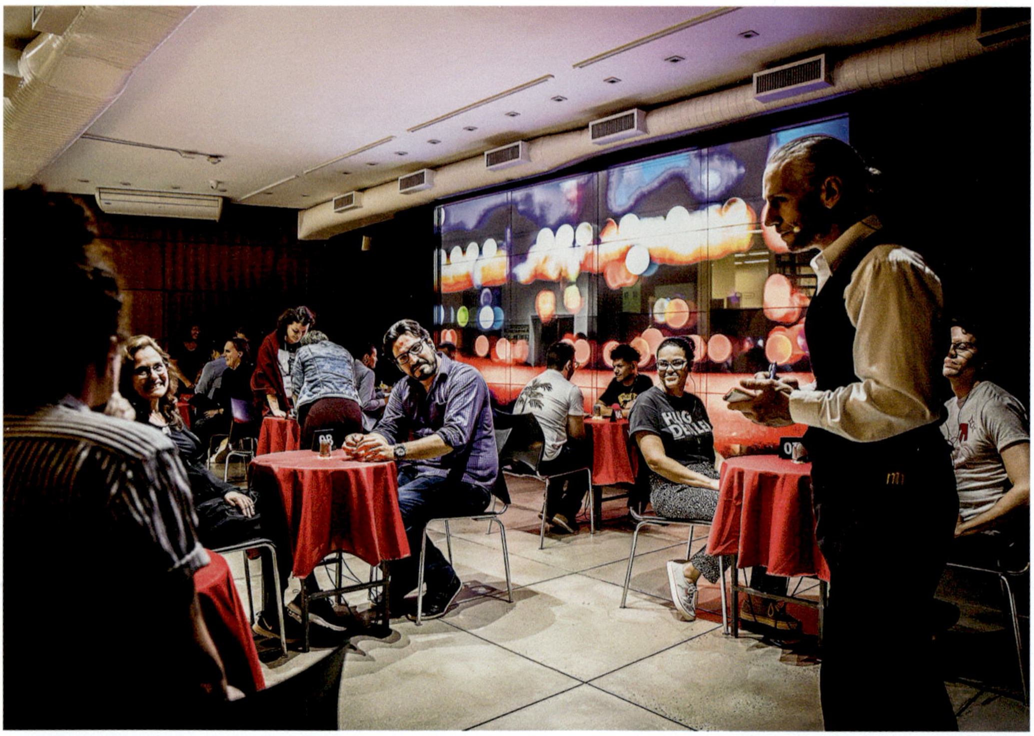

PLATE 4 The familiar conventions of restaurant-behaviour are activated by setting and simple signifiers. W performed by James Turpin, *Binaural Dinner Date*, Oi Futuro, Rio de Janeiro, 2022 (© Renato Mangolin).

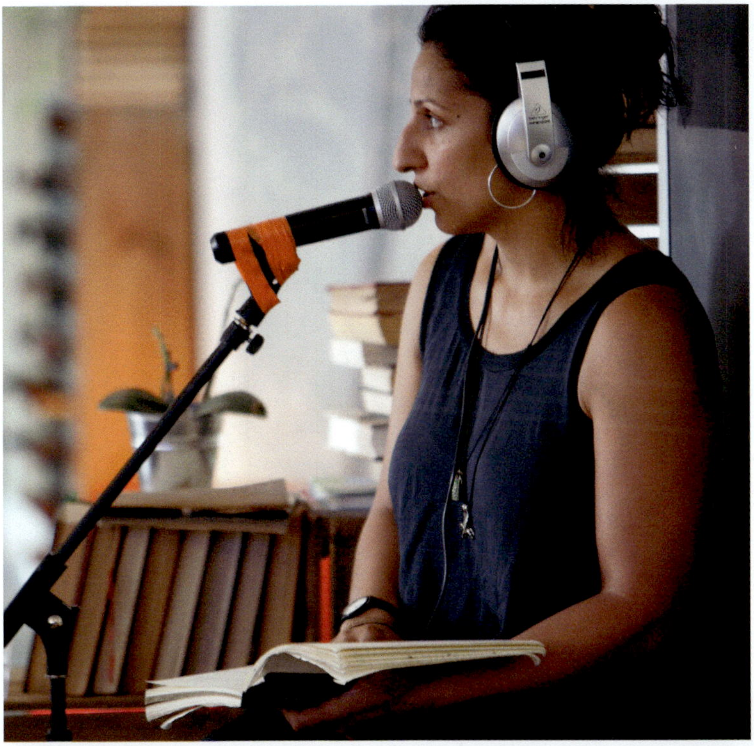

PLATE 5 The vanished body: Chef, hidden from view, performed by Persis Jadé Maravala, delivers lines scripted moments before live into the audiosystem, *Binaural Dinner Date*, Gerry's Café, Theatre Royal Stratford East, London, 2017 (© Ludovic des Cognets).

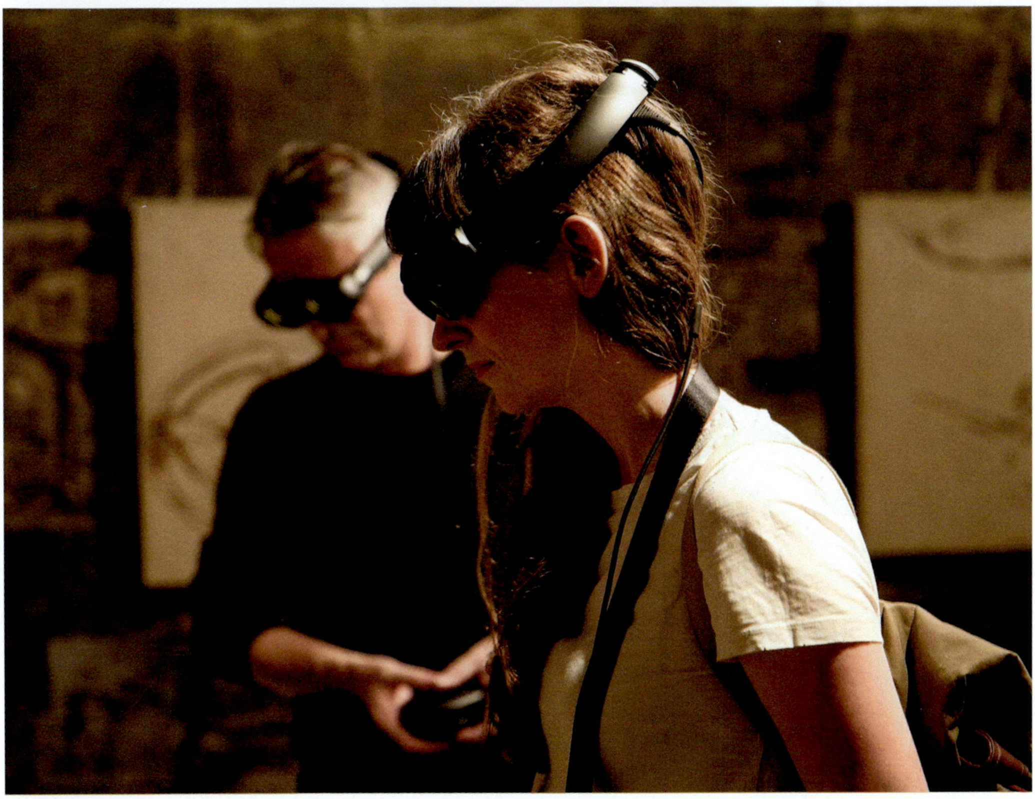

PLATE 6 Two immersants watch *Augmented Play* wearing Magic Leap glasses, perceiving the digital representation as being present in the same physical space, 2019 (© Néill O'Dwyer).

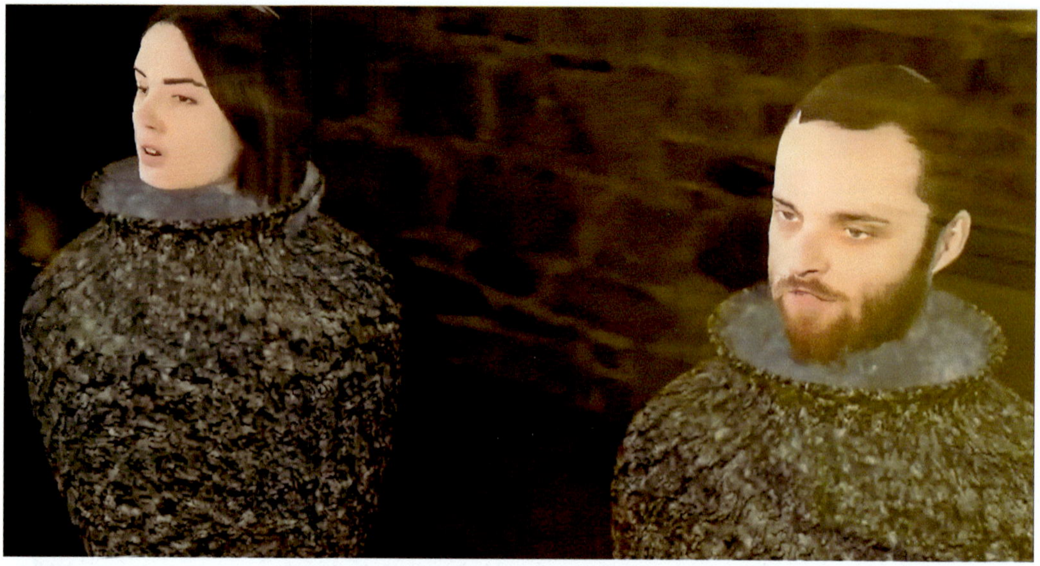

PLATE 7 *Augmented Play* (Screenshot) W2 (Caitlin Scott) and M (Colm Gleeson) as viewed in the Magic Leap AR glasses. The physical stone wall is visible in the background, and the virtual characters are superimposed onto the foreground of the viewer's field of vision, 2019 (© Néill O'Dwyer).

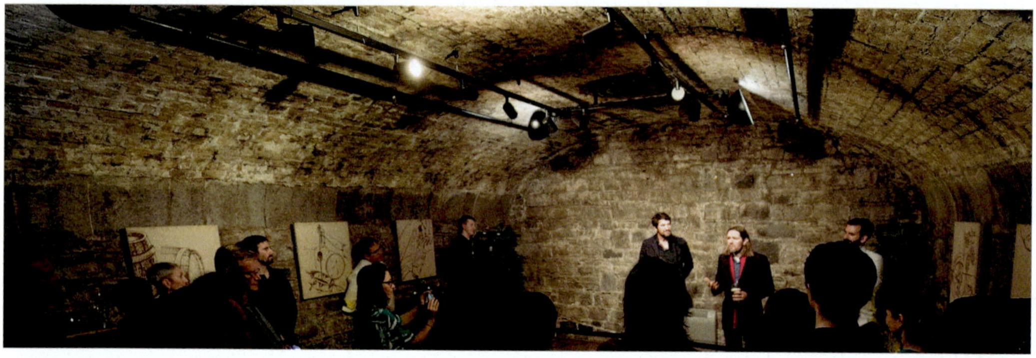

PLATE 8 Launch event venue for *Augmented Play*: an eighteenth-century stone/brick vaulted cellar. The virtual urns were positioned at the end of the room, where the speakers are standing. Speakers: Aljosa Smolic (Principal Investigator) and Nicholas Johnson (Director), 2019 (© Néill O'Dwyer).

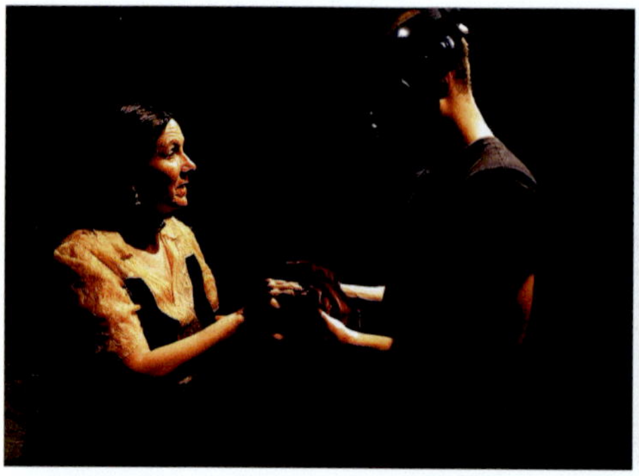

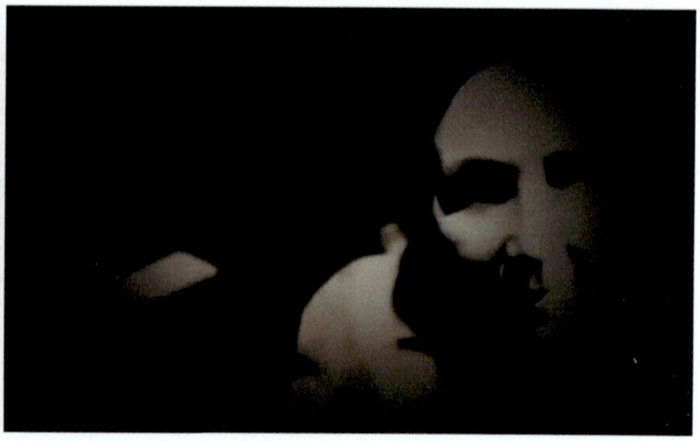

PLATE 9A&B *Bury the Wren*, 2019, 9a (left): 'I have something special I want you to see', says Annie (Valerie Campbell) as she hands the immersant the scarf. (© Beth Kates). 9b (right): an image from the modified pass-through camera, where the immersant sees Annie for the very first time, mediated through filters. (© Neil Christensen and Beth Kates).

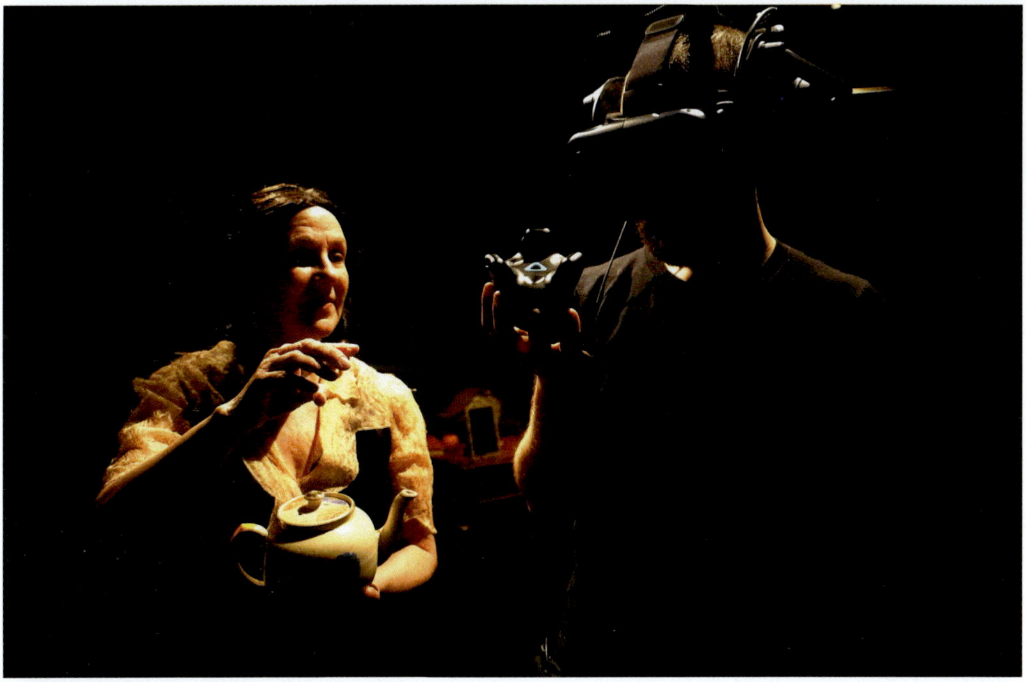

PLATE 10 *Bury the Wren*, 2019, Annie Donnelly (Valerie Campbell) draws the immersant's attention to the different colours painted on the teapot, as seen in VR. The colours are each connected to a portion of the story of her and Robert's courtship and wedding. She holds the original CR teapot, which was used to create clinking sounds in the performance space (© Beth Kates).

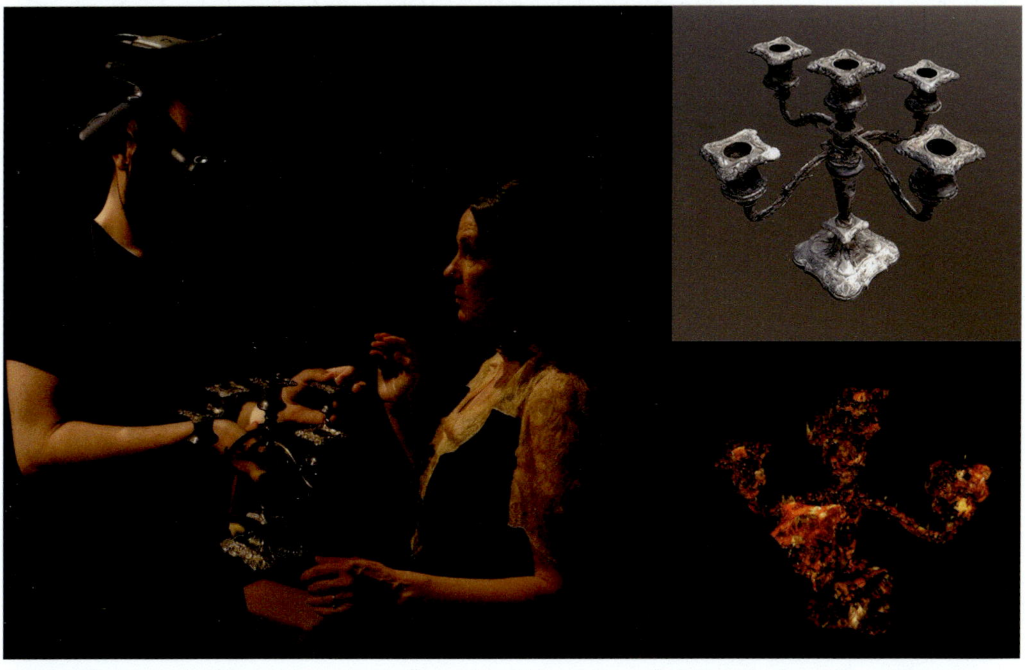

PLATE 11 *Bury the Wren*, 2019, Annie Donnelly (Valerie Campbell) hands the cold and heavy CR candelabra to the immersant (left). They cannot see the CR object; instead they experienced the virtual object (top right) burst into flames (bottom right). In VR the flaming candelabra is still sitting, burning, on the floor of the virtual space (© Beth Kates).

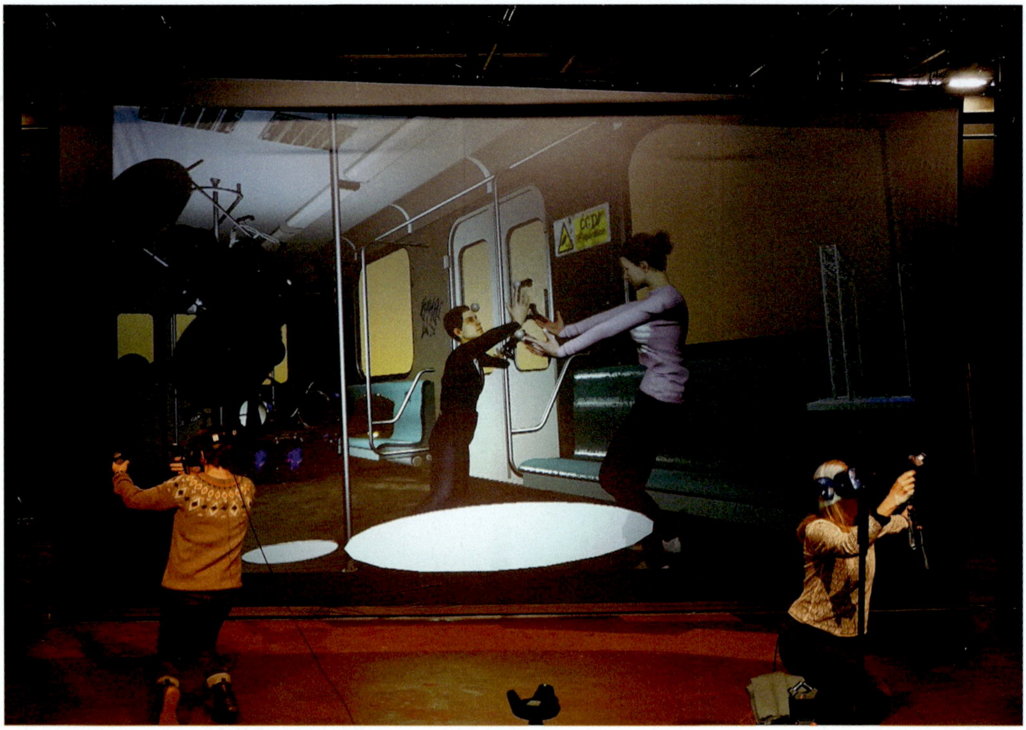

PLATE 12 Gob Squad's *1984: Back to No Future*, in Leipzig, a technical 'error' becomes meaningful while doing a spontaneous 'Hello' scene improvisation, 2020 (© J. Weijdom).

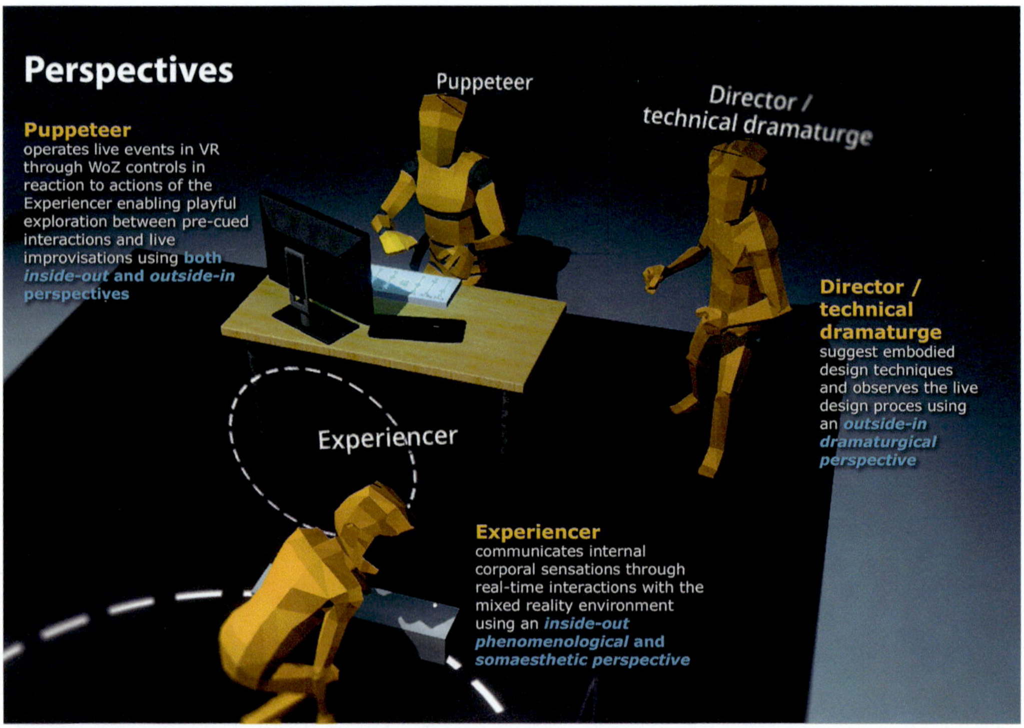

PLATE 13 Three key roles for an XR experience design team, combining inside-out and outside-in perspectives, 2020 (© J. Weijdom).

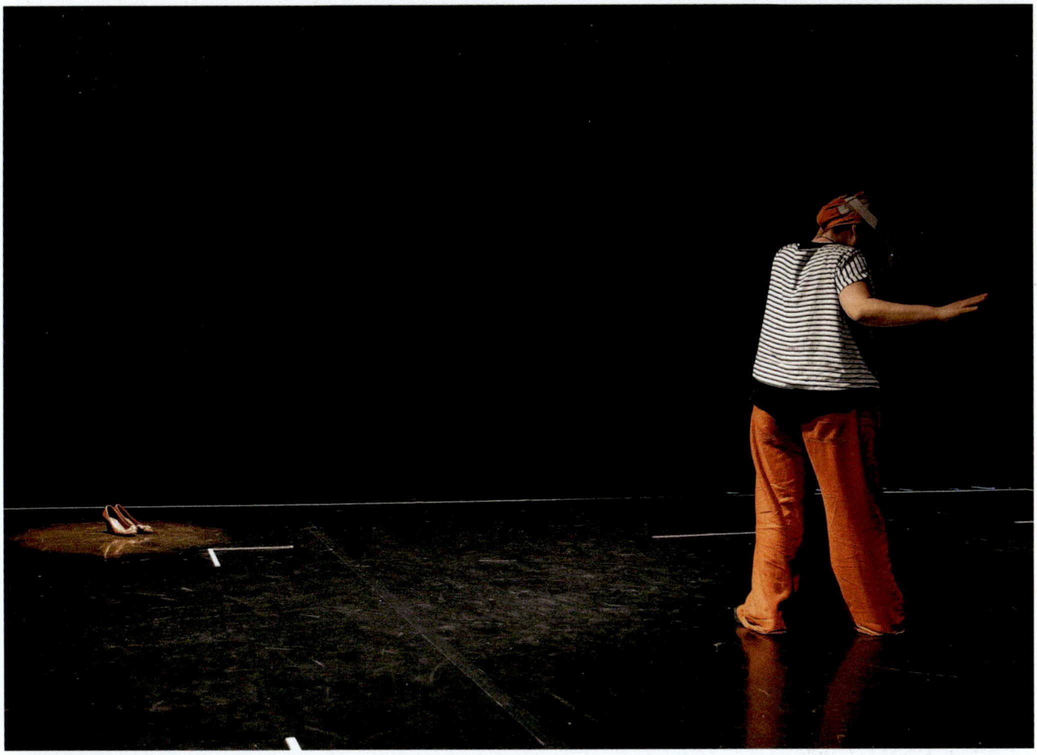

PLATE 14 *Facades* audience, 2021 (© Julian Hughes).

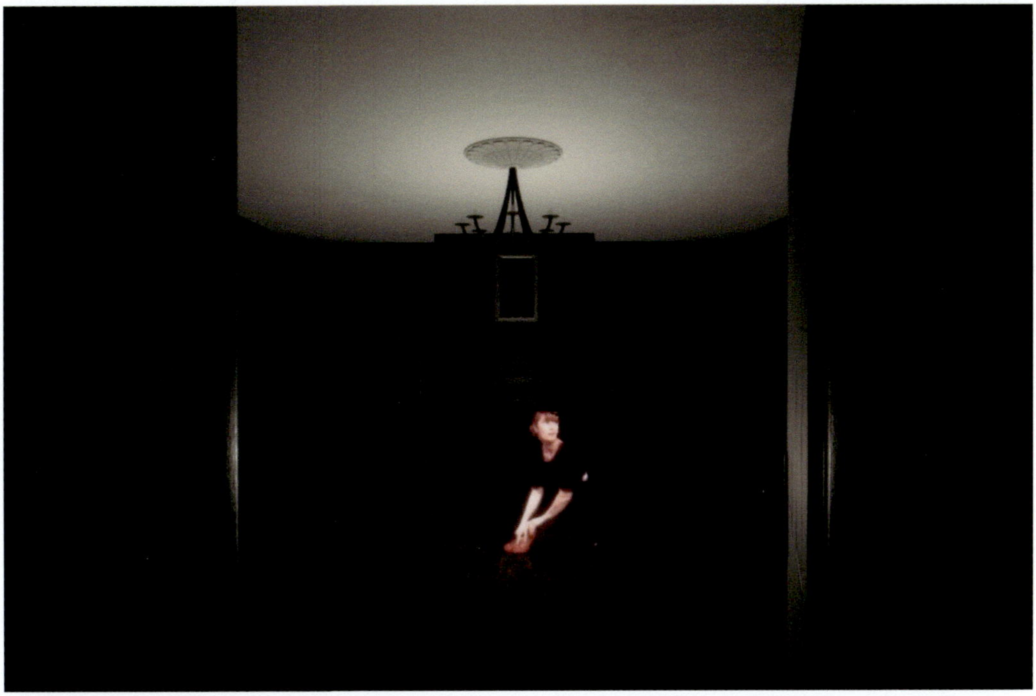

PLATE 15 Still from VR showing doorway, *Facades*, 2021 (© Kerryn Wise/Displace Studio).

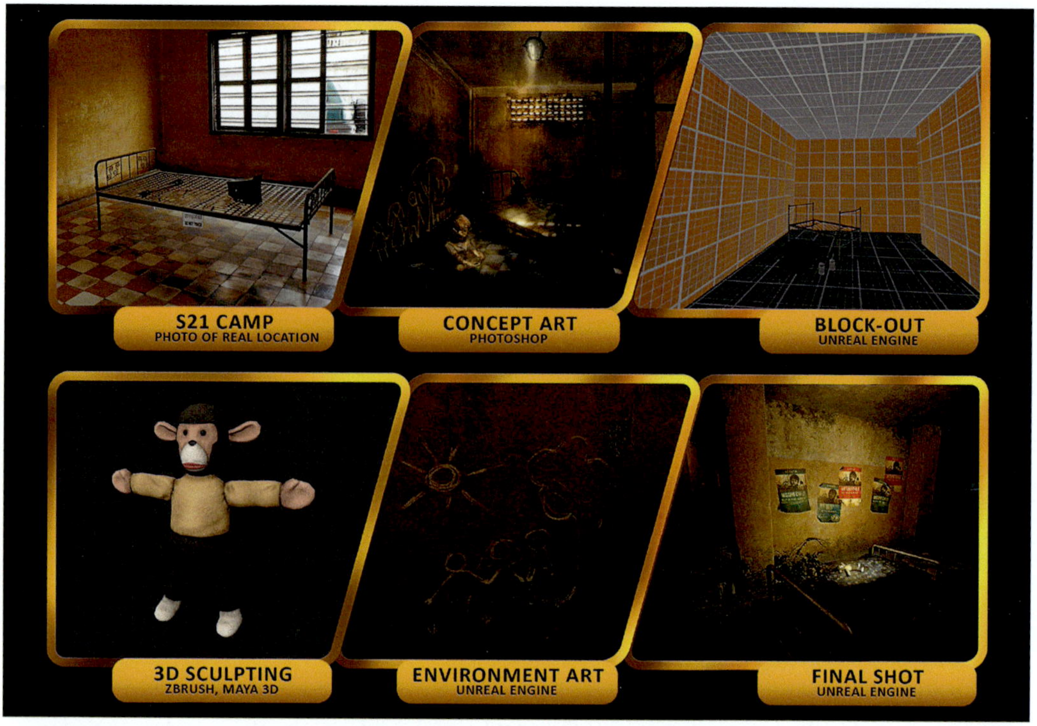

PLATE 16 World-Building & Asset Creation Pipeline, 2021–2024 (© UME Studios & Victoria Bousis).

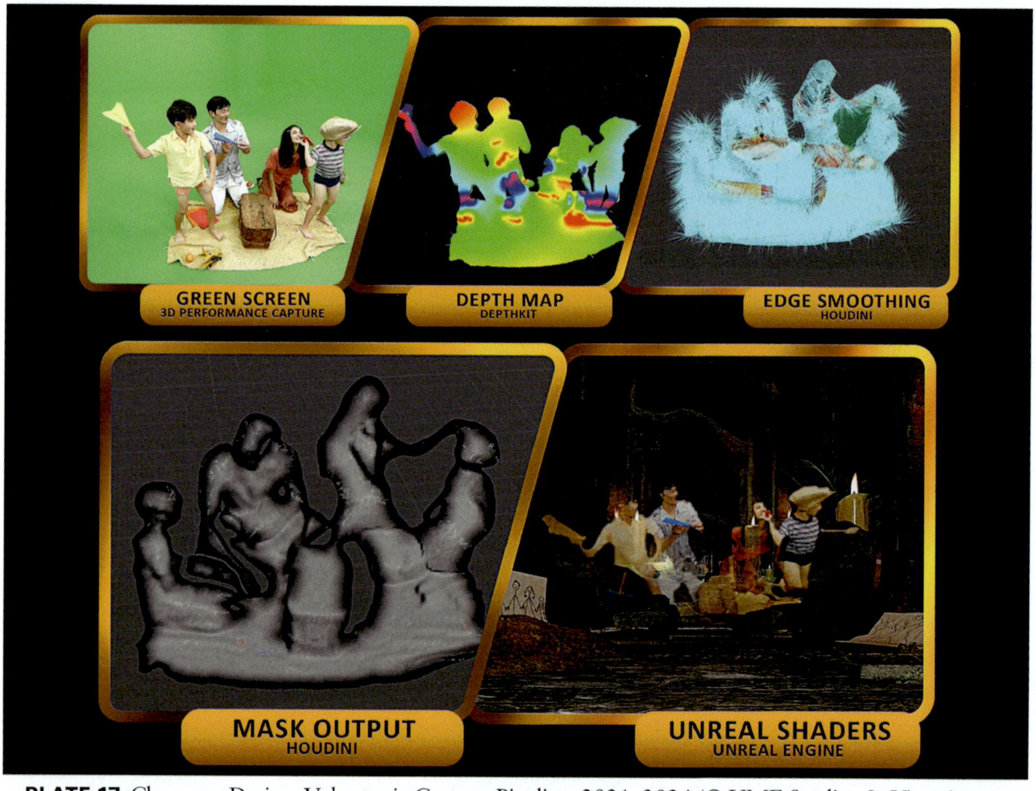

PLATE 17 Character Design: Volumetric Capture Pipeline, 2021–2024 (© UME Studios & Victoria Bousis).

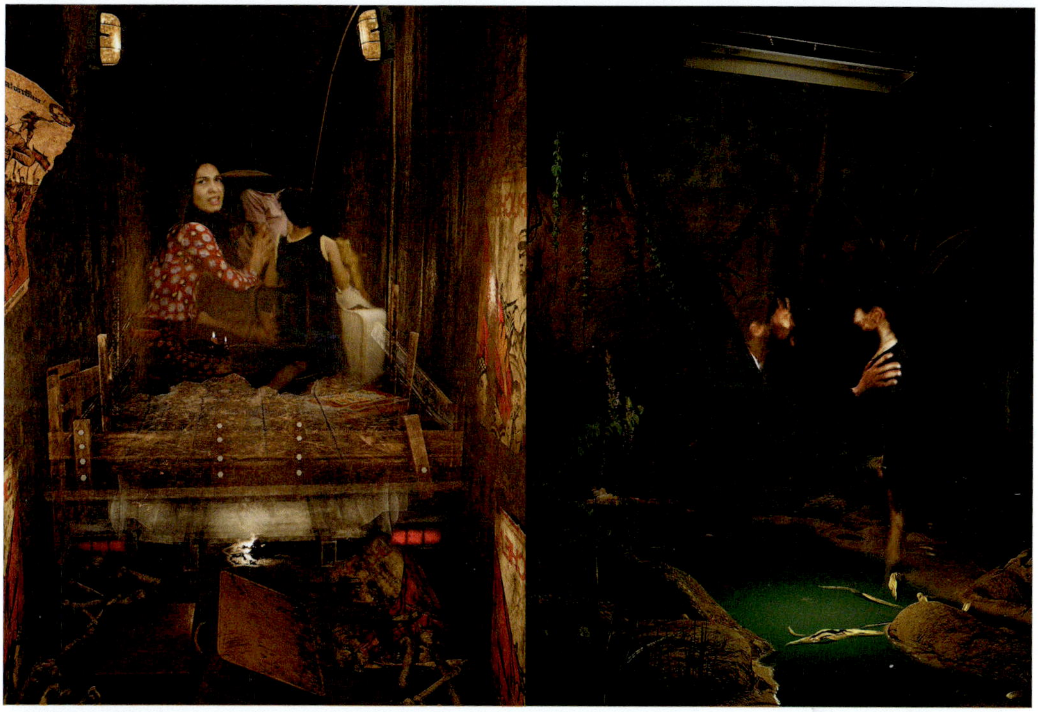

PLATE 18A&B 18a (left): *Stay Alive My Son* – in-game Screenshot: The Truck Scene, 2024, (UME Studios & Victoria Bousis). 18b (right): *Stay Alive My Son* – in-game Screenshot: The River Scene, 2024 (© UME Studios & Victoria Bousis).

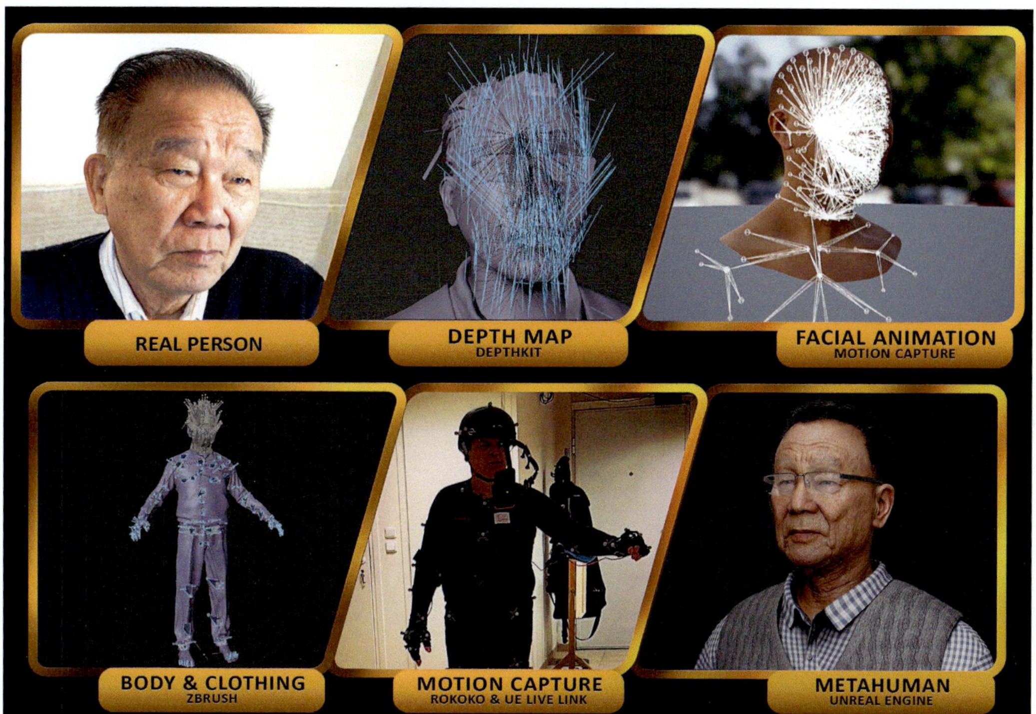

PLATE 19 Character Design: Digital Human Creation Pipeline, 2021–2024 (© UME Studios & Victoria Bousis).

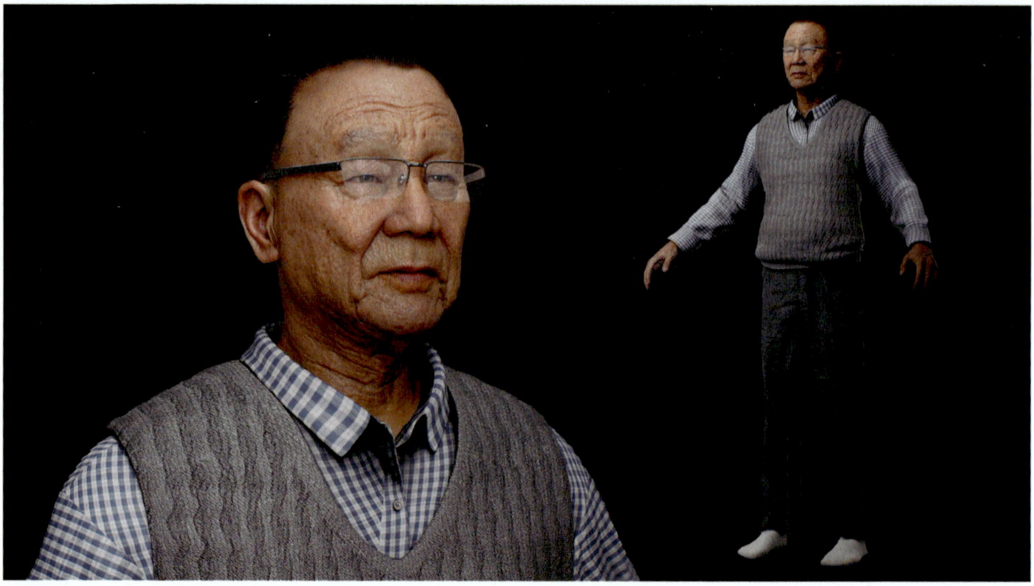

PLATE 20 Digital Yathay Pin: Front View & Side View, 2021–2024 (© UME Studios & Victoria Bousis).

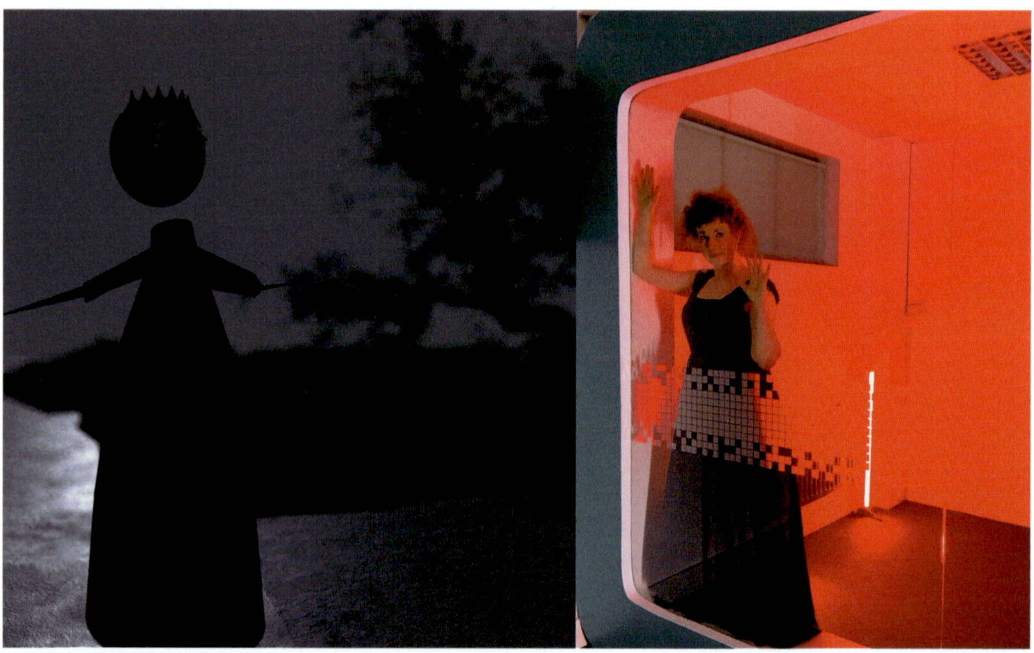

PLATE 21A&B 21a (left): Character 'C' played by Caitríona Ní Mhurchú, *Emperor 101*, 2021, (© Leon Butler, Jo Mangan, Peter Power, Tom Swift). 21b (right): Caitriona Ni Mhurchu in a pod or 'bubble' in The Performance Corporation's *Emperor 101*, 2021 (© Jo Mangan).

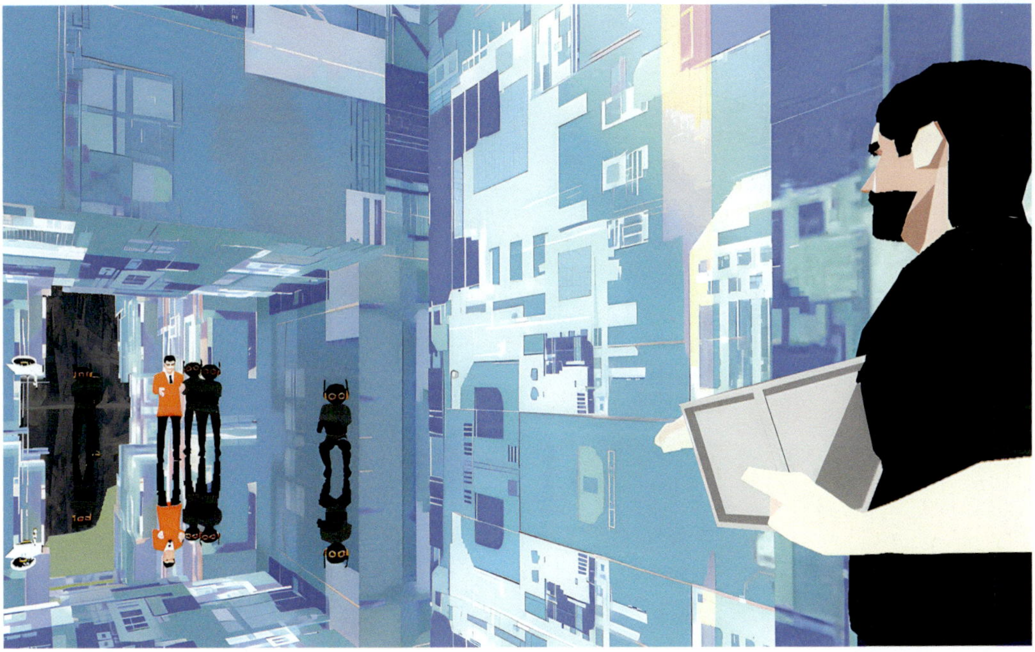

PLATE 22 Chief Yang and former CTO Han are facing each other in a glitchy space where the data is not fully loaded, 2023 (© Mina Hyeon).

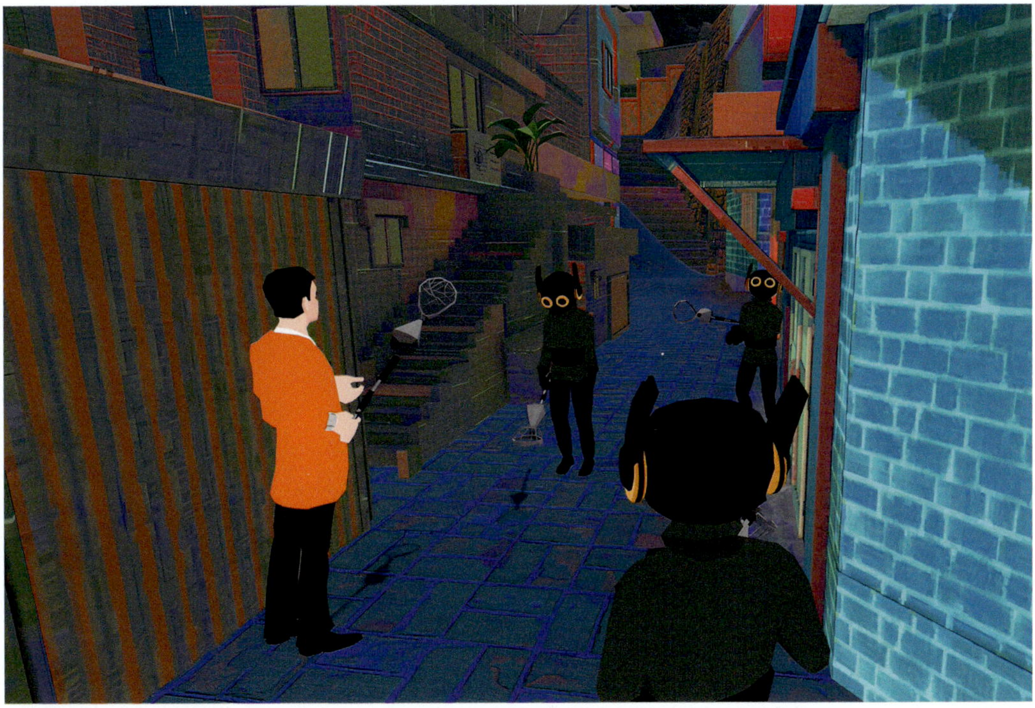

PLATE 23 Chief Yang is instructing the newcomers on how to use the *WiiLii* collecting tool, 2023 (© Mina Hyeon).

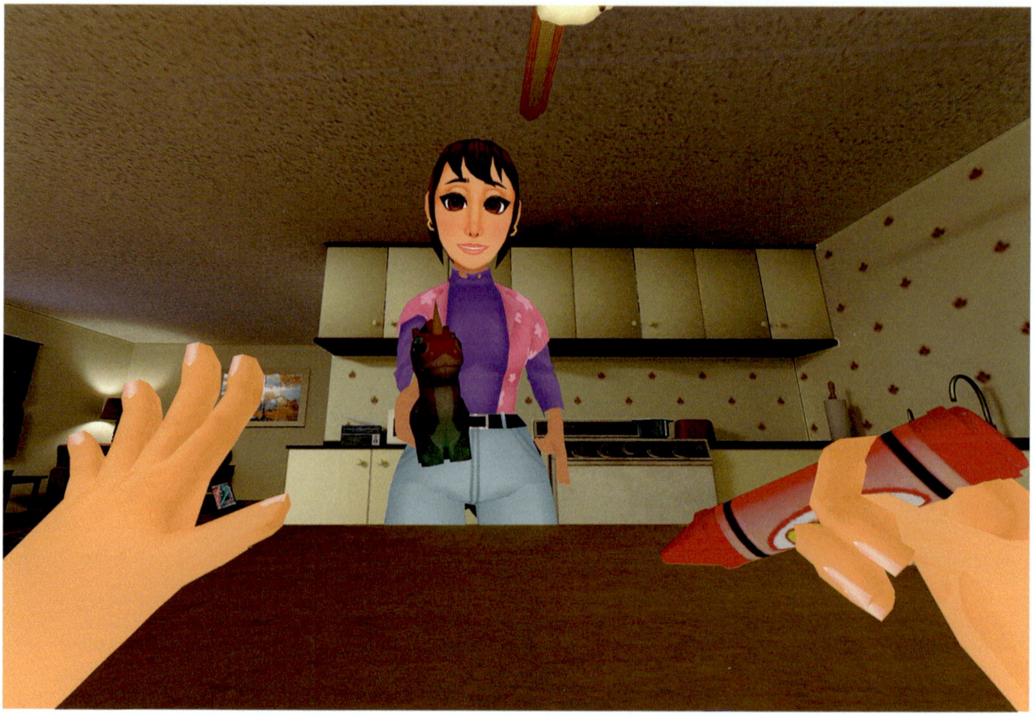

PLATE 24 *Welcome to Respite*, Mom from Alex's point of view (POV), 2024 (© Stephen Butchko).

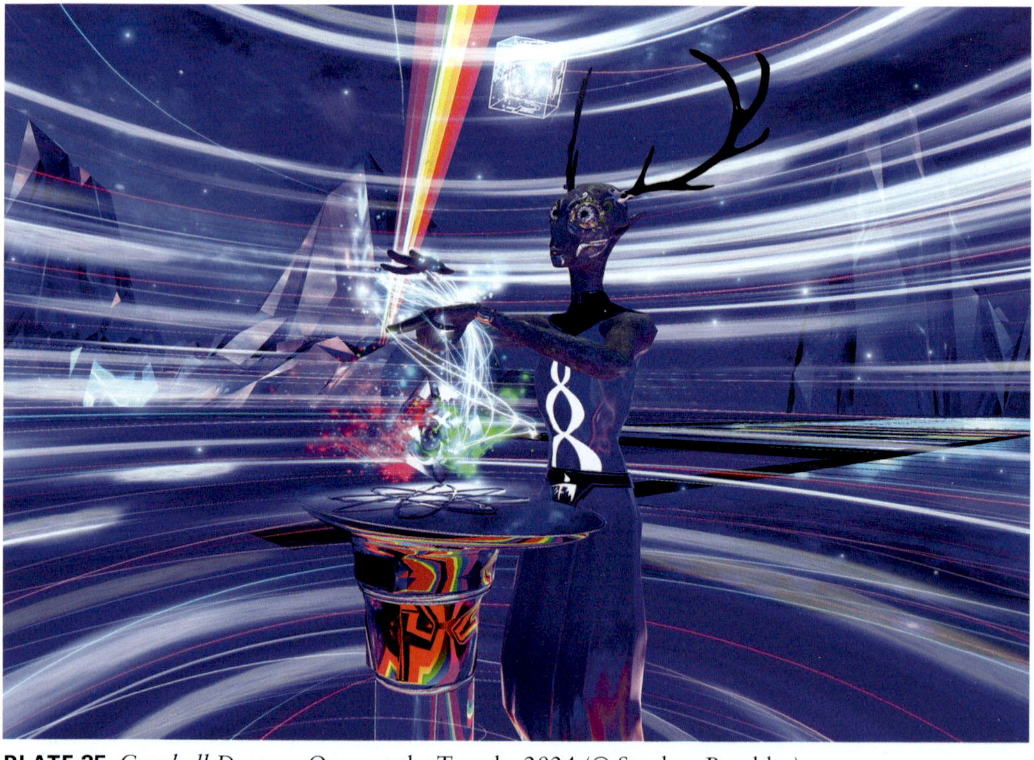

PLATE 25 *Gumball Dreams*, Onyx at the Temple, 2024 (© Stephen Butchko).

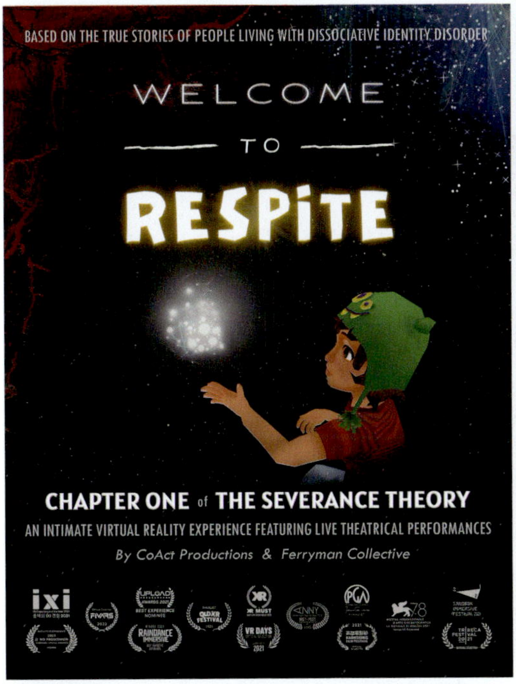

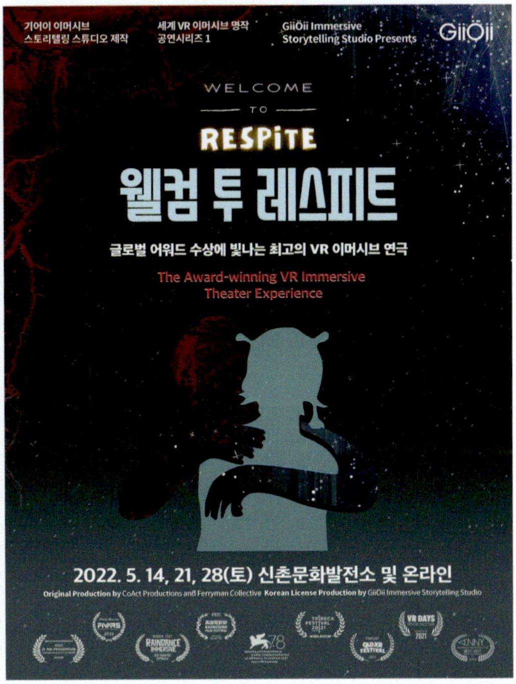

PLATE 26 *Welcome to Respite*, (left) English Poster, 2021 (© CoAct and Ferryman Collective) and (right) Korean Poster, 2020 (© GiiÖii Immersive Storytelling Studio).

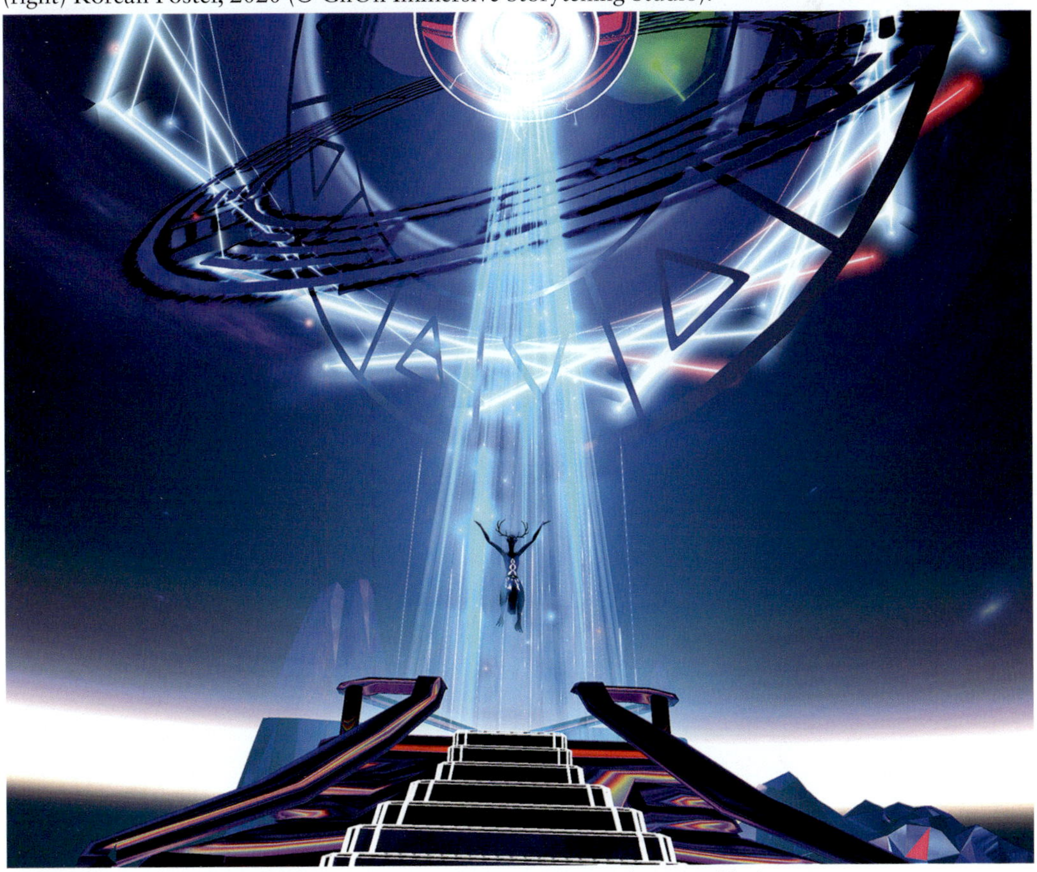

PLATE 27 *Gumball Dreams*, Onyx Ascention, 2024 (© Stephen Butchko).

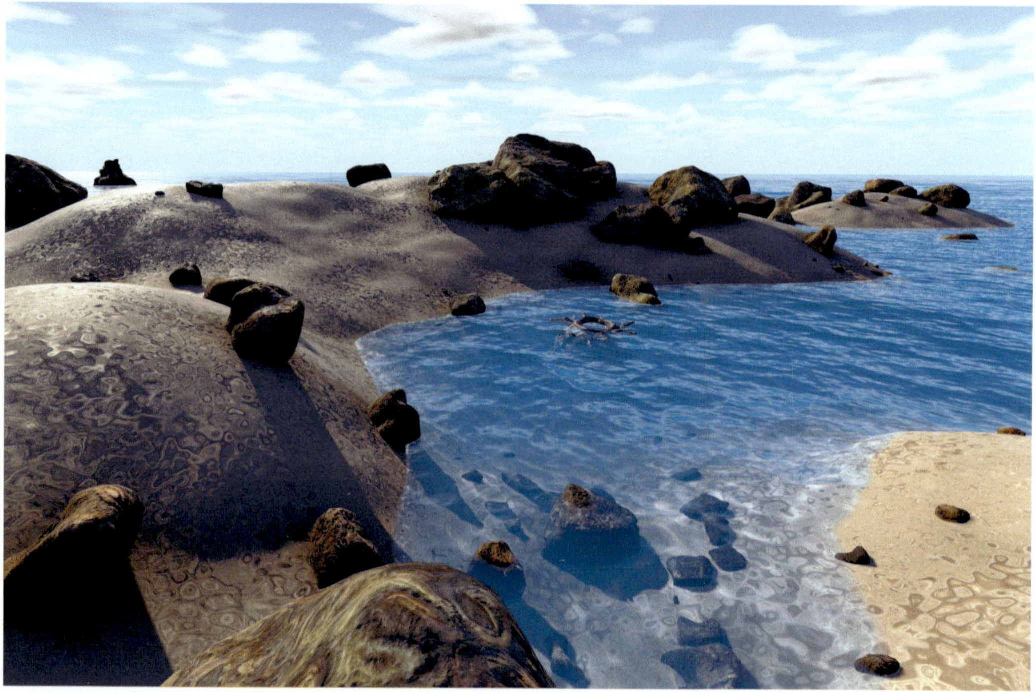

PLATE 28 Landscape view of *Namuanki*, 2022 (© Kevin Mack).

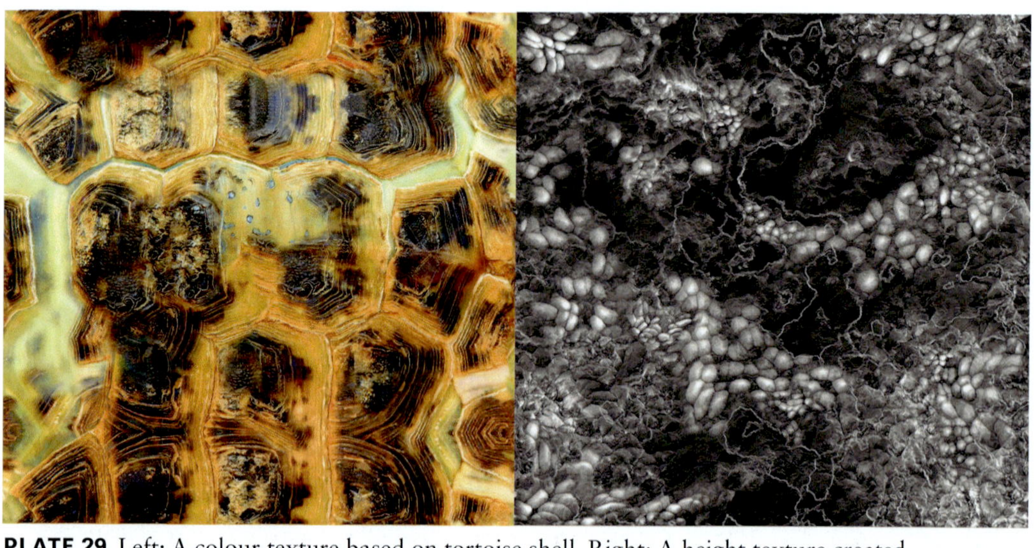

PLATE 29 Left: A colour texture based on tortoise shell. Right: A height texture created procedurally, 2022 (© Kevin Mack).

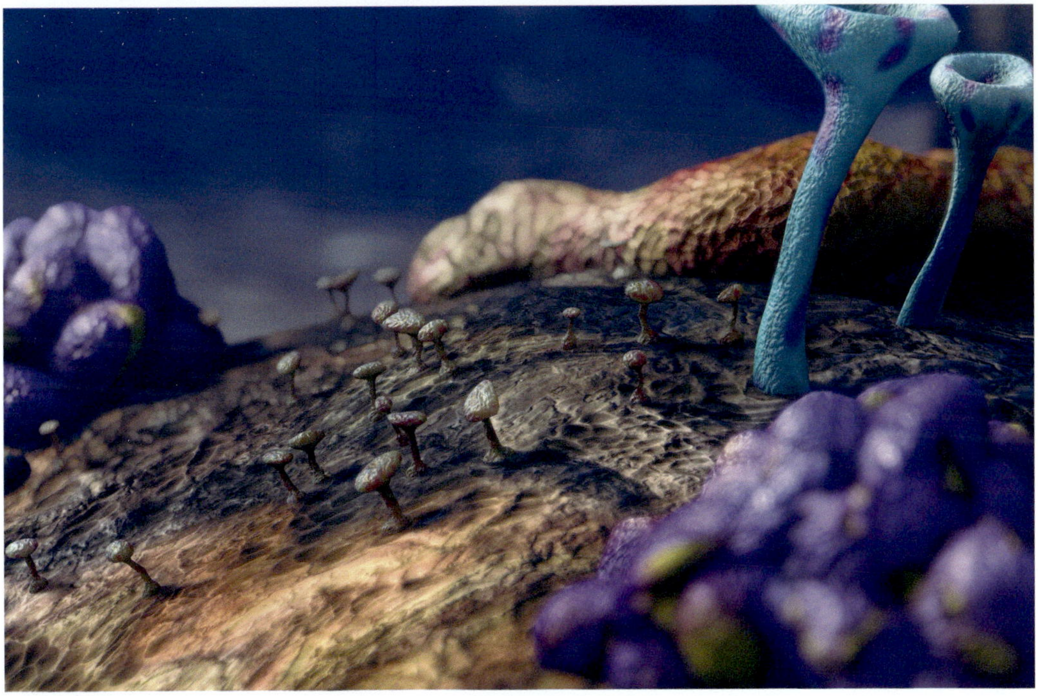

PLATE 30 Procedural reef life, 2022 (© Kevin Mack).

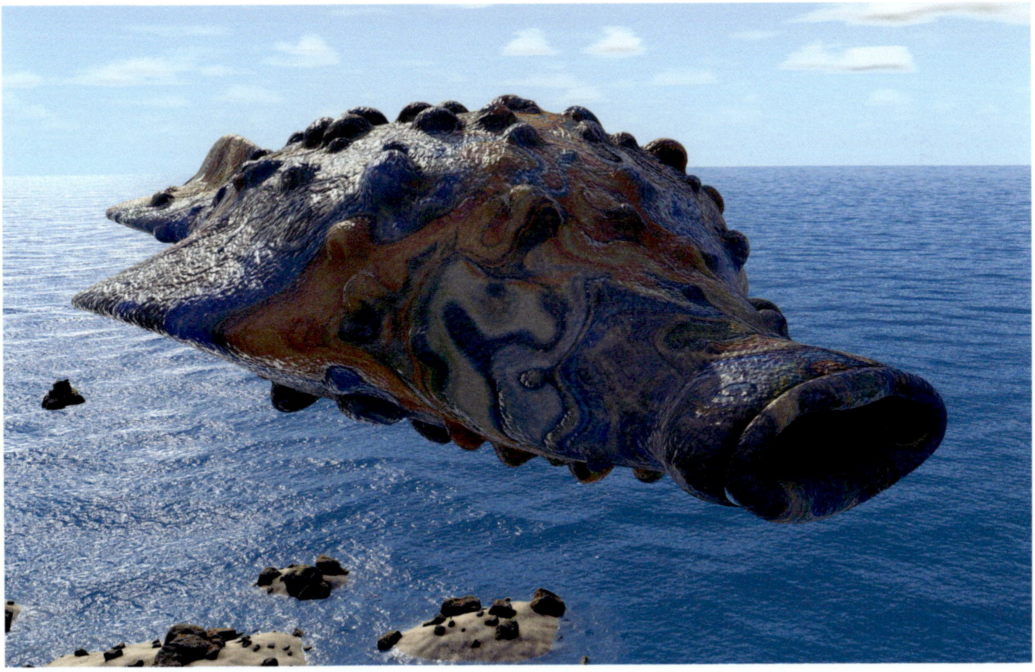

PLATE 31 'An', the Sky Whale, 2022 (© Kevin Mack).

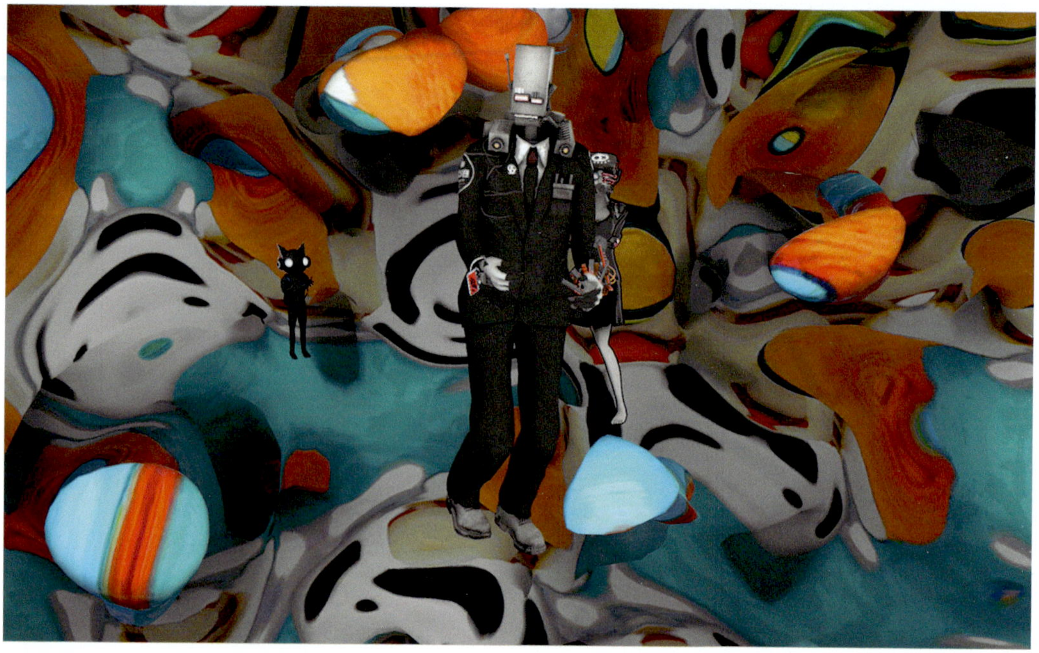

PLATE 32 Visitor Avatars inside a 'mystical vision', 2022 (© Kevin Mack).

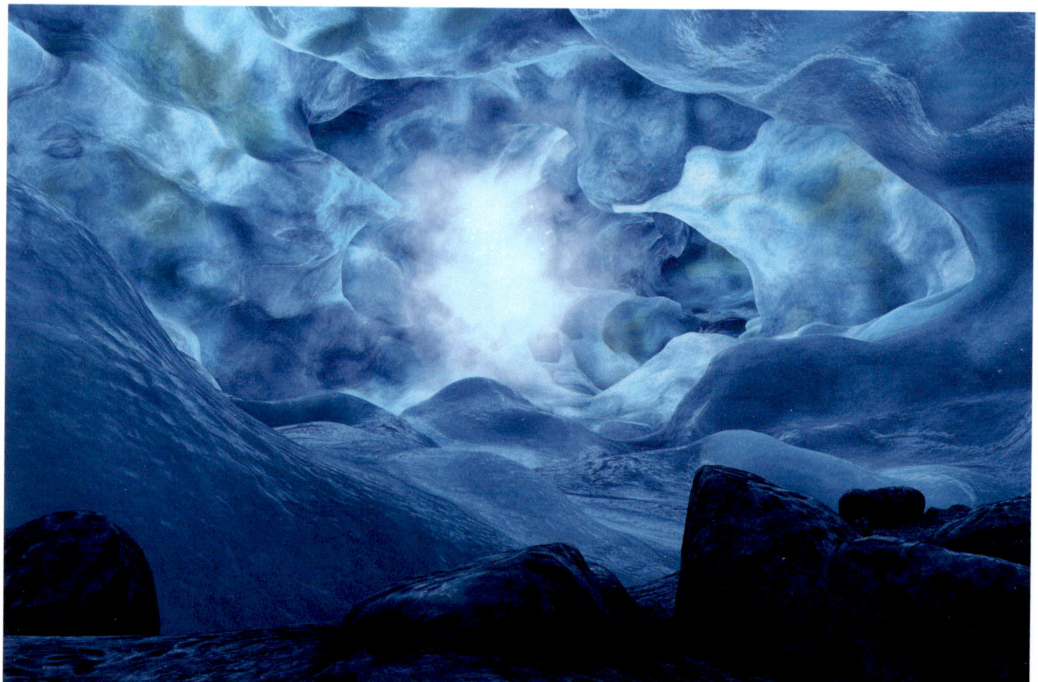

PLATE 33 The Ice Cave of Feth Fiada, 2022 (© Kevin Mack).

7

Live music, motion capture and VR: Creating new immersive environments for music performance and composition

Sophy Smith

Introduction

This chapter draws on practice-based research undertaken as part of the Audiences of the Future demonstrator project, which explored the creative potential of immersive technologies in live performance (funded by UK Research and Innovation through the Industrial Strategy Challenge Fund). This practice-based research explored virtual environments as a space for improvisatory composition, as well as an environment within which to engage and interact with the completed piece. VR is an emerging environment for sonic projects, highlighted in the popularity of recent VR audio experiences. However, little research has been carried out concerning how the affordances of virtual environments can offer new modes of creation for composers and new modes of engagement for music audiences. By foregrounding practice, specifically the voice of the practitioners and their reflections upon their practice, this chapter documents and analyses both process and product, drawing on interviews with the transdisciplinary collaborative team. In doing so, the chapter discusses the making of the piece, analysing and reflecting upon the transdisciplinary creative process and the prototyping framework used, which integrated devising methodologies from performance disciplines into a transdisciplinary design process. It also discusses and analyses the completed piece and outlines the implications and possibilities for future performance practice in this area. This chapter will be relevant to those interested in making new work in virtual environments – not only in relation to the new performance environments that are offered but also to how these environments are beginning to change the way work is made, and in doing so, changing the nature of the work itself.

Background to the practice-based prototyping labs

The Audience of the Future live performance consortium, led by the Royal Shakespeare Company, was a group of fifteen specialist organizations and pioneers in immersive technology bringing together their expertise in theatre and performance, the music industry, XR and virtual production, gaming and the research sector to explore what it means to perform live using technologies such as virtual reality (VR) (a fully immersive virtual world), augmented reality (AR) (the physical world with an overlay of digital elements) and mixed reality (the physical world with an overlay of digital elements where physical and digital elements are able to interact).

The Audience of the Future (Performance) (AOTFP) consortium was funded within the Audience of the Future programme by UK Research and Innovation through the Industrial Strategy Challenge Fund. One of the research partners in the project was the Institute of Creative Technologies (IOCT) a transdisciplinary research institute based at De Montfort University, Leicester. The IOCT's role was to explore and develop transdisciplinary prototyping processes for immersive performance and this practice-based research was carried out through a number of prototyping labs, developing proof-of-concept immersive performance experiences.

The labs took place within two work packages relating to Intensive Practice Research Labs that worked in consort – one focused on transdisciplinary lab-based investigations to explore proof-of-concept performance work relating to future audiences and immersive technologies, and the other focused on working with focus groups to evaluate engagement and accessibility. The objectives, woven across the two work packages, included: to understand the nature of the potential future audience and their modes of interaction and engagement, to use this knowledge as a framework through which to develop experimental proof-of-concept performance work focusing on user experience (UX) to 'fold-in' audience feedback to the creative process, to evaluate the audience's accessibility to and engagement with immersive content and, finally, to develop a framework of practice, arising from the findings of the practical research. To enable the approaches to develop without constraint, the prototyping labs did not follow any pre-prescribed methodologies but developed organically. The process was then analysed in retrospect, supported by observations recorded at the time and by user-testing and post-project interviews with the transdisciplinary team. A key role within this approach was that of the 'noticer', a researcher independent of the wider project, who observed the process and 'noticed' any micro or macro occurrences relating to the research foci, allowing the researchers working within the experience to fully concentrate on the developing the prototype. It is important that the noticer has significant expertise in the area of practice – the noticer for this project was Kerry Francksen, an independent researcher with expertise across performance, technology and interdisciplinary collaboration.

Practice review

In his 2019 book *The Digital Musician,* Andrew Hugill describes the transformational effect that digital technologies have had on music practices, reflecting on how they have 'transformed the way music is created and heard, composed and performed, produced and distributed. The world that surrounds the musician, the cultural context, has changed in many ways' (p.2). This in turn, Hugill reflects, has created a 'new' type of musician who embraces the possibilities of 'digital tools and devices which enable musical invention and discovery' (p.4). To be a digital musician, Hugill continues, one needs a combination of four interdependent factors – aural awareness, cultural knowledge, musical abilities and technical skills (p. 4). Hugill reflects on the promises offered by Virtual Reality to the digital musician:

> The embodiment of the performed within the virtual space offers real possibilities of gestural and haptic interactions that may be creatively exploited ... Motion capture, bio-sensing, machine intelligence and similar technologies may be effectively combined with VR to build a musical experience that is genuinely new.
>
> (p. 225)

XR, more widely, is an emerging environment for audio experiences, and a wide range of practices has been developed in recent years. To date, a number of large-scale music performances have taken place within existing computer games, including *Fortnite* (Marshmello, Travis Scott and Ariana Grande), *Roblox* (Royal Blood and Lil Nas X) and *Minecraft* (BTS). In 2022, the MTV Music Video Awards added a category for Best Metaverse Performance, which was won by Korean pop girl group Blackpink for their in-game performance made in *PUBG: Battlegrounds* (previously known as *PlayerUnknown's Battlegrounds*), a battle royal game developed and published by PUBG Studios. The company Wave produces interactive virtual concerts, merging gaming, real-time motion-capture and live musical performance into an immersive interactive experience (Aswad 2021). Musicians including John Legend, The Weeknd and Justin Bieber have performed live shows on Wave, their movements captured and transmitted to a digital avatar in real time before being broadcast to a remote audience tuning globally on wave.watch and across social and gaming platforms including YouTube, Twitter, Twitch, TikTok, Facebook and *Roblox* (wavexr.com). In 2022 Epic Games Publishing produced the *Kid A Mnesia Exhibition*, available on Mac, PC and PS5, an exploration game based on the music and artwork of the Radiohead albums *Kid A* and *Amnesiac*.

In terms of headset-based audio experiences, in 2018, Sigur Rós collaborated with Magic Leap Studios to create *Tónandi* (2018), an interactive mixed-reality music experience where the user can manipulate sounds by interacting with visuals around them. Audio experiences specifically for VR have included game-based experiences such as *Beat Saber* and *Audio Trip* and more exploratory creation experiences with virtual instruments such as *Virtuoso* and *Unplugged*. In addition, artists such as French electronic pioneer Jean-Michel Jarre and rock guitarist Slash have created performances in VR – Jarre performing the concert 'Alone Together' in VRChat, with Vive body tracking and real-time audio streaming and Slash performing work via Soundscape VR, utilizing its Magic Mirror tool that enables 2D content to be experienced in VR.

Specifics of the PBR prototype

While the commercial artists discussed above have embraced the opportunities afforded by XR, these performances/experiences have tended to focus on new distribution platforms and experiences for existing musical content. As Hugill reflects, although the potential of VR for music performance is immense, many VR music performances merely replicate existing performance experiences, for example, the live concert experience (either filmed in 360-degree video – for example the Philharmonia Orchestra including *Beethoven's Fifth* and *Mahler's Third* or avatar-fronted game-based concerts in *Fortnite*, *Roblox* and *Minecraft*) – missing the opportunity for a *'new creative element that is aligned to the characteristics of the technology itself'* (p.225). Little practice or research has been carried out concerning how the affordances of virtual environments can offer new modes of creation for composers and new modes of engagement for music audiences.

The proof-of-concept prototyping lab discussed in this chapter focused on live performance in Virtual Reality. The prototype drew together a transdisciplinary team across music performance, spatial audio, motion capture and games programming. The proof-of-concept piece was founded on capturing a cellist's motion in performance and the live processing of the motion capture data in the Unreal game engine. This enabled the movement of the cellist to have a visual relationship with the Unreal environment. The prototype did not aim to represent the live physical presence of the performer in a virtual space through an avatar. Instead, it used the movement generated by the live performer to affect the virtual environment. This approach offered a new mode of improvisatory composition, where the musician and environment were symbiotically linked, each affecting the development of the other. The selection of the cello as the musical instrument within the motion captured environment was deliberate, as the cello necessitates a great deal of body movement in performance, which would generate a good amount of data to be created for the reactive visuals.

Process (environment, structure and collaborative relationships)

The discussion of the process of creating the VR prototype expands beyond the order in which things took place. The process of creating a transdisciplinary prototype was wider than what happened. It expanded into where it happened (the creative environment) and how it happened (the collaborative relationships).

The proof of concept prototype was made over one month, including establishing the transdisciplinary team, pre-project planning and an intensive R&D week, incorporating user-testing. Team members included a collaboration lead (with overall project management and producing responsibilities), a Cellist (a musician with experience in improvised practice and live performance), a motion capture specialist, a spatial audio engineer and a creative technologist working with the Unreal game engine. The starting points for the lab were very open – to work together to explore the potential of a reactive environment to create a new space for composition and performance. The lab broke down into two distinct foci: firstly, to take the motion capture data generated in performance and to use them to develop an engaging and beautiful experience to be experienced in VR; and, secondly, to experiment with the live streaming of this experience in VR and, thirdly, to test the experience on users.

Environment (where)?

To support this organic prototyping, for the majority of the lab, the team worked together in one shared lab space, which supported what Alistair Cockburn describes as 'osmotic communication' (2004), where team members work in the same room and information flows into the background hearing of team members. They receive information as though by osmosis (p.40). Questions and answers flow naturally, and with little disturbance; therefore, knowledge is disseminated quickly (p.40). This was supported by the arrangement of the lab space (see Figure 7.1), where all team members could see and communicate with each other at all times. The cellist (A) was situated in the centre of the motion capture volume, wearing the motion capture suit and seated with the cello. An amp and pedals were placed at their feet. To their left was a monitor showing the feed from Unreal incorporating the motion capture data. To their front were the other team members. The cellist was able to adjust their movement to focus either on the monitor, the team members or across the two. The spatial sound specialist was situated in front of the cellist but out of the volume, to ensure that any recording was as un-invasive as possible. The motion capture specialist and the creative technologist (C and D) sat side by side, behind their separate computer workstations with simultaneous visibility of the motion capture data, the Unreal build, the feed from Unreal (incorporating the motion capture data) and the cellist in the volume. This enabled them to work across the workflow directly, with visibility of each other's actions. By sitting together, they could discuss approaches, challenges and solutions directly. The cellist was constantly in eye-line, so communication between the three was easy. The Lead Collaborator, Sophy Smith (PI on the AOFTP project), was also present in the room throughout the process, situated apart from the process, but able to see the whole workflow across the collaborators:

> [the cellist] is sat centre-stage playing; their movements are being captured by numerous infra-red cameras positioned above their head height, whilst copious amounts of wires scatter away from them in various directions … Covered in tracking markers, surrounded by cameras and wires, you can imagine how tricky it must be to move the bow gently backwards and forwards across the cello's fingerboard. And yet, the air is charged, and the room filled with magical tones. As the cello sings, the wires, the cameras and the computers all seem to disappear into the background, leaving the room to fill with dulcet notes and imaginary textures conveyed by the sounds of the cello.
>
> (Francksen 2021)

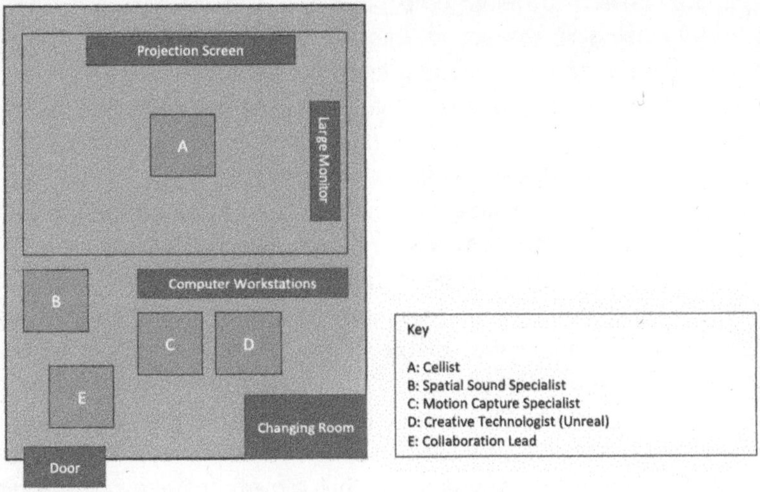

FIGURE 7.1 Lab layout, including position of collaborators (© Sophy Smith).

Structure (what)?

While the prototyping was fluid, there was a clear structure to the week, designed and maintained by the Collaboration Lead, through which a working prototype could be achieved. The Collaboration Lead supported the team to explore their ideas while keeping them focused on the completion of the prototype. Key to the success was the pre-project planning stage, where the Collaboration Lead met with collaborators separately in advance of the lab to outline the rationale for the project and begin to scope out opportunities and challenges. During this time, the collaborators shared past work with each other to contextualize their practice. The motion capture specialist and Unreal developer also met to discuss and establish the technical workflow, and the cellist and creative technologists both developed work in advance of the lab, enabling initial ideas to be workshopped quickly. The cellist Dave Dhonau reflected:

> In terms of music, I had a number of sections with different dynamics and hopefully a variety of movement and each part could be extended or shortened as needed or joined together in different ways. I also had a loop pedal, so one potential approach was to build layers of sound, which could somehow be represented or blended visually. Motion capture and VR was a completely new world for me so I was much looking forward to learning how it works …!
>
> (Dhonau 2022)

The cellist was asked to develop some material in terms of physical movement, rather than focusing on the sound – small medium and big – and was also asked to prepare a range of textures, timbres and velocities, to explore how these may affect reactional visuals. The duration of the piece was restricted to three minutes due to the amount of data that would be generated and the length of time it would therefore take to process.

The intensive lab took place over five days. The transdisciplinary team worked together in the lab for two sets of two days, broken by a day where the Unreal developer worked alone to build the interactive environment. Day 1 focused on experimentation and exploring the potential of the digital space. This included establishing the relationships between discipline areas and collaborators. Different marker set-ups were used for motion capture, and various ways of integrating these into the Unreal environment were explored. Most of the time was spent allowing the cellist to explore performing during motion capture and how the impact of his movement affected the digital environment. The cellist was asked to develop some material with a range of physical movements to explore the effect that different performative dynamics would have on the reactive visuals. The cellist came up with ideas, which were developed through improvisation in the reactive environment.

It is important to note that the process of calibrating the motion-capture system and ensuring that the performer, bow and cello are mapped precisely is a lengthy one, taking around an hour. However, while time consuming, this methodical procedure of wanding, calibrating and checking marker placement established a systematic and procedural process that was both meticulous in its aims and clear in its focus. The cellist wore a motion capture suit and could see the Unreal environment his performance was affecting on a large screen in front of himself. This had an immediate effect on the cellist's creative practice. Different sounds and movements were explored, to see how they affected the environment. As an improvisatory performer, the cellist was able to collaborate with the system, 'playing' the environment. At first, it was difficult for the cellist to feel relaxed in the motion capture suit, but this quickly became part of a new routine (Dhonau 2022). As the day progressed, the cellist spent lengthy periods of time exploring the relationship between the physical movement, the digital environment and the different timbres and motifs that arose from this physical/digital relationship. This tension between the internal world of the composer and the external world of the physical performance is discussed in greater detail below, in relation to the different collaborative relationships that emerged during the prototyping process.

Day 2 focused on capturing both the movement and the audio. An early iteration of the environment included 3D geometric shapes, which changed in colour dependent on the movement of the cellist and the environment was developed, incorporating trees and rocks, initiated by the Unreal developer.

Following the explorations in day 1, the cellist formulated parameters for his improvisation based on what had interesting effects within the environment. Three movement data sets were explored: rigid bodies (the bow and the cello fingerboard), skeleton (the performer), and rigid bodies and the skeleton. The term 'rigid bodies' refers to where the motion capture markers are placed on inflexible objects where the positions of the relative markers do not change, in this case where they are placed on the bow and the fingerboard. Skeletons are markersets for the human body, where the markers position in relation to each other has been pre-programmed.

Experiments relating to how best to add the motion capture markers to the cello and bow were solved with Velcro hats being placed at the top and bottom of the fingerboard and attached with gaffer tape to the bow. The performer began to be very aware of their movements and the relationship between the movement and the sound generated. The cellist remarked:

> an interesting part for me was seeing how the developing visual elements would change the way I was approaching the music. it just had geometric forms – a sphere and a cube – and my motion was affecting the light and shadow and some of the colour as well. For each iteration of the reactive visuals that was applied, suddenly a certain type of motion was having a different effect, and that was very interesting. That was not like anything I've ever played with. Strange, but really quite fascinating. Quite immersive ... in an unusual way.
>
> (Dhonau 2022)

Day 3 saw the Unreal developer working alone, needing time to develop the responsive environment further, in response to learnings from the first two days. This need for a collaborator to retreat to their disciplinary environment and practices to develop elements of the work that would then be brought back to the whole group as part of the development process is referred to by Cockburn as a 'caves and common' arrangement (p.43). In this approach, part of the Agile Methodology, 'common' describes an open plan area, where teams collaborate in close physical proximity and 'caves' as individual working areas apart from the commons, but in close proximity. By being able to move between collaborative space and individual space, team members were able to incorporate shorter time-outs while retaining Osmotic Communication.

Day 4 brought the team back together again. Most of the day was spent enabling the performer to fully explore the developed responsive environment and continue developing the environment in response to the performer's use. The performer and Unreal developer collaborated to develop the most effective performance and environment, developing the environment in response to the way the cellist engaged with the environment, thereby developing the relationship between movement and visuals. Francksen noted:

> The translation of [the cellist's] musicking in the dystopian forest takes on a hybrid fusion of physical practice (the playing), and technological translation (the creative technologist's interpretations) … I imagine that the very act of being in the sound world must have had a qualitative effect on the creative technologist and I therefore can't help wondering if the Forest creation was in part influenced by the haunting, melancholy sounds of the cello. In one improvisation, I was struck by how the sound grew and then retreated in intensity. Deep, guttural tones became intermingled with the soft sweeping higher notes as [the cellist] continued to make the instrument sing. I was interested to notice how this rich intensity then became translated digitally. The character of the sounds in the room were enchanting and the experience, even for me as an observer, was utterly transfixing. This is interesting in terms of identifying an overall creative intention. Was it in fact the sound itself that enhanced the characteristic qualities in the VR world too?

Francksen describes how the creative technologist's developing visualization was having an identifiable impact on the cellist's process of creativity, as each time the cellist re-experienced his musical gesturing in VR, it was clear to see a physical adjustment in the way he was playing and moving (Francksen 2021). The cellist reflected:

> It's almost like a simulated kind of synthesthia, because a movement or a kind of a sound does have a colour or a change in shape … Having that visualization was a really interesting aspect to it, but it would change very dramatically. I remember it went from that very stark geometry into this kind of video-game like environment, to an environment with trees and leaves … you feel like you're part of a bigger process … you're aware that there's this technological thing happening with data that's then being thrown back at you very directly, with colour and form.
>
> (Dhonau 2022)

Day 5 focused on experiencing the live performance in VR. First the performer was placed in VR to explore the effect that such full immersion would have on his improvisation. The cellist performed while wearing the VR headset and could see himself as an avatar in the VR environment. For the cellist, this was an incredibly intense experience and presented the possibilities of performing within VR. The second part of the day included testing the user experience of engaging with the live performance in VR, with the user wearing the headset and being placed in the Unreal environment while the cellist performed the piece. A Wizard of Oz (WOZ) approach was used for this testing to work around networking and audio latency issues. WOZ is credited to usability expert Dr Jeff Kelley (1983), where developers create a basic model of the completed product, which may either use every-day objects to represent parts of the finished product or it may be a working model, that has some of the affordances of the final product. Users can then role-play with the WOZ prototype to see how it would work in practice (Laskowski 2014). In this project this approach was applied to initial user testing. Rather than setting up a network over which the user could experience the work remotely, the user was placed in VR within the same room as the performer. The purpose of the testing was to evaluate the user's experience of the prototype rather than testing the reliability of a network, so the WOZ approach was deemed sufficient.

How (collaborative relationships)?

Francksen reflects that as the days progressed and as the work being developed, moving from the calibration stages towards the capturing and translation of data into Unreal, the distinct disciplines of music, motion capture and programming began to overlap and inform the resulting artwork:

> the resulting artwork was an amalgamation of processes that were both creative and technological. In other words, the utopian-singing and dancing forest became a hybrid realization of the physical craft of music making in tandem an augmented amplification via VR processing. The resulting interactive sound and visual VR environment was only possible because of the exchanges and varying collaborations that were evolving in the room.
>
> (Francksen 2021)

The relationship between the collaborators, and the characteristics of those relationships enabled the team to operate with 'real care and attention'. This was especially important due to the complex experience for the cellist:

> such a process requires real stamina, especially for [the cellist] who had to keep his performance quality operating at a high level for a sustained length of time. The technological situation, therefore, required him to repeat gestures with enough precision and exactness, which presented a different challenge from the normal processes involved in rehearsal. Add

> into the mix the restrictions placed on [the cellist's] movements, as well as the system being able to stream clean data, the demands on them as a performer were tangible.
>
> (Francksen 2021)

Stamina and patience were key characteristics, as each member had to be attuned and open to trying and re-testing things many times over, working within their own disciplinary parameters, yet also working beyond them. Francksen reflected:

> In my conversations with the creative technologist, it became clear that the technicalities involved in processing the data were the foundation for his decision-making process. As an expert in his field, it was evident that he knew exactly what could be achieved technologically. Listening to him describe some of what he was doing in terms of his workflow, highlighted the distinction between processing data via comprehensible procedures and the sometimes messy and chaotic nature of creativity. In and of itself, this was interesting to observe and supports the idea that producing fruitful VR work comes from a fusion of these two things.
>
> (Francksen 2021)

The selection of collaborators, in terms of approach as well as expertise, is key to the open development of prototypes. Francksen commented:

> I wonder, if another cellist, or another programmer, or another sound engineer hadn't been as generous as those present in the room, would this project have been as successful as it was? In summary, this type of work almost dictates a certain level of collaborative working ethics – each element needs to come together in such a way that every step of the process is supportive, open, and honest.
>
> (Francksen 2021)

Sue Broadhurst, in *Digital Practices* (2017), discusses the tensions that exist 'within the spaces created by this interface of body and technology' (p.1), reflecting how 'the virtual body (as any other body) inscribes its presence and absence in the very act of its performance, leaving gaps and spaces in its wake. I suggest it is within these tension-filled spaces that opportunities arise for new experimental forms and practices' (p.1). The point of tension within the cellist's exploration of creative practice within a virtual environment lies in the dual focus required from the performer, both on the musical performance itself and on the application of that performance within the reactive environment. As the team moved from calibration to creation, Francksen noted the significant relationship between the cellist's physicality and the objects in the screen world:

> The translation of the cellist's movements and sounds via their avatar counterpart felt inextricably connected because every action that occurred in the physical world (the music making) and in the virtual world (the mirroring avatars), was being continually influenced by the other. In terms of a creative practice, this indeed highlights a very particular need to manage physical execution at the same time as mastering any digital translation.
>
> (Francksen 2021)

The cellist explains:

> I still have that other focus, which is trying to hear what I'm doing and try and make it sound as good as I can. So then there's always that more traditional part of it, so I can't completely get lost in the VR, you know, the motion and the visual of that ... it's just different ... if you're performing, you're aware that there's a physical, gestural aspect that's outside of just playing the notes. If you're performing with other people, there's always an interaction that's outside of yourself, so it's a different kind of collaboration.
>
> (Dhonau 2022)

This relationship between the physical execution of performance and the digital translation of that physicality proved to be a key challenge for the cellist. Understanding this will be key when looking to develop digital environments such as this for music creation and music reception. In *The Merging of Musician and Music Instrument*, Luc Nijs posits how musical expressiveness arises from the 'push-and-pull' process between a musician's internal (self) and external world (non-self) (p50). The internal world, she suggests (citing Leman 2007 and Nijs et al. 2012), is 'motor trajectories, internal thought processes relating to the self, musical intentions and feelings'. A key element of this internal world is the internal model of the music, created through practice and previous experience, that guides the musician's actions during performance. The external world, is constituted by the space of sensory trajectories that arise from the interaction with the musical environment (Leman 2007). The way this push-and-pull between internal and external worlds shapes the performance depends on the relationship between musician and instrument (Nils, p.50). For the cellist, the push-and-pull between the internal and external worlds are more complex because the external world involves not only the traditional musical environment but also the new reactive digital environment which, in turn, impacts upon the cellist's internal world relating to musical intentions.

Nijs states that attention should be focused on the musical environment (external world) rather than on the technicalities of handling the instrument (internal world), but the complexities of encountering and developing new technicalities may pull the musician's focus away from the musical environment, especially where the cellist encounters two layers of the external world simultaneously – the cello and the reactive environment. This push-and-pull experience was articulated by the cellist:

> I preferred the first really simple reactive environment, which was just the lighting and the colouring of shapes ... I could tell that Ryan was having loads of fun building it [the forest], but to be able to track what each gesture is doing, it was really helpful to just to see a spotlight getting brighter ... that simplicity [is] quick to absorb and feed into what I'm doing. When there's something very immersive in its own right, it's more aesthetically complex and it's a little bit harder to integrate that into playing. So it's better when I see strongly the input that I'm having on it [the environment], because that became not just the playing of the cello, but whole body movement affecting it.

Additionally, the newness of the external environment makes it challenging for the cellist to display Leman's paradigm of embodied cognition (Leman 2007), where 'expressive performance relies on the degree to which the body can play its role as a natural mediator and freely enact the musical intentions'. To achieve this, the musical instrument needs to disappear from consciousness and become a 'natural' extension of the musician by being incorporated into the 'natural mediator' of the human-music interaction – 'the human body' (Leman 2007; Nils et all, 2013). This is tricky, where the musician is extremely conscious of the body's role in the external world and is exploring these new relationships between the internal and external worlds and also the musician is being pulled back to the physicality of their surroundings, making any unconscious action difficult. Francksen reflected on how the digital nature of the VR environment began to expose the cellist's physical attributes that may otherwise be hidden when they play:

> Consequently, the cellist seemed to be hyper aware of the physicality of playing. I'm sure they have improvised and repeated musical sequences thousands of times over. Yet, in this world (one where he was making music in both real and virtual space), they were seemingly re-engaging with the physical act of playing. This was, in part, a purely practical response as they tried to keep the markers in place. However, the very process of having to try and move with enough clarity and precision to allow for a

> clean capture as described earlier, magnified their movements tenfold. For example, the slight movement of their fingers, even the tapping of their foot was significant for their paralleling avatars.
>
> (Francksen 2021)

Final thoughts

The experimental lab outlined and discussed in this chapter was the cellist's first experience of VR in any capacity. Francksen reflects on how working in the reactional digital environment enables an experienced musician to experience their craft in a new way:

> It was striking to observe his intrigue as his movements and sounds were being translated in real-time – his curiosity, as the avatars moved in tandem with him, was palpable. I remember thinking how precious this moment was and how important the initial experiential stages of any new process are for advancing creativity.

The cellist acknowledged that experimentation with the potential uses of musical instruments goes hand in hand with musical creativity, reflecting, 'I don't see it as a sacred thing … it's a thing to do a job … why not use it in different ways?'. The experience was, at first, unsettling for the cellist who commented that he was *'freaked out'* by his duetting avatars /environment and felt that his brain didn't 'know what's real and what's not' (Francksen 2021). The system was asking him to do something different in performance terms, offering a 'fresh perspective and new sensibility' for the performer (Francksen 2021). The cellist remarked how the lab was 'a bit of a learning curve, a bit of a push out of the comfort zone', commenting, 'I don't really have any experience with VR so it was a strange moment … it was a completely different experience … I can see the potential of it' (Dhonau 2022).

The cellist also described the experience as 'tantilizing' (Dhonau 2022) and spoke about the potential of future explorations relating to networked live VR performance for an ensemble that they are part of:

> Maybe each member could have a few sensors … forms in a in a 3D space. I'd be interested to explore it a little bit more. I'm really interested in the immediacy of it as a live event that could be kind of experienced in real time.

The prototype was originally envisaged as an environment for a different kind of live experience of music performance for audiences, but what transpired was a new environment and tool for creative music practice, demonstrating how the affordances of VR can offer new modes of creative practice. The cellist reflected;

> I think that it's very exciting ... it felt like it was new. Something that could be really explored and has loads of potential. Everything was sparking new ideas.
>
> (Dhonau 2022)

The beginning of this chapter cited Hugill, who states how a digital musician requires a combination of four interdependent factors – aural awareness, cultural knowledge, musical abilities and technical skills (Hugill, p4). In terms of creative music practice in VR, musical abilities and technical skills are more interdependent than ever, as the musicality of the performance and the development of that performance within the technical system are symbiotically linked. While the musicality of the developing composition is still of paramount performance, this must also take into account what works in terms of data. This fascinating interplay between creative and technological practice offers exciting possibilities where VR can offer not only immersive environments for performance but for the creation and reception of new kinds of musical experience.

8

Volumetric capture in VR dance-theatre: Encounters with self and other in *Facades*

Kerryn Wise

Facades

This chapter presents critical practitioner reflections and analysis of audience feedback,[1] gathered through the development of a virtual reality (VR) experience entitled *Facades* (2021). *Facades* is a fifteen-minute room-scale VR experience where the audience member is subtly guided through different domestic spaces. Within this virtual house, participants encounter a volumetrically captured[2] (VolCap) performer playing different versions of herself. This unique, theatrical dance journey invites solo audience participants to engage with digital representations of a female performer, who when viewed frontally looks complete; however, when looking around the edges of the illusion, she becomes a fractured concave shell – a spectral facade.[3]

Facades begins with a doorway which the participant is encouraged to enter. A miniature house appears, inside which a woman is curiously dancing with a pair of red shoes. The next scene transports the participant to the scaled-up version of the house, where they are positioned outside a large window, peering in at the performer inside. The house unexpectedly starts to rotate, revealing another doorway which the participant is encouraged to enter. Later, the walls expand to reveal the performer running outside, caught in a windstorm. The walls gradually disappear to leave a vast blackness with just the lone performer reaching out, yearning to touch the visiting participant. The final scene returns to the house that has now aged, where the performer and her double perform a melancholy duet. *Facades* is an atmospheric and sometimes challenging VR experience that leaves audience members questioning their place on the virtual stage.

Facades is inspired by iconic film scenes that use the architectural features of mirrors, windows and doors as metaphors for duality, reflection and portals. The visual work is influenced by the cinematography of the chosen film clips which include scenes from Hitchcock's *Rear Window* (1954), Flemings's *The Wizard of Oz* (1939) and Tarkovsky's *The Mirror* (1975). The choreography in *Facades* explores domesticity and loneliness through unusual, repeated gestures including abstracted movement, themes and settings inspired by the chosen film scenes. Throughout the work, the isolated performer seeks to find a connection by reaching out to the visiting viewer. In one scene, the performer approaches from the dark – grasping out towards the participant, yet she constantly remains out of arm's reach, slowly spiralling around the user based on their head movement. These interactions between the participant and performer create an unsettling narrative that exposes themes of vulnerability, trust, disembodiment and isolation.

Facades aimed to explore the potential for using VolCap, alongside established strategies from contemporary performance and immersive theatre practices to create an intimate and engaging performance in VR. Specifically, we captured a performer using a single Microsoft Azure depth

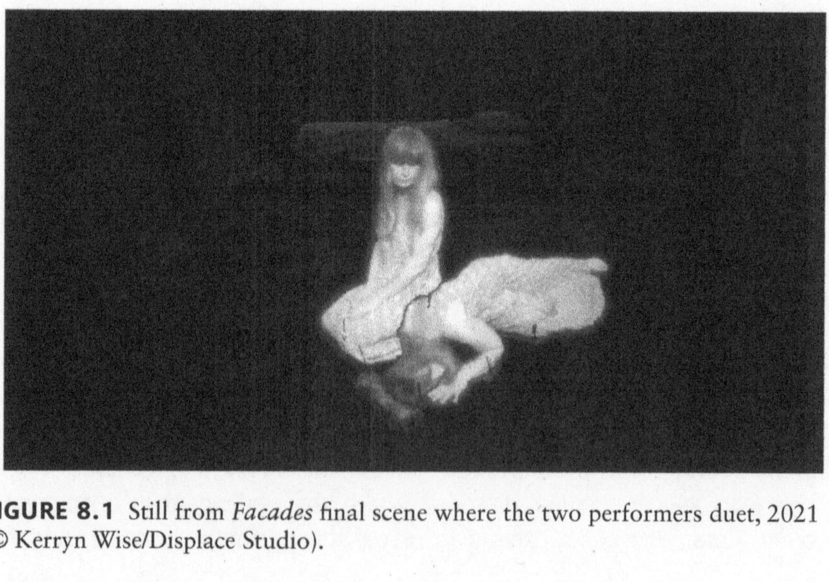

FIGURE 8.1 Still from *Facades* final scene where the two performers duet, 2021 (© Kerryn Wise/Displace Studio).

camera with a software called Depthkit,[4] which is used to generate volumetric video for three-dimensional (3D) environments. The captured clips appear more recognizably as video, thus seemingly closer to cinematic VR, which usually comprises a 360-degree video that spectators can look around from the fixed point of the camera. VolCap offers a cinematic aesthetic yet with the added potential of six degrees of freedom (6DOF): 6DOF allows participants to traverse through a virtual space moving forward/back, up/down, left/right, and pitch, yaw and roll.

My proposition was that capturing an actual performer using VolCap could encourage a heightened emotive and embodied response from the participant, beyond the scope of motion capture (mo-cap) with its potential for uncanny[5] computer-generated graphics. While mo-cap has been used extensively to allow performers to provide animated avatars with natural movement qualities and has been a popular technology with dance artists;[6] VolCap is offering new opportunities for extending the possibilities for immersive content that is closer to film. The video appearance of the captured VolCap dancer seems to offer an enhanced connection between the spectator and the performer. The knowledge that the performer is an actual person further increases this sense of intimacy. In *Facades,* the glitchy video imagery evokes nostalgia in the participant, akin to an old photograph. Through analysis of this practice, which evolved through a design-led process of prototyping, experimentation and user-testing, this artistic position chapter reveals new creative strategies and highlights the potential of using VolCap in Extended Reality Performance (XRP).

My examination of *Facades* will draw from critical practitioner reflections and qualitative audience data gathered via questionnaires.[7] I gathered sixty-two questionnaire responses to *Facades* and I have used elements of thematic analysis (Braun and Clarke 2006) to understand the audience responses to the work. I was fascinated by the individual qualitative responses which offered rich insight into individual participant's engagement, experience and interpretation of *Facades*. There were many instances after sharing *Facades* where a participant was visibly moved and in a heightened emotive state. Martin Barker calls these resonant moments collisions: 'a person "collides" with a moment of experience. It does something to them and leaves a trace, which is very important to them' (2022, 259). It felt important to document these moments to understand the effect of this technology on audience experience and I draw on several examples within my analysis.[8]

Within my discussion of *Facades*, I will elucidate how the approaches used challenge traditional engagement in VR, adapt the normative use of the technology and contest some established VR design processes. VolCap is often used with multi-camera set-ups to capture highly photorealistic 3D performances which involve minimal movement. Using VolCap to capture dance via a single capture set-up is a novel approach and leads to a particular ethereal aesthetic. Moving beyond VR's pursuit for full immersion (Fictum 2016), *Facades* deliberately blurs and breaks the boundaries of apparent realities using the shifting virtual mise-en-scene as a dramaturgical device. I will present reflections on how audiences responded to these intimate, theatrical, liminal spaces. I propose that the artist-led interlacing of techniques and effects, which playfully exploit the potentials of the VolCap technology alongside established strategies from performance, have generated a perceptually evocative experience for audiences that contributes towards new understandings of audience perception and embodiment in virtual environments (VE).

Context

Facades was developed in 2021 with a team of collaborators including Creative Technologist Ben Neal, Dramaturg Tina Carter and Sound Designer Daniel Frazer. The project was financially supported by Arts Council England and De Montfort University. The final VR artwork was shared online via Itch.io[9] and presented at several arts centres, theatres and festivals across the UK during 2021–2. *Facades* was presented at three international festivals, including the QLD XR Festival in Australia, The Festival of International Virtual and Augmented Reality Stories (FIVARS) in the United States of America and Canada and Moving Body Festival in Bulgaria, significantly widening the international reach of the project. Overall, around 600 people have engaged with the work directly and at the time of writing *Facades* continues to tour.[10]

VolCap for performance

VolCap is a process that involves multiple cameras capturing the volume of an object or performer from different angles, which are then combined to create a realistically formed digital asset that can be placed within a range of VR and augmented reality (AR) environments. VolCap allows creatives to capture actual performers digitally and transform them into photorealistic 3D, virtual representations – performers you can occupy the same space with, walk around and view from any angle.

Established creatives working with VolCap are hailing its potential. Cyril Tsiboulski, director of *Queerskins: ARK* (Tsiboulski and Szilak 2020), notes that VolCap allows audiences to find a closer, visceral connection to the performers, beyond the scope of mo-cap (2020). *Vestige* (2018) Director Aaron

Bradbury states that 'Volumetric capture allows me to create intimacy between the viewer and Lisa to connect them with her story in a way which is more visceral than any other medium' (Melnick 2018). These testimonials support the notion that VolCap could offer an alternative to mo-cap for performance makers working with VR.

Although many industry creators are utilizing this technology via expensive, large studios that offer high-end VolCap, involving hundreds of cameras, to create realistic virtual humans and avatars,[11] *Facades* uses a single camera set-up, capitalizing on the glitches that occur within the capture as an artistic effect. The type of set-up used in *Facades* offers an affordable and portable option for creating VolCap. These types of systems use depth cameras such as the Microsoft Azure with subscription-based software such as EF EVE[12] and Depthkit. As more artists experiment with these affordable options, an exciting new body of work will emerge.

Challenging normative VR design processes

Writing about VR experience design, Casey Fictum discourages breaking a user's sense of presence. He states that 'the moment you remind them that they are in a VR headset and they pay attention to the externalities of the real world … you have broken your design' (2016, 15). This perspective is concerned with game design which primarily engages the visual and auditory senses. In these experiences, the tendency is to ignore the other senses, such as proprioception,[13] smell, taste and touch (unless they are embedded within the design via haptic interfaces such as data gloves and bodysuits), which can distract and remind the viewer of their actual physical location. *Facades* differs from this approach and actively plays with a push/pull between apparent realities that are woven into the user experience (UX). Before putting on the VR headset and as part of the participants' acclimatization, audiences see the VR room-scale area taped on the floor, with red shoes placed in a pool of light, and they hear the soundscape playing (see Plate 14). This corresponds to features in the VE and highlights both the virtual and physical spaces, which are later disrupted. Within *Facades*, we wanted to encourage participants to cross boundaries, look through objects and break many of the behavioural rules of VR. We prompted audiences to walk through virtual walls or step inside a performer's virtual body. These actions can produce powerful physiological and emotional effects that can heighten the participant's consciousness of their own body and disrupt their sense of presence.[14]

Facades challenges normative VR design in the way we use the guardian system. The Meta Quest VR headset has an in-built blue safety grid guardian system which protects users from walking into physical walls. At the start of any VR session, a play area boundary is drawn which pops up as a blue grid if the user gets too close to the edge. We chose to incorporate this safety grid, which would usually be immersion-breaking, as part of the experience. This dimensional barrier changes the navigation and level of audience control within the VE. For example, audiences are encouraged to explore freely, yet may then have their movement limited. A participant said:

> I had a sense of being able to go where I wanted to but being very much influenced by the visual spaces even if I was able to step through objects ... I was reminded by the blue lines that there were limits that didn't feel like natural borders, they were surprising, sometimes restricting.

While building *Facades*, we used a system for identifying the position of the blue grid, thus showing where the participant could move within each scene, allowing us to direct the participants' navigation. We were able to manipulate this so that features could be just beyond the participant's reach, such as a doorway or window, toying with their sense of agency and adding to a process of unsettling that evolves throughout *Facades*.

There are various strategies for moving audiences through 6DOF VR experiences. Gaming approaches this via a risk and reward paradigm based on the premise that the user will continue to search for the next clue by moving forward in the game and interacting with characters, objects and features of the environment, eventually working out what to do next. I wanted to enact a journeying experience more akin to immersive theatre, where you have some agency to explore the spaces freely, although there are prompts used to move you forward. These prompts include having the virtual performer as a guide beckoning you to follow them, as well as lighting and sound cues. These techniques used in live performance to direct attention, are more challenging to control in virtual space with VolCap; as the VolCap data is pre-recorded, clips have a set duration with a start and end point. The main issue we experienced was transitioning between multiple Depthkit clips, as you cannot merge from one action into another. However, we used the head tracking of the VR headset to know the spectator's position in space and where they were looking, so we could trigger events accordingly. We also used the architectural features to hide clip transitions. As with much VR content, we also added visual cues, sounds and hints to encourage the viewer to stand in a particular spot or face a specific direction. Ultimately, we used a mix of theatrical prompts and devices afforded by the technology to move audiences through the experience.

Another issue that needed resolving in *Facades*, was how to move audiences through the work within a relatively small physical space.[15] After experimentation, we settled on a three-stage process to navigate audiences within the set space and timeframe. First, we offer an invitation for an action; second, we add a prompt; third, we force the action to occur. An example of this process can be found in the *Window* scene. After watching for a while on the outside, looking in through a window, we want the spectator to move inside the room. Due to the size limitations of the physical space, they couldn't walk from the window around to the door to enter. Our solution was to gradually rotate the whole room so that a doorway appears before them (the invitation), and a light comes on inside the room (the prompt), both these actions aim to encourage the participant to cross the threshold and move inside (see Plate 15). If they do not enter the room, they gradually glide forward (the forced action). This three-stage process helps to balance giving the participant some agency (or the illusion of agency), while still moving them through the experience.

Agency is a term with many different contexts depending on the discipline and philosophical approach. Agency is broadly defined as the ability of decisions and actions to alter a situation. In VR, agency can be understood as the level of control users have to manipulate and alter their environment. Astrid Breel's discussion of agency in participatory performance states that agency is something that everyone has, however, notes that 'agency exists within systems and structures (such as society) that can inhibit or conduct a person's ability to meaningfully exercise it'. Breel suggests that agency should be considered based on the specific situation and argues that agency cannot be 'given' to participants by artists (2022, 403). Breel highlights phenomenological perspectives of agency which focus on the participant's awareness of their actions, the connections between actions, the context and the effects of such actions. Breel's discussion of agency leads towards the notion of 'conducting agency' as an inclusive approach that offers an awareness that participants do not lack agency, yet the situation may be restricted by the performance context. In the feedback for *Facades*, most spectators suggested that they were aware that their agency was limited to mainly looking and positioning themselves, yet there was a consensus that this worked well within the context of the piece. Breel's insights are useful to the discussion of agency in *Facades*, where there is a sense of us 'conducting' the participants' agency within the experience design (2022, 407). One example of this is the dark scene when we lock the gaze of the participant to the VolCap performer's image, this means that every head movement made by the participant spirals the performer's body and turns this inside out. A participant noted that 'I found the room where the virtual dancer moved in response to my head movement more uncomfortable at first and then playful'. Another said, 'I absolutely loved playing with observing the dancer from the side and playing with the inside-out face'. Thus, emphasizing the way that agency is enacted in *Facades*.

In live theatre, a performer can improvise, responding in real time to the audiences they encounter. Using VolCap in VR, improvisation is more difficult to achieve. The journeying needs planning to get participants to follow instructions (often in an environment new to them) and to follow the prescribed route, while still having a sense of freedom. *Facades* conjures a tension between my control as director and the participant's control as the spectator. We added moments when the virtual scene shifts without the participant's control – a sudden shift in perspective or architecture moving towards or away from them. These shifts challenge and draw attention to the participant's awareness of their agency. Audiences seemed to respond well to this liminal state; one noted, 'I was intrigued by the unsettledness of being allowed to do whatever I want as an invisible observer but then was stopped and clear boundaries given.' Within *Facades*, we have tried to create an experience that draws attention to the audience's consciousness of the effects of their movements and positioning.

Contrary to many VR experiences, we decided not to give the participant hand controllers, which provide the ability to interact with objects and teleport through space. We made this decision so that the participant cannot freely teleport as their trajectory is mainly controlled by the directors' choices and guided by the technical and theatrical prompts previously discussed. The lack of controllers allows participants to focus on the movement content, characters and cinematic staging, and not be distracted by elements of object interaction. I suggest that for artistic, content-driven work, this type of interactivity is less important. A notion supported by the majority of audiences who gave feedback on *Facades*.

Towards a rethinking of embodiment in VR

In designing *Facades*, we utilized the aesthetic qualities that the single camera set-up offers, so that the dancer is shown with one particular perfect angle. As audiences step around the edges of the illusion, the performer's body morphs between realistic and abstract imagery. Additionally, rather than following set procedures for cleaning up the VolCap imagery through post-processing, we chose to highlight the fractured edges and glitchy appearance of the performer, enhancing the ethereal qualities and artistic effects of the illusion. This revealing highlights her digital-ness, her imperfections and her hollow shell, thus prompting the participant to consider how digital representation is created and exposed.

Facades cultivates an intimate and emotional connection between the participant and the performer. In the feedback, participants expressed a strong

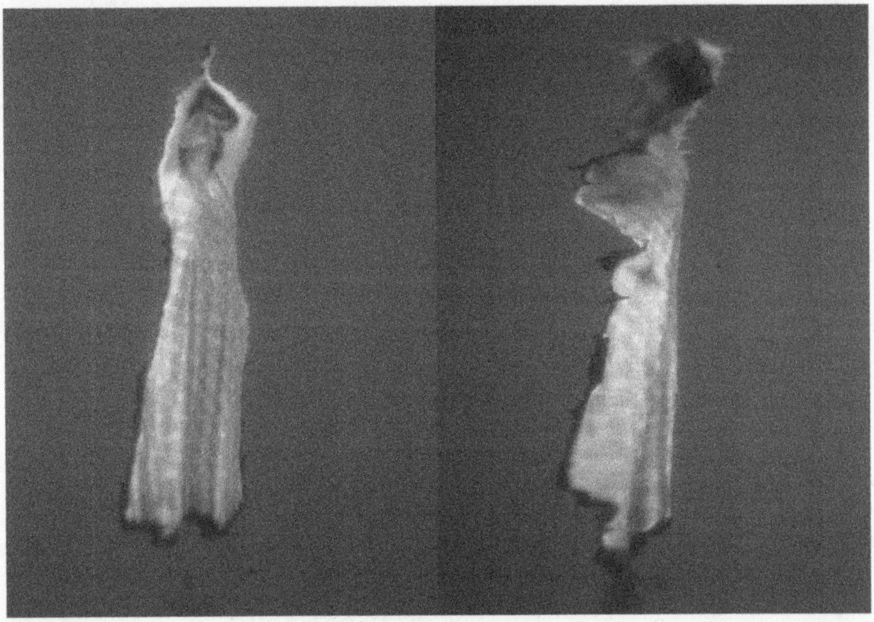

FIGURE 8.2 Still from VR showing the front and side perspective of the performer's body, *Facades*, 2021 (© Kerryn Wise/Displace Studio).

sense of connection to this imperfect, vulnerable woman and a yearning to care for her, despite her being a fractured, digital shell. Moving away from VR's pursuit for the perfect human replica through photorealistic avatars, *Facades* is interested in the audience's relationship to these fractured performers and what this evokes. One participant said that 'the flickering pixelated image, solid but not solid, made me think of them like digital ghosts', another said 'I found the breaking up of the image of [the performer] had an emotional quality'.

In *Facades*, we are inviting participants to inhabit positions and perspectives that shift and break their sense of presence which allows them to perceive the virtual world and performer differently. There are moments built into the experience design which act to blur the boundaries between the physical and virtual. Some examples include the walls and floor falling away, destabilizing the participant or the blue safety grid popping up unexpectedly showing the material space. These instants momentarily interrupt the participant's presence in the VE and focus attention on the participant's body. A participant said, 'I felt aware of my physical body being in the virtual world but also being in the physical. Partly sensing the actual room space as well as the visual landscape'. This shifting of the participants' sense of presence is also developed via their evolving relationship with the performer. There is a moment when the performer suddenly runs directly through the participant making them jump or when the participant is encouraged to step inside the performer's hollow body shell. These moments act to draw attention to the participant's invisible yet present physical body, reminding them of their liminality. In *Facades*, we do not place the participant inside an avatar's body, or ask them to play a role; yet, their invisible body is still reacting physiologically and emotionally to the evolving narrative and some powerful responses were noticed. After experiencing *Facades*, a participant said, 'A very physical sensation has been left with me. The only way I can explain it is the delicate hollowness of the virtual bodies leaves me with the sense of density, "realness", awareness of "liveness" in my own body.' Thus, suggesting that the ethereal aesthetic of the VolCap imagery used in *Facades* provokes a heightened awareness of the audience's own body, despite it being invisible in the VE.

Sita Popat discusses embodiment in VEs suggesting that:

> Experiences and interactions in, and with, VR environments can enable us to relocate ourselves as embodied beings rather than distancing us from our bodies ... The nature of action in virtual worlds is such that our bodies are both present and absent, experiencing agency and aspects of sensation even though there is no direct contact between flesh and world.
>
> (2016, 359)

Even without a visual representation in the VE, audiences described a sense of intimately connecting with the performer, yet in an altered state of being, somewhere in between Popat's 'flesh and world'. An audience member noted: 'Obviously, I couldn't see my body, or any kind of virtual representation of it, but I still felt my physical presence in the virtual space.' *Facades* invites audiences to become more aware of their bodies through a series of encounters that gently build and then break the layers of immersion and realities experienced. The strategies employed consciously played with the participants' sense of embodiment/disembodiment and awareness of the physical/virtual spaces they inhabit. They highlight the participants' shifting agency and relationship with the performer, provoking them to question their own (invisible) presence on the virtual stage.

Susan Kozel, Ruth Gibson and Bruno Martelli propose, in their discussion of affective experiences in VR, that:

> Current artistic works in VR ... have such shifts in attention designed into the fabric of the experience, actualised through a play with modes of participation, performance or witnessing. Along with a revitalisation of attention, the simple definition of the term embodiment is no

> longer sufficient to unfold the corporeal and cultural complexity of these various experiences.
>
> (2018: 4)

Facades plays with these 'modes of participation', by inviting participants to move beyond perceived and behavioural boundaries. Participants are prompted to cross thresholds, become voyeurs, witness, dwell and explore the place where their sensate yet invisible virtual body meets the performer's increasingly fragile body. During *Facades*, the performer's body becomes increasingly fragmented. This is mimicked within the architecture which progressively becomes dilapidated. Throughout the work, there is a gradual *unsettling* for the participants, with each scene taking them further from the solidity and physical laws of the material world. Walls move, rooms rotate and floors drop away, performers appear and disappear, bodies dissolve and combine. The architectural changes accompany the narrative progression, which gradually becomes more emotive and dreamlike. A participant reflected that 'time slowed down and I was transported to a different place … one that felt familiar and otherworldly at the same time … otherworldly, but the connection to the characters made it feel familiar … this sort of betwixt and between'. The combination of the fractured aesthetic of the performer resembling an old faded photograph and the invisible body of the participant, which is both present and absent, leads towards a mode of participation that can be characterized as an ethereal embodiment. This sense of ethereality is captured in the words of one participant, 'in a way I existed, but also not'. The term 'ethereal embodiment' also acknowledges the participant's relationship to the fractured quality of the Volcap performer's body, which has a ghostly aesthetic.

Conclusion

In conclusion, I propose that the VolCap techniques developed through this practice offer audiences a unique and intimate VR performance experience contributing to what participants described as 'a beautiful journey into intimacy and self-awareness' and a 'delightfully unnerving experience'. The use of VolCap alongside approaches taken from immersive performance and choreographic practices has produced an experience that reconfigures the participants' experience of their own body and contributes to expanded notions of embodiment highlighted by Popat (2016) and Kozel et al (2018). Furthermore, by disregarding some established VR design protocols –

in terms of the aesthetic treatment of the captured footage, lack of VR controllers, breaking the user's sense of presence and the use of the Guardian System as a navigational device – we created an experience that playfully toys with the audience's sense of space, presence and agency. I propose that the combination of unique approaches used in *Facades* acts to destabilize the participant, encouraging a series of perceptual shifts that enable embodiment through disembodiment towards a mode of participation I am calling ethereal embodiment.

At the time of writing, there were currently a handful of performance artists experimenting with VolCap and time will tell if this becomes more prevalent in the fast-moving technological landscape. As more performing artists experiment with VolCap, new approaches will emerge that could offer an alternative to mo-cap as the leading VR movement capture technique. The reflections in this chapter offer creative strategies and insights into how this technology can affect audience experience. As an interdisciplinary artist working with VolCap, the potentials seem rich and ripe for further artistic investigation.

Notes

1 Audience feedback was gathered via written questionnaires and engaged with three audience test groups: culturally engaged adults over fifty and new to VR, performance practitioners with mixed prior experience of VR and expert VR users. I also gathered feedback from public audiences from the initial tour to four venues. Overall, I gathered sixty-two feedback forms analysed within this writing.

2 VolCap is a process that involves multiple cameras capturing the volume of an object or performer from different angles, which are then combined to create a realistically formed digital asset that can be placed within a range of VR and augmented reality (AR) virtual environments (VE).

3 This effect was created by using a single Microsoft Azure depth camera.

4 See www.depthkit.tv.

5 The Uncanny Valley is a concept first developed by Masahiro Mori in relation to robots, which has since been developed to describe animated versions of humans used in games and film. As the visuals become increasingly realistic, any slight defect could result in feelings of repulsion in the viewer and a lack of emotional connection with the animation (Sparks 2019).

6 Some UK examples of dance artists using mo-cap include Alexander Whitley and Gibson & Martelli.

7 The questionnaire design offered open and closed questions and used sections of Witmer and Singer's questionnaire, *Measuring Presence in Virtual Environments: A Presence Questionnaire* (1998).

8 Two of the audience comments used within this writing were gathered via an interview for the marketing film.

9 Itch.io is an open platform to upload independently made video games.

10 See www.facades.info.

11 See Dimensions Studio in the UK.

12 EF EVE: https://ef-eve.com/.

13 Proprioception is sometimes referred to as the sixth sense, it allows us to perceive the position, movement and action of parts of the body (Taylor 2009).

14 There has been an abundance of research exploring presence in virtual environments in different contexts as explored by Sanchez-Vives and Slater (2005); Giannachi and Kaye (2011); Jarvis (2019), which I do not have the scope to discuss here.

15 *Facades* has three versions depending on the setting: the on-location space is five-by-five metres, the at-home version is three-by-three metres and the seated version is one-by-one metres.

9

Embodiment of a digital human: Cineplay and the transformative power of immersive storytelling in *Stay Alive My Son*

Victoria Bousis

Introduction

This chapter examines the capacity of immersive storytelling and virtual reality (VR) to revolutionize narrative techniques, by focusing on *Stay Alive My Son* (SAMS) (Bousis 2021)[1] as a paradigmatic example. SAMS, an award-winning immersive and interactive film, exemplifies VR's ability to intensify human connectivity, enrich emotional depth and catalyse societal transformation.[2] Hailed as a technical 'masterpiece of storytelling and emotion' (Baillargeon 2024), SAMS explores human endurance by leveraging immersive storytelling and gameplay interactivity to shape culture, shift perspective and drive social impact.

By reimagining the hero's journey from a third-person to a first-person perspective within a digital environment – integrating cinematic elements and interactivity – SAMS facilitates a profoundly emotional narrative experience. In this chapter, I introduce a novel genre termed 'cineplay', which leverages this unique narrative approach to advocate for social change by chronicling the survival and redemption of Cambodian genocide survivor, Yathay Pin. The chapter delves into SAMS' inception, narrative formulation, visual development and the intricacies of gameplay mechanics, alongside character design through the pioneering creation of hyper-realistic digital humans and volumetric capture technologies to reinforce its narrative impact. It concludes with reflections on SAMS' international impact on global policy regarding family reunification and refugee dignity.

Chris Milk characterizes VR as an 'empathy machine' (2015). Propelled by rapid technological progress in game engine development, immersive storytelling and interactivity through VR head-mounted displays (HMDs) and immersive spatial computing HMDs, for example the Apple Vision Pro, VR advances empathy elicitation techniques. Immersive storytelling is emerging as a powerful medium for individualistic transformation and altruistic-centred societal change. The medium enables audiences to transcend their reality and intimately engage with others' stories, with lasting effects amplified through agency and interactivity within the immersive world. As active participants of the story, audiences embody characters, traverse digital worlds, interact with digital characters and affect the narrative. By re-envisioning the hero's journey through an immersive, first-person perspective, SAMS ventures into unexplored territories of technical and narrative innovation.

Stay Alive My Son: The experience

SAMS is a fifty-five-minute immersive film and interactive VR experience that chronicles the life of Yathay Pin, a Cambodian genocide survivor. Written by Victoria Bousis (2021) and based on Yathay's memoir, *Tu Vivras Mon Fils* (Yathay Pin 2000), SAMS transports audiences into true events, allowing them to uniquely participate as Yathay in an emotionally complex and metaphorical narrative, where every decision unfolds a poignant story of family separation, survival and resilience.

The participant's journey begins in modern times, outside Yathay's home in France. Participants meet an eighty-eight-year-old man, represented by the first hyper-realistic and interactive digital human in VR enhanced by artificial intelligence.[3] Through light gameplay mechanics, participants move through the digital world and interact with key objects in his home, delving deeper into the psyche of a father haunted by past choices and loss. In a ceremonial rite intertwining their fate with his, participant's hands become his. They see the world through his eyes as his memories and dilemmas flood their consciousness. In a surreal twist reminiscent of *Alice in Wonderland*, participants fall through his living room floor and into the depths of his harrowing memories, initiating a quest for redemption and understanding.

Transitioning to the second act and now embodying Yathay, participants navigate a cavernous labyrinth digitally representing the Cambodian concentration camps. This design symbolizes the recesses of Yathay's mind, uncovering Cambodia's rich culture and harrowing history. Within this mental prison, participants trigger poignant moments from his novel that defined his life, including his decision to abandon his son. His family is brought to life through the novel use of volumetric capture of real actors.

Participants are then carried to the mystical echoes of Angkor Wat, a metaphorical beacon of hope and healing. Inside the candle-lit sanctuary, they uncover the final, elusive memory of a father and son. Emerging back in Yathay's home, now as themselves, participants experience the final moment of revelation: Yathay's unyielding spirit shines brightest, revealing a tale of enduring love and the transformative power of forgiveness.

Fostering change through storytelling

Driven by personal experiences of family separation and global stories of genocide, my team at UME and the cast[4] embarked on a mission to go beyond empathy and bring Yathay's harrowing tale to life through immersive technology and innovation. Re-envisioning the hero's journey as an immersive first-person experience in VR, we amplified the heightened sense of immersion by giving participants complete freedom of movement, allowing them to embody a real person and interact with the digital world with consequence.

Our goal was to redefine storytelling by creating a new audio-visual genre to inspire, educate and empower audiences. Uniquely combining classic cinema's three-act structure with interactivity, SAMS established a new mimetic genre I call *cineplay*.[5] Prioritizing narrative followed by interactivity, cineplay blends cinematic storytelling and organic gameplay mechanics, mirroring natural behaviour to allow audiences to step into the protagonist's reality and *live* their story. Game-engine technology and game development pipelines augment participant's presence within the story, enabling free movement within digital worlds and interactivity with characters. Through a customized pipeline for creating hyper-realistic digital humans and volumetric capture, participants experience a deeply human narrative, forming profound emotional connections with stories that resonate beyond the headset. Cineplay's unique blend empowers audiences, not as mere spectators of a narrative but as active participants influencing the narrative.

Audience members, now as active participants with agency inside the headset, are compelled to take positive compassionate actions of change outside the headset, driving SAMS' social impact mission for family unity. This endeavour, coined as 'CompAction' VR during my TED talk (2023), represents a commitment to utilizing VR not only as a tool for empathetic storytelling but as a catalyst to drive compassionate action. CompAction aimed to transform a conventional book into an extraordinary narrative experience, underscoring the potency of immersive storytelling for internalizing the human experience by embodying characters and fostering a compassionate response to real-world events, thereby inciting real-world change.

Reconceptualizing the hero's journey within VR: Advancements in narrative immersion and personal transformation

For millennia, hero tales have captivated humanity, resonating deeply with our intrinsic aspiration for self-improvement. The archetypal heroic journey, as portrayed in cinema, often mirrors our own introspective and transformative experiences, imprinting lasting psychological and parabolic insights. The monomyth, or hero's journey, a narrative structure identified in narratology and comparative mythology, serves as a universal template for stories wherein a hero embarks on an adventure, triumphs over a crucial challenge and returns home transformed (Campbell 2008). In *A Hero of A Thousand Faces*, Joseph Campbell deconstructs this journey into distinct phases, proposing that a hero sacrifices their own needs for a cause greater than themselves. Through an arduous and transformative odyssey a hero faces trials that test their character and resolve, emerging altered and wiser for humanity's betterment (2008).

SAMS explores redefining the hero's journey within immersive storytelling, aiming to enhance presence and emotional engagement. What if, rather than passively observing a hero's journey, audiences could inhabit the hero's world, directly influencing the story through interactive design? Although modern role-playing games (RPGs) and interactive films have used some elements of interactivity, immersion and freedom of movement, this has not yet been satisfactorily achieved for full-length interactive, cinematic VR experiences. This chapter posits that experiencing the narrative in a more intimate and immersive manner could profoundly impact personal transformation, potentially inspiring individuals to effect change beyond the digital experience. The concept was not merely to adapt, but to *reinterpret* Yathay Pin's autobiographical narrative, offering audiences the opportunity to *live* his experiences, thereby fostering a deeper connection to the narrative and encouraging reflective personal transformation. Through SAMS, we endeavoured to transcend traditional storytelling boundaries, offering a new paradigm for narrative engagement in the digital age.

Background of the virtual reality adaptation of *Stay Alive My Son*

The inception of *Stay Alive My Son* was not a matter of the director finding the story, but rather, the story imposing itself upon the director. In the year 2016, the escalation of the Syrian conflict precipitated a humanitarian crisis of unprecedented scale, displacing approximately 13 million people. This episode, emblematic of a series of geopolitical crises culminating in significant human displacement – evident in the resurgence of the Taliban in Afghanistan (2020), the Russian incursion into Ukraine (2022) and the Israeli-Palestinian conflict (2023) – propelled a profound interrogation of the ramifications of forced migrations. Yathay's narrative (encountered during a sojourn in Cambodia) concerning a family's ordeal during the Cambodian Genocide (1974–9) resonated as a poignant testament to these themes, prompting a re-evaluation of themes concerning family separation within the ambit of modernity and emerging technological media.

Rooted in the real-life experiences of Yathay, SAMS recounts the immediate circumstances surrounding his decision and delves metaphorically into the protracted aftermath of his forty-five-year separation from his son through a psychological journey of the interior self. My vision was to fabricate a narrative experience within VR that not only narrated Yathay's story but also facilitated an immersive engagement with the Cambodian cultural context and the moral and emotional complexities of his decisions. This narrative approach necessitated a nuanced integration of cinematic storytelling with interactive gameplay elements to foster a personalized narrative journey, encapsulating the emotional spectrum of Yathay's experiences in a deeply profound manner unachievable in traditional cinema.

The architectural framework of the narrative was predicated upon honouring Cambodia's rich culture and history while underscoring universal themes of love, loss and redemption. SAMS' narrative journey was structured around two primary quests: (1) a physical odyssey marked by witnessing and experiencing Yathay's trials and tribulations through key scenes from his book and (2) a metaphysical voyage through an emotional labyrinth, navigating the vicissitudes of guilt, hope and eventual reconciliation. This dual narrative structure was designed to deeply engage participants, fostering empathy and a profound understanding of Yathay's resilience and capacity for forgiveness.

In summary, the directorial impetus and narrative strategy underpinning SAMS leveraged the immersive potential of VR, forging deeper, more meaningful connections with human narratives by allowing audiences the unique ability to *become* the hero and *live* the transformative journey.

Conceptualization, script and development of the game engine in 'cineplay'

Interactive storytelling through RPGs, interactive films and immersive VR experiences has evolved because of technological advancements and audience curiosity. Starting in the 1980s, text-based RPGs like 'Zork' (1980) allowed participants to navigate a narrative through text commands. This format was followed by advancements in graphics and the rise of adventure games, like 'The Legend of Zelda' (1986) and 'Final Fantasy' (1987), which provided richer worlds and deeper narratives with puzzle-solving and character interactions. Later, movies such as *Night Trap* (1992) introduced interactivity, blending video footage with gameplay elements and using full-motion video (FMV) to create a cinematic experience where audiences made real-time decisions that influenced the narrative. More recently, Netflix's *Bandersnatch* (2018) popularized the interactive film genre on TV by allowing viewers to make choices that affected the storyline. With the rise of VR technology, a new level of immersion emerged, with experiences like *Beat Saber* (2018) and Meta's *Vader Immortal* (2019). The former offered interactive environments and physical engagement, whilst the latter allowed participants to embody a smuggler character. In a continuation of this evolution of entertainment through interactivity and immersion, SAMS' cineplay paradigm is another historical benchmark.

Cineplay is a new genre that merges cinematic storytelling, interactivity and the classic three-act structure – where narrative dominates and gameplay mechanics enhance presence and immersion in VR – allowing users to become the protagonist and interact with the narrative world first-hand. Unlike traditional RPGs, cineplay promotes a first-person perspective with full VR immersion, making users feel as if they are inside the story while offering narrative control through mechanics. RPGs often offer more open-ended exploration and character development. Interactive films like *Bandersnatch* offer choice-based interactivity within a linear film, starting and ending in a scene-by-scene framework viewed on a TV. Cineplay provides a guided narrative experience akin to a film, while allowing continuous, real-time interaction with the environment and characters, similar to gaming experiences. Additionally, cineplay leverages VR technology to provide a fully immersive experience within the world. Furthermore, unlike immersive and interactive games – such as *Vader Immortal* where gameplay leads and narrative follows – cineplay integrates cinematic foundations with game design, creating an unparalleled experience where participants' actions directly influence the narrative, giving audiences a higher sense of agency through decisions and physical movements within the VR environment.

Studies have shown that VR enhances immersion by making participants feel present in the virtual environment, heightened through multi-sensory inputs, including visual, auditory, olfactory and haptic feedback (Slater and Wilbur 1997). In SAMS, presence was enhanced visually through the participant's exploration of the virtual worlds, sonically through spatialized sound and haptically through controller-vibration feedback during key moments. Likewise, the choice to embody Yathay was based on studies reporting that VR can elicit strong emotional and empathetic responses, enhancing the impact of a story through first-person perspectives and realistic environments, making participants feel more connected to the narrative and characters (Milk 2015). Studies have also shown that VR influences cognitive load and attention through interactivity and engagement within environments (Li, et al. 2013). Interacting with hyper-realistic characters, moving freely in the VR environment and using a flashlight to trigger historical information improved participants' focus and reduced distractions compared to traditional media.

The Unreal game engine was chosen for real-time rendering – including dynamic lighting, high-quality textures, realistic physics (Sweeney 2015) – and its scalability in designing complex environments through optimization and asset creation (Gregory 2014). Likewise, the creation of a hyper-realistic digital replica of Yathay was possible through the game engine's advanced animation and physics systems, allowing for realistic character movements and character interactions, enhancing the cinematic quality of the experience and improving effective storytelling in VR (Lai 2017). Presence throughout the narrative via interactivity was also possible via game-engine technology to give weight and consequence to the participant's actions and decisions. Therefore, despite SAMS use of linear versus branching narratives, each participant has a unique and personalized experience based on their movements, which trigger audio cues like voice-overs or sound effects and the pace at which they advance the narrative.

Defining the narrative scope and visual conceptualization

The narrative development phase focused on delineating a narrative arc centred on the familial unit, juxtaposing themes of loss, love, guilt and redemption to craft a poignant emotional journey with dramatic tension. Key scenes from Yathay's book were extracted, anchoring the historical narrative within a contemporary context that echoed present-day conflicts and family separations. Engaging with Yathay, the narrative's protagonist, was essential to bridging the temporal divide, as his personal experiences provided a vital connection between past and present. A defining moment involved presenting Yathay with a digitally aged photograph of his son, Nawath, using artificial intelligence to age him from six to fifty-two years. This unveiled the unresolved nature of Yathay's past and his persistent search for a son he failed to recognize as now a grown man.

The narrative arc, designated as the 'A' storyline, encapsulated a father's quest to find his lost son, moving from the present into the recesses of memory to recount pivotal moments leading to their separation. Yathay's revelation of his treasured possessions, including a photograph depicting his escape and remnants of his journey, highlighted the compelled separation from his son – a decision borne not of choice but of necessity. This narrative was enriched by a 'B' storyline, exploring psychological undercurrents, introspective reflections and the pursuit of atonement, allowing for the expressionistic representation of interior moments through VR.

In crafting the screenplay, these dual storylines structured the narrative and emotional trajectory. The completed screenplay prompted the visualization process, detailing transitions across scenes, levels and acts and consolidating visual references for Yathay's homes in France and 1970s Phnom Penh and iconic Cambodian locales such as Angkor Wat and the S-21 concentration camps. This visual repository, encompassing costume designs, lighting concepts, character design and thematic soundscapes, laid the groundwork for the narrative's cinematic and interactive realization.

Transitioning from conceptualization to format and game engine

Prior to the development of SAMS, numerous 360-degree video experiences using three degrees of freedom (3DoF)[6] emerged, which created promise and excitement. However, with recent technological innovations, 3DoF formats now underutilize VR's potential, barely scratching the surface of what can be achieved by storytelling through cineplay. Driven by an ambition to redefine VR and forge a novel, immersive narrative pathway, I chose to adopt the six degrees of freedom (6DoF)[7] format by leveraging game-engine technology. In addition to the dual narrative, participants were given a profound sensory journey amidst photorealistic scenes through autonomy, immersive presence and interactive engagement.

The visual development of each level was integrated into an asset creation strategy, setting a new standard for scenographic innovation in VR. Using Google Maps and VPNs to explore Cambodian media, we gathered environmental references to represent emotional transitions and contextual depth. By implementing a modular asset design strategy, we improved efficiency without sacrificing quality, allowing dynamic scene assembly to build an immersive and engaging experience in 1.5 years.

World-building inside the Unreal game engine started with the 'blockout' phase. Blockout entails the use of rudimentary geometric constructs to craft an interactive three-dimensional mock-up of each environment, allowing for spatial considerations that align with participant movement. Using screenshots of blocked out scenes, the concept art team created overpainted call-outs and key art as blueprints for the level design team. Furthermore, detailed hero objects were incorporated into each space to underscore key narrative moments. This systematic approach ensured narrative flow and interactive consistency while allowing for a methodical execution of each environment with cultural authenticity, visual coherence and spatial precision. The aim was to take participants on a journey into Yathay's emotional psyche – riddled with complex emotions of guilt, shame, love and hope – interwoven metaphorically with real, physical places from Cambodian history.

After appearing outside Yathay's home, participants progress into his mental prison depicted by a re-creation of the Cambodian (S-21) concentration camps. The prison was intentionally built to feel like a labyrinth with dark corridors, separated by prison doors and haunting assets to intimately explore Yathay's psychological landscape. Laden with locked memories of his family's separation and the abandonment of his 6-year-old son, Yathay's mental labyrinth becomes haunting and claustrophobic. By interacting with key objects that advance the story, participants actively learn about Cambodian history. Plate 16 showcases the world building process of Yathay's mental prison.

In contrast, Yathay's metaphorical heart was treated differently and intentionally created in an open colourful sky. To signify this transition, a mythical silk branch carries participants to the magnificent Angkor Wat temple, a symbol of Yathay's heart. As sunlight breaks through dried tree branches, participants feel Yathay's resilience, love and unwavering hope to find his son. Against its enormity, every statue and mural is crafted for performance, cultural authenticity and meaning. Participants explore with agency, learning, making the story their own and emerging with feelings of personal accomplishment, understanding and compassion. By placing a golden brick at the base of the Apsara statue, the doors to this temple open, revealing a sanctuary of healing and Yathay's path to redemption.

Stay Alive My Son transcends the conventional boundaries of immersive films by integrating gameplay mechanics that allow participants to embody Yathay and navigate his past and present experiences. Fundamental movement mechanics such as walking and turning were implemented to reflect natural locomotion. Although teleportation was recommended to mitigate motion sickness, the decision to refine the walking mechanism – focusing on acceleration and deceleration – was made to preserve the narrative's emotional depth. Teleportation, while easier, was considered to hinder the immersive experience. For instance, in the Second Act, as a participant traverses the sombre corridors of Yathay's mental representation of the S-21 concentration camps, the goal was for each step to convey the dread, fear and uncertainty that Yathay faced, with ambient sounds of footsteps, distant cries and gunfire intensifying the experience. This approach aimed to replicate the harrowing choices where every step could mean life or death and to bring a heightened awareness and understanding to audiences of the dire circumstances faced by others as a pretext to the inhumane choices forced upon them.

The second layer of gameplay centres on interactions with objects in the environment, utilizing grab and release actions. These interactions – ranging from ringing a doorbell and answering a telephone to more symbolic actions like throwing a paper airplane or opening doors with a flashlight – were designed to reinforce participant immersion. By mirroring real-world actions, these mechanics enhance the sense of presence and serve as poignant narrative tools, inviting participants to engage more deeply with Yathay's story through exploration and discovery.

The third tier of mechanics, involving the triggering of the memories, required a different process and presented one of our greatest challenges. The developmental phase of Chapter 1 coincided with the escalation of the Ukrainian conflict, directly affecting nearly half of our team. Faced with the impending deadline for the Venice Film Festival submission and with limited personnel, we integrated puzzles to activate cut-scenes within a three-dimensional environment. This approach inadvertently shifted the tone, diminishing the intended emotional depth of the narrative as participants' focus diverted from a moralistic essence to a logical one posed by the puzzles.

In response to audience observations from various festivals, and recognizing the necessity to maintain narrative immersion, the development of Chapter 2 involved a comprehensive revaluation and rework. We built a new pipeline, reconstructed scenes and soundscapes and overhauled the programming architecture. This enabled intuitive interactions within the virtual environment, akin to the natural recollection of a memory triggered by voiceovers, allowing participants to authentically engage with and inhibit critical moments from Yathay's life story.

Character realization: Stylized volumetric capture techniques and hyper-realistic humans

The graphic stylization used to represent Yathay's family emerged as a pivotal technological innovation, due to the constraints of volumetric capture. It was important to honour Yathay's family by memorializing their lives and enduring presence within his heart. Real actors were cast to portray Yathay's family, breathing life, possibility and dignity through gripping performances by: Elodie Yung as 'Any' (Yathay's wife), Arnold Chun as 'Young Thay', Abraham Sigler as 'Sudath' (Yathay's eldest son), Lucas Sigler as 'Nawath' (Yathay's lost son). Vincent Rodriguez III's haunting portrayal of the Khmer Rouge Chief provided historical context and dramatic tension (see Plate 17).

To enhance the poetic essence of the family, Houdini was used to stylize the volumetric videos using a complex watercolour-like shader, making them appear ghostly and nostalgic, leaning into the imperfections of volumetric capture to symbolize imperfect memory. Raw depth kit data was meticulously processed in Houdini to craft dream-like sequences for a VR experience. These data were transformed into alembic files with masking parameters and integrated into Unreal Engine using a custom material shader. This shader, refined for high fidelity and precise edge control, adjusts vertex colours and opacity, managing green spill from the original footage and enhancing dimensional effects from multiple angles. A depth fade feature and a Houdini-generated distance mask finely tune the opacity, crafting a surreal, immersive experience where participants feel present in a three-dimensional, dream-like virtual environment. This technique brought Yathay's precious family to life with poetry and beauty against a grim historical backdrop (see Plates 18a and 18b).

The next pivotal innovation was the creation of the hyper-realistic digital human of Yathay. It was narratively and emotionally imperative for participants to meet and interact with Yathay, prompting the decision to recreate an interactive digital avatar of Yathay within the game engine. A month after production began, Unreal Engine's Metahuman Creator[8] software was released, enabling the creation of digital humans, using a fixed library of face and body assets. However, the limited generic library only yielded likenesses that deviated substantially from the real Yathay. His hands, which become the participant's hands, lacked the worn, crooked aspect of a concentration camp survivor. His face did not reflect the suffering and resilience of a man who had defied the odds. His body did not represent an elderly frame, hunched and muscle-atrophied. His clothing did not match the meticulous clothes of an engineer, dressed in a shirt, sweater-vest, dress slacks and dress socks. The result was unusable and lacked the elements that made Yathay uniquely human.

As a solution, UME Studios spearheaded the creation of a customized digital human pipeline (patent-pending), enabling the generation of a customized high-fidelity Metahuman replica of Yathay, through an extensive six-month process involving various software. Yathay's face and clothing were sculpted in Zbrush,[9] texturing and material work through Substance Painter[10] and advanced clothing sculpting and texturing through Marvelous Designer. These elements were then reimported into UE via Mesh Morpher.[11] The face and body sculpt had to adhere to the morph targets of a complex Metahuman rig of over 1200 bones for the motion capture data to translate into workable animations. Complimented by the powerful performance of actor, Kostas Filippoglou, captured using a VCON optical camera motion-capture system and Live-Link facial capture software, Yathay slowly came to life before our eyes.

When we imported digital Yathay into UE and tested the first meeting between digital Yathay and the participant there was a lack of connection, placing the interaction in the realm of the uncanny valley.[12] To resolve this, we programmed nodes of artificial intelligence in his neck and eyes to track the participant's movement, solidifying and deepening their human connection. Henceforth, digital Yathay was complete and became the first hyper-realistic, interactive customized digital human in VR history, setting a new benchmark for naturalistic character realization within interactive narrative experiences (see Plates 19 and 20).

Social impact and ethical considerations

Stay Alive My Son has had a profound impact on its audience, driving awareness and empathy towards the refugee experience across communities and countries. In official partnership with UNHCR, this project has screened at notable events such as the Family Reunification Network and the Global Refugee Forum in Geneva to policy makers, Heads of State, NGO's and refugees. These screenings have sparked discussions on refugee rights and family reunification procedures, influencing policy advocacy. Pre- and post-experience feedback from surveyed participants indicated a significant increase in awareness, understanding and compassion, with many expressing a newfound commitment to supporting family reunification and advocating for policy changes.

Post-experience surveys revealed that 95 per cent reported heightened empathy towards refugees, gaining deeper insights into their challenges. In terms of engagement, an overwhelming 90 per cent of participants expressed a newfound commitment to supporting refugee causes through actions like signing petitions, volunteering or donating to related organizations. Over 90 per cent of participants described the experience as transformative and influential in reshaping their perspectives on refugee issues. These measurable results underscore the effectiveness of SAMS in engaging its audience, fostering empathy, shaping policy discussions and driving positive societal change within and beyond the headset.

The creation of *Stay Alive My Son* also prompted reflection on the ethical responsibilities of VR creators to avoid unintended consequences, particularly as we delve into hyper-realistic digital humans and immersive environmental designs. This realism, while enhancing user engagement, also necessitates careful consideration of ethical implications, especially when digital humans are modelled after real individuals.[13] The potential for misuse or misrepresentation of digital humans can lead to issues of consent and privacy. Without proper legislation and ethical guidelines, digital humans created from real people could be used in ways that the original person did not consent to, leading to significant ethical and legal challenges.[14] This is particularly relevant in the context of emerging technologies like AI and VR, where the boundaries between reality and digital representation are increasingly blurred. To address this, as the creator, I attained legal consent from Yathay to create a digital replica of him for the limited use in SAMS to ensure protection of his privacy. Additionally, we added notations on the SAMS Steam Store 'About This Game' page disclosing the use of artificial intelligence to empower the digital humans in the experience.[15]

The ethical responsibilities of immersive and VR creators extend beyond the creation of hyper-realistic digital humans to the immersive experiences involving hyper-realistic environments that can have profound psychological impacts on participants. This is particularly true when VR is used to depict challenging and emotional stories, such as those involving genocide or extreme violence. Numerous studies highlight the potential dangers of extreme realism in VR, warning about the neurological and emotional effects of such experiences, including lasting memories and significant psychological impacts on participants. For example, Studies found that VR simulations used for treating PTSD in military veterans can be highly effective due to their realism, including military weapons, explosions and simulated war scenarios, but also pose risks of re-traumatization if not handled properly (Rizzo et al. 2011). Similarly, Madary and Metzinger discuss the potential for VR to induce strong emotional and psychological responses. They argue for the necessity of ethical guidelines in VR development to mitigate risks such as trauma, addiction and the blurring of reality and virtual experiences (2016). Their work underscores the importance of warnings and appropriate content ratings to inform participants, especially when experiences involve traumatic events. As research continues to highlight the risks associated with extreme realism, it is imperative that creators prioritize user well-being by implementing these safeguards to ensure the intended impact is achieved, one that elevates society rather than harms it.

The Journey Ahead: A farewell and a homecoming

The creation of *Stay Alive My Son* was both a challenging and transformative journey – one that profoundly impacted me personally and professionally. What started with a book in a Cambodian bookstore evolved into an immersive experience that has travelled the world, fostered compassion, influenced global policy and inspired dialogue about memory, justice and healing. Its true success lies in its ability to bridge generations through its emotional resonance and to give a voice to a story once silenced.

On the 50th Anniversary of the Fall of Phnom Penh, *Stay Alive My Son* returned to Cambodia for its most meaningful premiere at the Cambodia International Film Festival. A farewell and a homecoming to the country and the people who inspired its creation. In partnership with the United Nations in Cambodia and The Extraordinary Chambers in the Courts of Cambodia (ECCC), the project will live on as a permanent installation at the ECCC's Resource Center, serving as a space for education, awareness and remembrance.

Stay Alive My Son sets a new benchmark for the future of VR, challenging boundaries by turning viewers into participants and making history a more tangible experience. It epitomizes the synergy between human connection and technological innovation that can empower a new generation of truth seekers, healers and storytellers, helping ensure history is carried forward and human stories are not forgotten.

Notes

1 Since 1 May 2024, *Stay Alive My Son* has been available on Steam for global audiences to experience in their homes. https://store.steampowered.com/app/2806890/STAY_ALIVE_MY_SON.

2 To date, *Stay Alive My Son* has premiered at over twenty-eight film festivals and technology conferences globally. To quantify the impact of SAMS, we conducted pre- and post-experience surveys to document the effect and impact of immersive and interactive storytelling. The detailed results are explained later in the chapter. On a global level and in collaboration with the United Nations High Commissioner for Refugees, SAMS was screened in Geneva at the Family Reunification Network (FRUN) events and the Global Refugee Compact Forum (GRF). Here, heads of state, NGOs, advocacy groups and members of the United Nations experienced the story, humanizing the legal challenges preventing family reunification and securing pledges in support of reunification. To foster a collaborative and collective dialogue, we are partnering with key museums and cultural spaces to create an exhibition of SAMS called 'SEEN'. This exhibition aims to further

discussion and awareness about the issues faced by refugee families, using immersive storytelling and technology to incite compassionate action and change.

3 In 2021, building upon Metahuman software, UME Studios developed a patent-pending pipeline to customize a hyper-realistic digital replica of Yathay Pin. Digital humans have been created by companies such as Digital Domain, but the use of hyper-realism, interactivity and artificial intelligence to respond to the participant's presence was not previously achieved.

4 *Stay Alive My Son*'s Lead Cast: Elodie Yung, Arnold Chun, Vincent Rodriguez III, Abraham Sigler, Lucas Sigler and Kostas Philippoglou

5 I introduced the conceptual term 'cineplay' in 2022, officially publishing it in 2024 in a *Variety* article, 'Immersive Doc *Stay Alive My Son* Uses Compassion to Spur Action', by Ben Kroll. Available at: https://variety.com/2024/digital/festivals/stay-alive-my-son-victoria-bousis-1235983152/

6 3DoF (Three Degrees of Freedom) refers to rotational movement used in 360-degree video experiences, which is limited to head-movement along three axes: the vertical axis (yaw), the lateral axis (pitch) and the longitudinal axis (roll). 'Degrees of freedom (mechanics)'. *Wikipedia, The Free Encyclopedia* https://en.wikipedia.org/wiki/Degrees_of_freedom_(mechanics).

7 6DoF (Six Degrees of Freedom) includes 3DoF rotations and locomotion along the: longitudinal axis (forwards and backwards); vertical axis (up and down); and lateral axis (side to side). 'Understanding 3DOF vs 6DOF Tracking in VR'. *Unity Blog*. Available at: https://blog.unity.com/technology/understanding-3dof-vs-6dof-tracking-in-vr.

8 Metahuman Creator Software: https://www.unrealengine.com/en-US/metahuman.

9 Zbrush Software: https://www.maxon.net/en/zbrush?gad_source=1&gclid=Cj0KCQjwv7O0BhDwARIsAC0sjWMfBXGOIJpgfRaTZsjQ4pUnJzowC9_ONdQMYFcXXj1lVu-wobJsyxwaApooEALw_wcB.

10 Substance Painter Software: https://www.adobe.com/products/substance3d/apps/painter.html.

11 Mesh Morpher Software: https://www.meshmorpher.com/?utm_source=google&utm_medium=wix-smart-campaign&utm_campaign=google-ads-campaign-1-2024-2-2-8ed195e7&gclid=Cj0KCQjwv7O0BhDwARIsAC0sjWOwd-oMGbcezPL7OtyW0t3pTuNq8t7ZgEkFMCJV2V2IHIVpyUXW1M4aAvKuEALw_wcB.

12 Uncanny valley is when the psychological and aesthetic relation between a digital object's degree naturalism and our emotional response to it varies.

13 'Creating Lifelike Digital Humans'. *Frontiers in Virtual Reality*, www.frontiersin.org/research-topics/15438/creating-lifelike-digital-humans. Accessed 10 July 2024.

14 HexTeach. 'Exploring the Universe of AI-Generated Virtual Reality: A New Frontier'. *HEX Teach*, 2024, hexteach.com/ai-generated-vr-content. Accessed 10 July 2024.

15 https://store.steampowered.com/app/2806890/STAY_ALIVE_MY_SON/.

10

Theatre and VR: Exploring the realities of virtual scenography in *Emperor 101*

Camille Donegan, Jo Mangan and Tom Swift

Introduction

The Performance Corporation[1] is a theatre company known for creating cutting-edge site-specific work in various unusual settings, often with the aid of new technologies. With a mission to create 'theatrical adventures in surprising places' very much at the forefront of their minds, in 2020, the company set out to develop a new play involving the actors and audience entering an immersive virtual reality (VR) space – encompassing all creative aspects of the process. The outcome was the play *Emperor 101*, which premiered at the Dublin Theatre Festival in 2021 and was later performed at South by Southwest (SXSW) in Austin, Texas, in 2022. This chapter discusses the artistic processes that create the VR experience. It reflects on a practice-based approach to immersive scenography in performance practice, exposing this emergent theatrical performance area for further scrutiny.

Motivations

Emperor 101 was built on The Performance Corporation's previous site-specific works, which sought to immerse the audience in a '360-degree' experience.

For example, in *Drive-By* (2006), a drama about car culture, the audience drove to a derelict shipping yard where actors in 'boy-racer' cars revved and skidded around them. Similarly, in *Dr. Ledbetter's experiment* (2004), a promenade piece in Kilkenny City, the final scene found the audience shut into a musty prison cell and abandoned in total darkness.

Before creating the work presented here, the creative team was inspired by several contemporary VR theatre performances, including the Royal Shakespeare Company's *Dream* (2021). The company wished to build on what these novel performances had achieved by creating a VR experience where the audience members have agency and can converse and interact in real time with the performers in a specially designed virtual world or 'set'. Moreover, the Performance Corporation's artistic director, Jo Mangan, was fascinated with the crossover between performance and tech, which led to the creation of a SPACE Programme Arts and Tech residency (2018). This annual 'R and D' programme brings together technologists, creatives and performers to collaborate and try new approaches to theatre and art-making that harness technologies such as VR.

Another inspirational factor was the current global issues with social media in 2020. Social media had become a dominant force in shaping public discourse, but it had also amplified the phenomenon of echo chambers, contributing to the polarization of politics (Pariser 2011). With the ability to curate our online experiences and connect with like-minded individuals, social media platforms unintentionally create echo chambers, exposing people to information that aligns with their existing beliefs and values, reinforcing their viewpoints and isolating them from opposing perspectives (Wu 2017). This effect leads to a deepening divide between ideological groups, fuelling polarization and making it harder to find common ground (Benkler et al. 2018). As a result, political discussions often become polarized, with individuals engaging in hostile interactions and the potential for meaningful dialogue and understanding is diminished (Tufekci 2017).

These inspirations, coupled with contemporary advances in untethered, wireless VR equipment such as the Meta Quest 2, have driven the company's immersive theatrical approach, and the learnings that emerged from VR experimentation in SPACE have all contributed to a new vision of creating a live theatrical experience in VR.

Developing the concept

Emperor 101 was to explore this world of conspiracy theories and theorists. It would be performed in 'real life' and a live and interactive VR world. The dramatic action centres on an imaginary high-profile conspiracy theorist whose extreme propaganda led her to be banned from conventional media platforms. She has resorted to building a VR space to induct recruits to her organization.

Emperor 101 was envisioned as an immersive experience for the audience to delve into an alternate world that reflects the minds and motivations of conspiracy theorists. In a time when the notion of truth or facts is called into question, the immersive environment was to reflect the multiple realities or 'bubbles' we live in. The piece was to riff on influences from ancient Greek mythology to *Alice in Wonderland* and ask if rejecting the 'mainstream' is a product of fear or the ultimate act of self-empowerment in an ever-complex media-driven world.

In developing *Emperor 101*, the core creative team consisted of Jo Mangan, Tom Swift, Camille Donegan, Leon Butler and Peter Power. They collectively resolved the thematic area they wished to explore, that is, conspiracy theorists. However, they found it hard to agree on the exact format and/or media to be deployed. As such, several practice-based research questions were developed.

- Could this be an entirely virtual experience and still be theatre?
- Should it veer towards an interactive experience more than a piece of drama?
- Should it involve any VR at all?

As often happens in site-specific or non-conventional theatre, the sites available began to guide the debate.

The dictates of space

Early on, the creative team had been given access to a large abandoned warehouse with a maze of interconnected rooms. This opening led them down a rabbit hole that suggested some immersive real-world experience full of interactive digital tricks and set pieces. In this version, the audience would wander (self-guided) through the labyrinth, with scenes that suggest the lies and the disinformation of conspiracy theories. Ultimately, they would be ejected from the building into a derelict courtyard where they would find a burning grand piano. This vision did not happen. The venue was withdrawn at short notice, and the team was offered a space in a dull 1970s office block across the street – this was when *Emperor 101* finally began to make sense.

On the ground floor of the office block, with its fading early noughties decor, was a large room with grey-green floor tiles. Three 'pods' – egg-shaped office cubicles with glass walls (see Plate 21b) – were in three corners of the room. The design was (presumably) intended to make them look slightly futuristic, but the effect was a bit odd and out of touch. It was perfect.

Thus, thematically, The Performance Corporation explored how people are 'living in a bubble' entirely separated from society today – within a feedback loop that reinforces their existing values and perception of the world and reality. The immersive experience could, therefore, place the audience member and two actors in separate 'bubbles' within these pods (see Plate 21b).

The discovery of this space guided the collective search for a dramatic form of the piece. This breakthrough inspired a work where the audience should be invited into a new area just off the societal mainstream and off the main street outside. The audience would be drawn into a world where truth and conventional meaning are gradually challenged and undermined and then invited to enter a new virtual world where the central character presents an alternative world, alternative facts and a skewed vision of reality.

Designing and building a virtual performance space

Peter Power and Leon Butler designed *Emperor 101*. Peter led the audio components, and Leon led the visual design. A multi-user VR platform was required so actors and audiences could converse in real time. Due to the non-user-friendly interface of social VR platforms of the time, the performance stage veered away from the onboarding friction of platforms like VRChat or AltspaceVR, which are only accessible to 'tech-savvy' people. Accessibility and user comfort were vital, hence the onboarding process with a dedicated facilitator described above. In addition, there were concerns about patch updates to those platforms that could affect the show without warning if relied on for their infrastructure.

Having previously worked with RETiniZE,[2] a VR Studio in Belfast, the project settled upon leveraging their Animotive[3] code for the tech infrastructure for *Emperor 101* – a real-time collaborative VR tool for 3D animation. Using this infrastructure meant the production had control over designing the environments/multiple rooms in Unity and hosting them for multi-user access on the Animotive platform. Animotive functionality handled visual and audio networking aspects for actors and audiences alike. Leon also worked alongside the Unity developers Jamie McRoberts and John Connor at RETiniZE.

Working together, the design and technical teams envisaged and built multiple VR rooms and environments in which the digital section of the immersive performance could take place. They also designed and created bespoke avatars for the actors to embody in the virtual world. These avatars were built in Blender and then brought into the Unity project. This highly technical process involved the iteration of multiple designs and builds of the VR world to perfect both the scenographic and dramaturgical elements and ensure the smooth functioning of the avatars within the VR spaces.

The actors could use Quest 2 controllers and head-mounted displays (HMDs) to embody their VR avatars within our specially created digital world. They could manipulate the movements of their virtual characters in real time, like how a puppeteer controls their puppet. With practice, the actors could fine-tune this manipulation of their avatars to ensure they moved dynamically and convincingly embodied the character. In this way, owning a virtual body has been shown to moderate emotional responses (Gall et al. 2021).

This networked multi-user VR platform had no noticeable lag between performance in real life and VOIP (Voice Over Internet Protocol) services allowed for seamlessly networked audio between all users, audiences and actors. Display lag degrades the illusion of stability and has been identified as a significant fault of virtual-environment systems (Allison 2001). This zero-lag factor was achieved even in a second production of the play at the SXSW festival (discussed further below), in which the actors entered the VR space from different global locations (one in Dublin and one in Spain). At the same time, the audience members were located elsewhere in Austin, Texas.

By facilitating the project in designing and building a virtual performance space, VR technology has transformed how actors connect and collaborate across geographical boundaries, enhancing their creative potential and expanding the possibilities of live and recorded performances. VR has facilitated real-time collaboration among our actors in different parts of the world. The actors could rehearse, interact and co-create arrangements using virtual environments regardless of location. This global connectivity has enabled diverse artistic collaborations, fostering the exchange of ideas and cultural influences that ultimately enriched the creative process.

Unique VR attributes

The *Emperor 101* application on HMDs was the same build for audiences and actors; however, the actors had a 'back door' button to another space where they would choose an avatar character to embody. Once embodied in C or K, they go through a portal to meet their audience. Audience members were guided to walk 'through the portal', which brought them to the first room where the show began.

The unique affordances of VR storytelling allowed the performers to play with some of their avatar attributes. For instance, the character 'C' (see Plate 21a) could press a button on the controller and become giant, approximately 50 times her original size. C becomes exceptionally intimidating to the audience at this large scale, so this was saved for her angry speech at the end of the VR section. Taller avatars are generally more aggressive than users given shorter avatars (Yee et al. 2009). Furthermore, both characters had a button to multiply and create 20 clones alongside their avatars' current position. This feature was applied at a specific point in the production to confuse the audience as they were led further into the mind of a conspiracy theorist.

During rehearsals, some unique 'happy mistakes' made their way into the final piece. For instance, before colliders were put on all the walls (a collider in Unity makes an object impenetrable), one of the actors realized they could see all of the rooms by putting their head through the corridor wall. This perspective change was such an interesting viewpoint that we decided to utilize it at the end of the piece, when an actor presses a button to turn the dome transparent, revealing a view of all previously inhabited rooms.

A walk-through of the *Emperor 101* experience

In *Emperor 101*, a single audience member arrives at the venue at an appointed time. They are greeted by a performer/technician, costumed in slacks and a green Fred Perry-type tennis shirt. They usher the audience into a bare, white-walled office with a white table. In the background, gentle harp melodies play. An array of white VR HMDs and controllers is on the table. The audience member is shown how to use the VR equipment and gets to explore a virtual 'training space' where those without experience in VR can learn how to use the controller, move about and get comfortable.

Once training is complete, the audience member is ushered into a larger room. It's pretty dark, and the lighting is dramatic, almost like some obscure late-night TV debate show. In three corners of the room, the pod rooms glow. The audience can see a technician operating a console behind a control desk at the room's far end. She wears the same uniform as the person who conducted the VR training. In the centre of the room are two leather swivel chairs. Behind the chairs, two large TV screens play a montage of scenes that include romantic Irish landscapes and imagery of Celtic High Crosses. This video is interspersed with scenes from protests, angry people demonstrating against 'elites' and vaccinations. The images are accompanied by a soundtrack inspired by Mise Éire, the well-known patriotic work composed by Seán Ó Riada.

A man wearing the uniform, but with the addition of a tweed jacket, welcomes the audience member warmly. This character is 'K'. Asking the audient's[4] name, K invites them to sit with him. At first, he is reassuring and empathetic. He talks about a person named C. He implies that she is an important person, someone we would like to meet. However, she is also a person who has been vilified – the subject of an unjustified witch hunt.

K changes the subject. Now he wants to know what the audient thinks and poses a series of questions: 'On a scale of one to ten, how much do you love your country? How much freedom have we lost on a scale of one to ten? On a scale of one to ten, how much do you agree with the following statement – in today's crisis, complexity is the enemy of the good?' K tots up the person's 'score' and decides that they are ready to enter a new phase of this induction. They are brought to one of the glass 'bubble' rooms and the performer/technician helps them to put on a VR HMD.

In VR, the audience member enters an expansive space populated with what looks like giant telegraph poles connected by wires. Overhead, fluffy clouds float by in a light blue sky. On closer inspection, the poles are oversized corkboard pins connected by red threads, reminding us of the obsessive need of conspiracy theorists to connect ideas, experiences and facts – even when those connections are not genuine or unfounded (Cassam 2019).

In this space, the audience member meets an avatar – a live VR representation of the real-life character K. The audience member is invited to move around the area to 'follow the thread'. As they approach each of the pins/poles, an audio track is triggered. The audience hears the voices of far-right demagogues whipping up anger and violence. K asks the audience members what they think about the voices: 'Do you hear the anger?' Throughout the piece, the audience members can speak to 'the avatars', engage them in discussion and respond to what they are experiencing.

The character 'C' then appears and talks to the audience member. She explains this is 'a space where we can talk freely about our common concerns, about the direction in which our country is going'. She also claims that Big Tech and Big Pharma 'control the narrative' and want to remove people's freedom. She claims: 'There is no reality, only narrative'.

C beckons the audience member to a portal at the edge of the space. We enter a second space, a high vaulted room with the feel of an industrial area. On one side is a giant TV monitor. Overhead, a bank of CCTV cameras seems to track the audience as they move from one place to another. A yellow corridor with a portal at the end leads from the space.

C tells us that 'they are watching you' and that 'they know everything before it even happens'. She claims that 'this is the future' and says, 'I don't want the future; I want the past'. She becomes upset and flustered when she begins to talk about the past. She walks away down the corridor and tells the

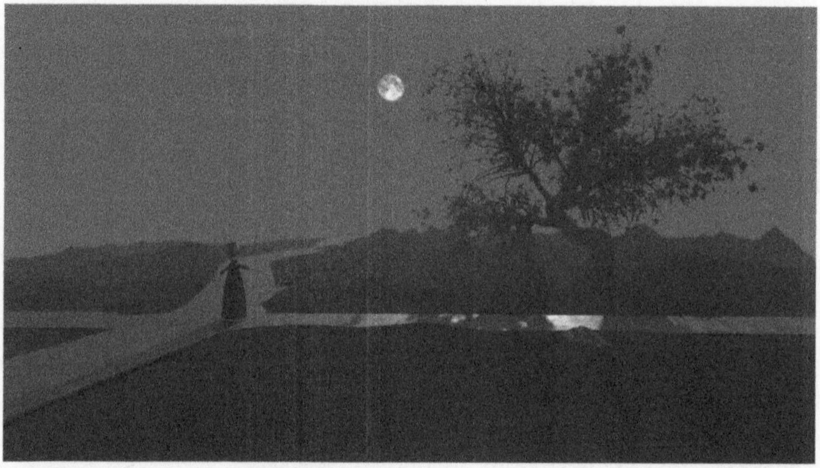

FIGURE 10.1 'C' played by Caitríona Ní Mhurchú in the 'Crossroads' virtual scene from *Emperor 101*, 2021 (© Leon Butler, Jo Mangan, Peter Power, Tom Swift).

audience to come with her. K becomes anxious and pleads with her not to go through the portal, 'let's not go there', he insists. But C ignores him and passes through the portal – the audient follows.

The audience member is in a barren moonlit landscape. The topography is reminiscent of the bleak beauty of Connemara (a region located on the west coast of Ireland). There is a ring of large mountains rising in the distance, and we are standing at a crossroads, but unlike in the other spaces, we cannot move about; we can only watch and listen. Next to the road is a gnarled old tree. From the tree, we hear C's voice. Her words are whispered, internal, slightly distorted. When she speaks, dead leaves rise from the tree and disappear into the ether:

This is where I live.
This is where I am trapped.
This is my story.
Two roads.
My blood and your blood.
The face, that face, those eyes.
Crucify, crucifix.
Brisance.
I'm losing him.

Go back.
Go back in time and change it.

There is a white flash. We find ourselves in another VR space. We are inside a giant dome structure. Inside the space, suspended in mid-air, are the smashed-up parts of a crashed car. K and C are here. C is angry. She begins to shout, her rant becoming more extreme, racist and unhinged: 'I will be the rod of St Patrick. Out, out, out, drive, drive, them out. Snakes, snakes, snakes, go back'. K tries to calm the situation, telling C: 'We've gone far enough, too far'.

Attempting to take control, K orders the audience to remove their HMD.

Back in real life, K is apologetic about C's strange behaviour. He enters the audience member's 'bubble' and helps them put away their VR equipment. Suddenly, there's a loud bang on the wall of the bubble. The real-life C is pressed up against the glass. She is wearing a large ball gown, and her long hair is tangled and unkempt. She tells the audience members that she is in charge now; she must be obeyed: 'People of Ireland. I give you my promise; I will be strong but fair, hard but even-handed. Fear. Believe. Obey. This is the narrative. This is your destiny'.

C tries to approach the audience member, but K physically intervenes. C retreats to her bubble, looking fragile and troubled. She returns to her narrative about the death of her husband in a car crash. She insists on what sounds like a fantasy – the impact wasn't her husband's fault. He wasn't drunk. A man with dark eyes veered into their path. He forced them to crash:

My husband hardly took a drink, hardly ever.
There was another car.
This was murder.

Go back now.
Go back and find him.
That's an order.
Go back and find him and punish him.
Go.

C seems crumpled and powerless now. K shepherds the audience members away from this spectacle, ushering them to a fire escape at the back of the room. Before even saying goodbye, K shunts them out the door and slams it shut. The audience member finds themself in a large courtyard. Cars are parking up, and people are walking in and out of an office block on the other side of the yard. There is a coffee stand, and small groups chat at tables.

Remounting *Emperor 101*

A few months after the initial premiere of *Emperor 101* at the Dublin Theatre Festival, the show was invited to be performed at SXSW as part of RETiniZE's showcase at the UK House. The main difference between the two presentations was that the SXSW show would be completely virtual, with no pre and post-VR physical theatre experience. The actors were performing from home, with one performing while on holiday.

The live VR and theatre show was designed to be performed to one audience member at a time. During development, we had built a 'spectator mode' in which the show was still committed to one primary audience member (who spoke and interacted with the actors); however, there could be several unseen and unheard spectators, similar to Tender Claw's Tempest (2020). This feature was utilized to increase audience numbers without retracting from a piece designed and directed to be performed intimately to just one audience member.

In April 2023, *Emperor 101* was remounted again for the LivePerformance360 festival[5] with the Boca De Lupo theatre company in Vancouver. On this occasion, none of the tech facilitators who had worked on the show previously would be providing in-person support. A detailed onboarding and user guide document was created, essentially an SOP (standard operating procedure) on how to run the show, a troubleshooting guide, etc.

Audience response

When working at the intersection of VR and theatre in these early days, audience feedback (often through their physical responses) is critical. The overall audience response was very positive. Most found it an exciting and sometimes unsettling experience, which is understandable and desirable given the subject matter and the immersive nature of VR.

Even after play-testing the app with many different demographics in advance, a live audience will inevitably surprise you. For instance, the term 'hoppers' was created for the audience members who would hop (teleport) away from the actors and the narrative, choosing instead to explore what the various VR rooms had to offer. One such hopper expressed:

> *'I didn't want to be brainwashed by C and K, so I headed to other rooms to look for more exciting avatars I could interact with'.*

During the induction process with the show's facilitators, an audience member would occasionally take the HMD off and say they felt claustrophobic or it just wasn't for them. To facilitate and let these audience members experience the show. The VR producer wore the HMD as their proxy, and the HMD viewpoint was cast to a large screen that the audience member sat in front of.

Technical challenges and solutions

Initially, *Emperor 101* had a hard deadline for premiering at the Dublin Theatre Festival in 2021. The design and code were fine-tuned until the opening day, and as the doors were opening, it hit its first technical challenge. For seemingly unknown and unpredictable reasons, the *Emperor 101* app crashed. Troubleshooting with an audience waiting outside the door was beyond nerve-wracking. The root cause was uncovered – a spike in activity on the network was causing the underlying port connections to drop. More evolved technology (like website infrastructure) has a fault tolerance where micro-drops in a network are hidden from users as the site poles multiply to gain a connection. This polling is not necessarily the case with more nascent technologies like the platforms we were using. The *Emperor 101* application required a more robust network, and the solution was to physically move the server to another building to resolve the issue.

Another issue appeared during the show's run that was intermittent and impossible to reproduce: the actors' audio would suddenly become disconnected. Through troubleshooting, it seemed the Meta Quest firmware would take control of the HMDs' microphone input. The team at RETiniZE coded a bespoke workaround patch – a 'magic' button that the actor could press to reset all of the app's VOIP services and return control of the microphone to the user.

Conclusions – recommendations, takeaways and learnings for VR theatre

With the creation of *Emperor 101*, The Performance Corporation was exploring uncharted territory in scenography and dramaturgy. Few other theatrical works in this area are performed in a bespoke virtual space with uniquely designed avatars. Retrospectively, the strength of the design elements served the piece's dramaturgy very effectively, creating an engaging, exciting and sometimes unsettling world. Designers Leon Butler and Peter Power were shortlisted for The Institute of Designers in Ireland Awards 2022 in the category of Experience Design.

The team learned a lot during the process, especially regarding the technical aspects of creating such work. In the future, all design, visual and audio development should cease at least two weeks before opening the show. Achieving this would help to ensure as much time as possible rehearsing in the finalized VR space. Also, guaranteeing robust Service Level Agreements with the VR developers is essential.

One of the keys to the project's success was the team's commitment to the experimental nature of this work. They were primed to expect the unexpected, which reared its head on many occasions! In particular, two hugely experienced performers were invaluable to the performance process. Namely, Caitríona Ní Mhurchú and Karl Quinn, who have track records of working on innovative and developmental projects, showed outstanding commitment, creativity and flexibility as they navigated this new theatrical form.

VR is poised to redefine the performance landscape through globally networked actors. As technology evolves, the boundaries between physical and virtual realms will blur, presenting new opportunities and challenges. VR has the potential to democratize access to theatrical performances, amplify artistic collaborations and revolutionize storytelling. However, careful navigation of ethical considerations and the promotion of inclusivity will be crucial in realizing the full potential of VR in the performing arts.

Notes

1 https://www.theperformancecorporation.com/.

2 https://www.retinize.com/.

3 https://www.animotive.com/.

4 The person who is experiencing the performance.

5 https://bocadellupo.com/projects/live-performance-360.

11

Find WiiLii and beyond: Exploring memory and reality in immersive theatre through extended reality – a conversation with Mina Hyeon

Yong Suk Yoo

Mina Hyeon exemplifies a multifaceted creative producer with a deep understanding of content creation, technology and immersive storytelling. With a background in international documentary co-production and a master's degree in multimedia video, Mina has honed her skills as a producer and storyteller. In 2020, she co-founded Giiöii Immersive Storytelling Studio in South Korea, leading initiatives to redefine storytelling boundaries. Among these, *Find WiiLii* stands out, recognized as an official showcase at the 2020 Marché du Film – Festival de Cannes XR Development. Mina's role as co-director and writer was crucial in shaping the project, which has evolved into the XR immersive theatre episode *The Gate-Crasher*, featured at the 2023 SXSW and BIFAN festivals.

This chapter explores Mina's innovative contributions to XR storytelling, mainly through *Find WiiLii*, a project inspired by her grandmother's Alzheimer's diagnosis and the family's differing recollections of shared events. Mina uses XR to blend past and present, designing emotional and non-linear narrative experiences that allow users to 'see and touch' memories in immersive virtual spaces. She balances technical challenges, like optimizing XR environments for various platforms, with the creative goal of fostering memory-driven engagement. Her work highlights the intersection of technological innovation and storytelling, emphasizing collaboration and experimentation across diverse media.

This conversation, conducted in Korean on 25 November 2023, and translated into English by the author, delves into Mina's career, creative process and vision for advancing immersive storytelling through interdisciplinary approaches and evolving XR technologies.

Yong-Suk Yoo (YY) Could you please briefly introduce your project, *Find WiiLii*?

Mina Hyeon (MH) *Find WiiLii* is a simulation system that allows users to see and touch the memories of others. In 2023, it produced its first episode as XR Immersive Theatre: *The Gate-Crasher*. The inspiration for this project originated in 2017 when my grandmother was diagnosed with Alzheimer's. While reminiscing with family over old photographs, I became fascinated by how we each recalled the same events and situations differently. This intrigue laid the foundation for the concept. I aimed to explore elements like external and internal contexts and emotions, which are not captured in 2D frames, using 6DoF XR and three-dimensional spatial experiences. The project was set in Changsin-dong, where the stark contrasts of a steep quarry, dense residential areas and Namsan Tower coexist within a single landscape. The objective was to design a non-linear narrative experience that stimulates emotions through the user's spatial perception and interaction.

The initial plan was to create a linear narrative for single or multi-user experiences. As the project expanded, it was divided into discrete episodes, with the inaugural one serving as Immersive Theatre despite a limited production cycle. The necessity of training actors unfamiliar with virtual environments necessitated an adjustment period. The design, modelling and construction of the space required several months. A virtual city was created for effective actor navigation and rehearsal, as an alternative to offline practice rooms, and to facilitate more efficient rehearsals.

The project commenced with a rough and personalized approach, exploring the concept of representing memories in a virtual space. Influenced by my interest in memory and dreams, as evidenced in my student films, I questioned the unique value of XR compared to traditional media. During the planning phase, the concept evolved from missing memories to memories lost in teleportation, inspired by Philip K. Dick's *Ubik* (1969), where characters communicate with the deceased, inspiring the idea of seeing memories.

Traditional media often depict memory in a manner that is almost identical to reality. However, I believe that actual memory and the act of remembering are two distinct phenomena. This idea has frequently occupied my thoughts.

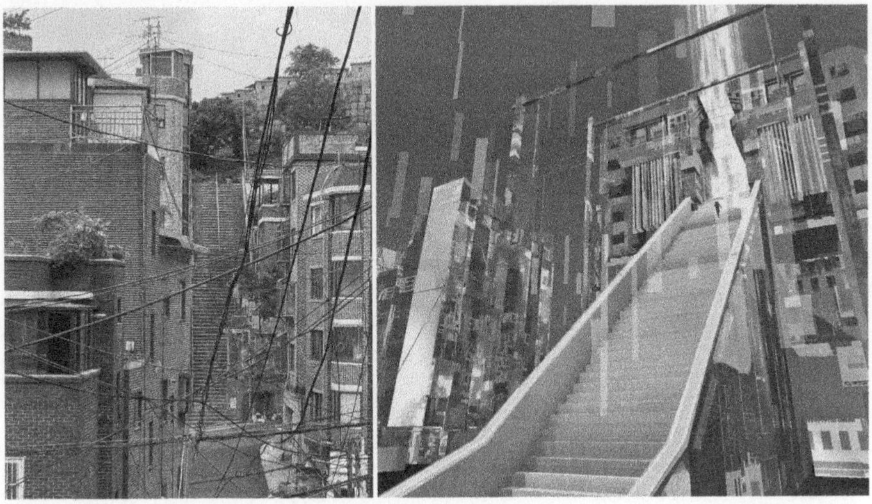

FIGURE 11.1 The real Changshindong stairs (left) and the virtual world of *Find WiiLii* (right), 2022 (© Mina Hyeon).

YY Could you please elaborate on the representation of memory in XR and analogue? Please describe any personal or social context that influenced your work with XR and any relevant events at the time. How did the portrayal of memory in traditional media, especially analogue video, as almost identical to reality, whereas remembering is more complex and nonlinear, inform your considerations and approach to building immersive storytelling through XR technology?

MH After my grandmother was diagnosed with Alzheimer's, as a family, we often discussed old photographs. We were intrigued by our differing recollections of the same events. This phenomenon piqued my interest, prompting me to explore memory further.

I defined memory as the totality of the subject, space and emotions that constitute the context of events within and outside a specific moment captured in a photograph. From this understanding, I envisioned a simulated world where forgotten memories exist and designed a virtual reality experience to see and touch others' memories. This three-dimensional spatial experience aims to express personal memories centred around emotions, blending exaggerated and distorted forms with the familiar and unfamiliar.

Find WiiLii tells the story of a father searching for his lost daughter (see Plate 22). The plot explores the biopolitical theme of a tech company's conspiracy to access memories without consent. The design objective was to transform participants from passive observers to active participants in the drama, aligning their personal experiences with the story's timeline. Experiments across spatial design, interaction and narrative were conducted

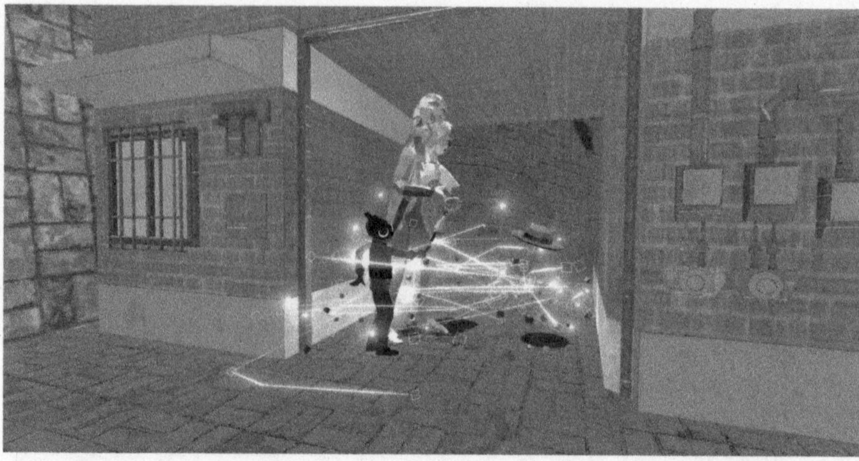

FIGURE 11.2 A scene capture of collecting *WiiLii*, 2022 (© Mina Hyeon).

to evoke emotions tied to individual memories, especially from childhood, allowing participants to integrate their unique experiences into the drama.

At the outset, participants are not mainly engaged with the form of *WiiLii* or the purpose of the actions. Instead, they become immersed in completing game missions. In addition to the *WiiLii* representing the daughter and father directly connected to the story, small plants are breaking through the pavement, elongated stray cats and unidentified *WiiLii* shapes are hidden throughout the alleys (see Plate 23). Participants quickly lose their way in the complex environment, and at the end of a cul-de-sac, they can see a large red building in the distance. In contrast with the prevailing ambience and style of the space, this edifice serves as the playground, the culminating stage of the drama. Participants who have become lost are informed by the concealed antagonist within the environment that this red structure is a playground. At this juncture, participants are queried about their own childhood experiences. The sensation of playing with the butterfly net evokes tangible memories, transferring emotions into the drama. Participants process and remember the experience in a manner similar to how memories are created in reality through the three-dimensional spatial experience.

YY Memory can be understood as an interaction between the past and the present. In this context, theatre can be considered a form of presented memory. Events on stage, even those depicting the past, occur in the same time and space as the audience, allowing for memory reconstruction through interaction and the merging of past and present. This process makes the essence of XR or virtual worlds akin to that of theatre. Additionally, virtual worlds enable experiences of previously nonexistent events, extending into future memory.

MH Indeed, the initial concept remained influential during the production, as evidenced by the discussion of presented memory. Despite the production having occurred last year, the virtual space enables the audience to act as a reality, thereby establishing a new memory.

What memories can be implanted within that audience experience? At what point in the narrative can sensory and visual information be implanted to have a meaningful impact on the audience's subsequent behaviour? These were questions that we considered extensively.

Furthermore, due to the nature of the performance, certain elements were feasible, while others were not. Alternatively, some elements were not fully considered due to the lack of the desired visuals, but some attempts were valid.

YY In immersive theatre, the concept of moving the audience through the space is often discussed. However, the critical aspect is the audience's psychological and emotional journey, which connects to the concept of immediacy. XR experiences frequently erase the space in between, resembling teleportation rather than a traditional journey. This instantaneous experience delivers a more powerful immersive impact, potentially making virtual experiences more impactful than real-world ones requiring physical build-up. Could you discuss how the identity and status of human audiences or actors are established or altered in your projects within this virtual environment, where digital media images are central?

MH Creators are still experimenting with how to invite the audience into the space. In my projects, the audience can be a first-person protagonist, a third-person observer or a second-person helper. XR narrative content is primarily experienced in the first-person, and while this allows for interaction, it cannot guarantee complete guidance according to the creator's intent.

I have found that a first-person perspective is not always practical for storytelling. In contrast, I frequently situate the audience as a second-person facilitator. This viewpoint allows for the presence of a protagonist while still enabling the audience to experience the narrative from a first-person perspective without assuming the role of the protagonist.

YY In your creative process, could you discuss how dramaturgical, choreographic and artistic/directorial decisions were influenced by technical agencies, both regarding the potential for new ideas and the restrictions they imposed?

MH Between 2017 and 2018, research on interaction and presence using motion capture technology was actively conducted, allowing participants and characters to interact in both virtual and physical environments. XR was anticipated as the next visual medium after film during this period. However, it became evident that hyper-realism and high-quality graphics alone were insufficient to achieve a sense of presence; instead, low-poly graphics or abstract environments rendered with particles provided greater immersion.

In 2018, I worked as a video designer for a contemporary dance project called *Namu*. Collaborating with the choreographer on movement aspects significantly influenced my approach to space-based work. My work focuses on designing experiences where the audience can move voluntarily, evoking nuanced emotions beyond primal feelings like fear. While many XR contents still follow PC game UI conventions, recent research has led to XR works that align more with how our brains perceive reality.

At Giiöii studio, in addition to my roles as director and producer, I led R&D efforts on production technologies, studying volumetric capture, motion capture and optimization. Overcoming technical limitations was a routine occurrence, and despite rapid technological advancements, maintaining curiosity and persistent research is essential. Typically, I consider the desired experience first, conducting technical research and prototyping during planning. However, I also plan items suited to specific technologies when available.

A consistent challenge in XR projects has been optimization. Elements that worked well on PC often broke or lagged in Android builds. Finding developers skilled in optimization was difficult. Prototyping during planning proved to be a practical approach. XR creative tools such as Quill and Gravity Sketch facilitated the rapid grasping of spatial scale and discussions on interaction, graphics, sound and other elements. For *Find WiiLii*, we uploaded spaces in VRChat to co-design the experience with team members, inviting actors to compose key scenes and experiment even before the world was entirely created.

When working on *Find WiiLii*, we were concerned with how to lead the audience naturally to the next step without disrupting their immersive experience in terms of interaction. Because the game engine primarily utilizes the interaction elements, employing a UI grammar in game development is often necessary. For example, if there is a cup in the space and the user is required to interact with an object to obtain a clue and progress to the next stage, it is possible to make the object glow, draw attention to it in some way or create a sound when the user interacts with it. This process is an example of interaction design. However, when the user is in a performance format and attempting to immerse themselves in the narrative, it is often distracting. It feels forced and artificial.

The distraction is lessened when connected to a PC because the user can navigate the space through mouse operation. Even if the user is not skilled, they can quickly find the clues. However, when wearing an XR device, the user must deploy a specific set of skills; they must be familiar with the controls. If the audience is unfamiliar with the device and the interface itself, and the UI is unfriendly, the story may not progress. Consequently, I have been contemplating the following:

In the case of *Find WiiLii*, we utilized an off-the-shelf XR platform, which precluded the complete elimination of cues to interact with it when approaching the operational tools it inherently possessed. Consequently, we retained these cues, but we were able to eliminate the text prompts. Instead, we intentionally created a performance for the tutorial session, utilizing actors in character. The objective was to have the actors demonstrate the actions essential to the play experience so that the audience could immediately imprint the fundamental interactions and use them whenever needed.

In addition, for spatial transitions, the project aimed to create a sense of teleportation in the story. This movement would allow the landscape to change around the viewer when they enter an alleyway suddenly.

YY To achieve a more abrupt and spontaneous effect.

MH Indeed, we attempted to provide an experience where the transition from one space to another is delineated as if one is turning into an alleyway and then looking back to find oneself in a different environment. At times, we would involuntarily relocate individuals to a different space. For instance, in one example, we would provide background information such as 'Some dark force or lurking force has forcibly transported the audience.' To achieve this, we would set the relevant scene as a background. To facilitate witnessing the phenomenon in question, we employed various techniques, including visual stimuli, to elicit a visual response or, in instances where this was not feasible, the forcible teleportation of the audience through the space itself. In other cases, we instructed the audience to remain stationary while the space underwent a process of deconstruction and reconstruction, resulting in the emergence of a new environment.

YY I am curious about your thoughts and practices related to liveness as an individual creator, which have been shaped by your work combining XR and immersive theatre.

MH When creating XR content, visuals are only half the equation; sound is equally important. In *Find WiiLii*, we used the VRChat platform, which inherently limits sound use. Despite this, sound is crucial for creating a lively virtual space.

Unfortunately, the platform's nature, which primarily facilitates conversations between users, precluded spatial sound design in *Find WiiLii*.

Our sound design efforts were limited to amplifying specific avatars' sounds or adjusting sound distances per object.

It is crucial to create stories that respond to audience diversity. Immersive theatre principles where actors and audience coexist, guide my approach. Future XR projects might include AI-driven avatars alongside human actors to reduce costs and network load. This human-machine collaboration could lead to more flexible storytelling, adapting to audience choices without breaking immersion. I am exploring ways to create an open-world experience where the audience can freely navigate and influence the story, using sound cues or actor guidance to maintain narrative coherence.

YY As an XR artist, could you discuss the benefits and challenges of interdisciplinary collaboration, considering factors such as participants' varied disciplinary languages, expertise and technical proficiency?

MH During interdisciplinary collaborations, we conducted a comprehensive review and discussion of references with artists for approximately one or two months to align our visions, particularly for those new to XR. This phase involved hands-on experiences in an office or on-site to inspire artists and integrate XR concepts such as perspective, scale and colour schemes.

We emphasized the importance of trial and error, research and familiarizing artists with XR tools, leveraging global communities that share pioneering experiences. We frequently employed motion capture technology in projects involving performing artists like dancers.

One significant challenge in XR is mitigating dizziness and motion sickness while maintaining compelling visual storytelling. This task involved addressing technical limitations in capturing detailed movements and optimizing equipment efficiency, often through extensive trial and error and equipment adjustments.

YY Could you share specific plans or concepts for your ongoing or future projects?

MH As an artist, my interest lies in identifying moments when reality suddenly becomes unfamiliar and reconstructing it into a form I can comprehend. By reflecting on events characterized by irrational choices and emotional upheavals, I aim to continuously explore how systems and user experiences in the technological era impact an individual's unconscious mind.

Currently, I am preparing a project called *Popcorn-phobia*, which aims to illustrate how social media recommendation algorithms, influenced by capital, induce collective anxiety and distort perceptions of reality, using the thermodynamic process of popcorn as an analogy.

The initial iteration of the project was created as a video with Generative AI. Intriguingly, the AI struggles with unconventional images, particularly in creating diverse representations of a single popcorn kernel. This challenge is reflected in finding these precise images online.

The project's ultimate objective is to evolve into a real-time interactive XR environment design. This shift in focus will move away from creating new meanings through image montages and cross-editing to exploring emotional and sensory changes through spatial form and texture.

12

Live performance in social VR: Using the affordances of social virtual reality to create audience-centred live performance experiences

Deirdre V. Lyons and Stephen Butchko

Today's audiences exhibit different tendencies to those of previous decades due, in no small part, to the evolving nature of telecommunications and screen technologies. Now most individuals in industrialized cultures have access to entertainment via a smartphone. People can step into the digital limelight and bask in the glow of social media stardom, or sit back and passively consume curated digital stories on the multiple entertainment options available to them, from TikTok to streaming services. Today, online goods and services are bought and sold, global communities are being built at breathtaking speed and art in all forms is flourishing.

While experimenting with these new tools is rife with challenges, it is only natural that artists are at the forefront pushing the boundaries of what is possible as the next invention comes along, such as virtual reality (VR), where a computer-generated three-dimensional environment allows users to perceive a virtual surrounding in a way that approximates reality.

> The user becomes engulfed in a virtual environment that simultaneously engages multiple senses, in ways similar to how we are accustomed to experience things in our daily 'real' lives. This is distinctly different from

> other media experiences, which only capture fragmented aspects of what our senses can detect … When you look at something in VR, it is not framed by the dimensions of a monitor, or television set, or movie screen. Instead, you see the virtual world as you see the real one. When you look to the left or right, the virtual world is still there.
>
> (Bailenson 2018, 40–1)

It is a wholly different medium.

And in this new simulated space theatrical performances have sprung into digital life in ways that are dazzling audience members, from traditionally staged proscenium plays where the audience watch actors on a stage behind a real or imagined 'proscenium' (usually abiding by a 'fourth' wall and ignoring the audience) such as in *Neverland Live!* (Nickle 2020) a VR theatre production based on Peter Pan, to immersive plays that invite participants to experience up-close and personal interactions with the actors, as in *Gumball Dreams* (2022). While these experiences can affect audiences profoundly, there is a cost to working at the cutting edge of tech, where performances rely on the stability of Wi-Fi, the challenge of teaching audiences how to arrive in the digital theatre lobby or cybersickness for sensitive individuals. But in our experience, when it all works, magic is created.

For classically trained theatre performers with extensive immersive theatre experience, entering the expanse of VR was like stepping onto the biggest immersive theatre stage in the world – confined only by one's imagination and the limits of technology. Technology allows for both proscenium and immersive theatre to coexist within VR, but is one form more effective than the other? It has been our experience that immersive theatre, particularly when using its interactive elements, is the most impactful genre of live theatre within the realm of VR. We will explore some of the reasons that have led us to feel that way.

Live theatre in VR is a relatively new phenomenon. VR has been around since the late 1950s but consumer-grade head-mounted displays (HMDs) only became commercially viable during the last ten years. It was shortly after artists had access to these consumer-grade HMDs that experimentation and live performance in the 'Metaverse' began to bloom. Such creative endeavours reveal the challenges, affordances and opportunities of this nascent technology.

Background and related work

Cinematographer Morton Heilig patented the first HMD, the *Telesphere Mask* (Barnard 2022), in 1960, which boasted 3D images and stereo sound. Fifteen years later, Myron Krueger's VR platform, *VIDEOPLACE* (Barnard 2022), premiered at the Milwaukee Art Center. In this installation, participants were immersed in a virtual world of recorded human silhouettes that they could interact with; however, the machine's position-sensing technology and video displays did not require the use of an HMD. In the early 1990s, the Virtuality Group premiered *Virtuality* (McCauley 2016), a pod-like arcade machine, complete with HMDs, where players would play games in a 3D world. Slowly VR made progress. Then, in 2010 Palmer Luckey developed the Oculus Rift and in 2014 Facebook purchased the company and virtual-headset technology began to take off, allowing many more people to explore the possibilities of VR (Barnard 2022).

One of the earliest live performances in VR is *Placeholder* (Dixon 2006) premiering in 1993 and created by Brenda Laurel and Rachel Strickland. When social VR platforms started appearing in the early 2010s, this presented an easier solution for staging live theatrical productions in this digital space. One of the first companies to mount such a production is The Orange Bucket Acting Troupe, with their production of *The Princess Bride* (Carson 2018), hosted on Rec Room, by developer Against Gravity. Audiences entered the social VR platform Rec Room, then gathered in the same digital lobby before moving to a viewing box for this well-received proscenium play.

The above examples evince that this new (VR) performance genre is still at a very early stage of development of this new category of entertainment. It took over 100 years to get to the point in film that we are at today, where fast cuts, over-the-shoulder shots and computer-generated graphics define the current sophisticated grammar/language of standard filmmaking. When Palmer Luckey was asked if VR was the next iPhone, he responded

> We're kind of starting from scratch here. It's unlikely that the first things to come out in that range of consumer devices are going to be the iPhone. The iPhone moment is going to take longer, and it's probably not going to be such a huge, radical jump, it's going to be more gradual. The [Oculus] Rift is not the 'iPhone of VR.' Nothing out there is 'the iPhone of VR.' They're almost like the Palm Pilots and the Treos of virtual reality.
>
> (Johnson 2016)

We can only imagine where we will be with VR a hundred years from now and what VR theatre will look like in the future.

Adaptation of new technology is often thought of as an upward slope, progressing steadily to mass adoption, but it is more often like a stair step, with leaps and plateaus. One of these leaps was when the untethered Oculus Quest headset was released in May 2019. This headset allowed participants, at a relatively low price point, to experience VR for the first time. *The Under Presents* (Damiani 2019), a VR game developed by Tender Claws, was released in November 2019, featuring live actors creating devised theatre within the game. Originally slated for a three-month run, due to the pandemic of 2020, the actor run was extended and another show developed out of this crisis, *The Under Presents: Tempest* (Hayden 2020). The pandemic was the catalyst for new theatrical experimentation, including in VR with our work at Ferryman Collective, which started as a group of four creators – Stephen Butchko, Deirdre V. Lyons, Braden Roy and Brian Tull – with a twenty-minute proof of concept, *PARA* (2020), and continued on with *Krampusnacht* (2020) when others joined the collective, Whitton Frank and Christopher Lane Davis (AKA Screaming Color), to create the award-winning productions of The *Severance Theory: Welcome to Respite* (2021) (Welcome to Respite) followed by *Gumball Dreams*. We were witness to the first steps of *The Meta Movie's* work, *Alien Rescue* (Pietrobon 2020) and *Scarecrow* (Melnick 2020), originally a hybrid experience with both in person and VR aspects; they were forced to pivot to a completely VR show due to the pandemic. All of these productions were well received, particularly with the added visibility of major film festivals giving credibility to this new storytelling genre which is at the intersection of gaming, film and theatre.

When asked to think of theatre, you may picture a form of proscenium theatre as outlined above. As the play unfolds, audiences are allowed to absorb the story in a passive way, mercifully free of the danger of having to be vulnerable in the moment. Alternatively, there is the lesser-known immersive theatre, sometimes called playable theatre, environmental theatre or site-specific theatre. These genres of theatre discard the traditional stage and fourth wall, and place productions in myriad locations, anywhere that gives credence to the setting within the story of the play. Audiences become part of the performance with the division between actor and audience less defined. Moving outside of the constraints of traditional proscenium theatre, the 360-degree nature of immersive productions, along with the up-close performances, lays the groundwork for profound personalized audience connection. Having exploded in the 1960s, Richard Schechner's work experimented with 'Environmental Theatre' (Eckersley, 2014) including sets that were constructed in front of the audience, encroaching on their space to encourage greater interaction between audience and performers and inviting audiences to participate in the performance. In *The Commune* (Gussow 1970), they were even asked to remove their shoes.

Arthur Sainer (Sainer 1997), a drama critic for the Village Voice in New York, had seen so much experimental theatre in the 1960s and 1970s that he wrote thus in his book *The New Radical Theater Notebook*:

> What are the virtues of the non-theatrical interior (the church, the laundromat)? A certain enriching tension is set up when the space is employed as itself but is simultaneously something else: the church isn't

> transformed into a theater for a night but in which theatre nevertheless happens, and the laundromat in which theater suddenly erupts both demand that the spectator understand that life is less capable than usual of protecting him from art, that the demands of the imagination, with its audacious risks and its disturbing confrontations, have pursued him as it were into his own home.

This long history of 'audacious risks and its disturbing confrontations' continues today with companies like JFI Productions and their beloved show *The Willows* (Martens 2022) and the work of The Speakeasy Society, including *The Kansas Collection* (Winters 2019) among many others.

During immersive performances, audiences are absorbed into the story, often interacting with the actors, resulting in a dance of scripted and unscripted storytelling magic. Along with the fourth wall being discarded, bringing the audience closer; the mercurial nature of the immersive genre, and, more specifically, virtual reality performance, opens the door to almost limitless staging, offering even more exciting possibilities, and makes every iteration as unique as a fingerprint.

Many immersive theatre productions will choose to incorporate group and/or personal interaction into the experience with the actors, by casting the audience as a character or even assigning them roles in the play. For example, audiences may play the part of mourners, art gallery attendees or candidates interviewing for a job. In our live VR theatre production *Welcome to Respite* by CoAct Productions (CoAct) in collaboration with our company Ferryman Collective, directed by Lyndsie Scoggin, we cast our audience as alternate aspects of Alex's (the main character's) personality. *Welcome to Respite* was adapted from an award-winning physical production presented in Silverlake, CA, by CoAct Productions (Pawlowicz 2019) about a child, Alex, who has returned from an extended stay with their aunt while their parents worked out their marital problems during which an unknown trauma happened. As a result, Alex began to experience symptoms of dissociative identity disorder.[1] It was a three-actor show: two playing the parents and one actor played the part of a real estate agent, the shadow, as well as handling stage manager duties; each show allowed only one audience member per performance.

We were able to take this single-audience show and, in VR, transform it into one that allows ten audience members to experience the performance at the same time, by having nine of them embody invisible avatars. The remaining audience member plays the role of seven-year-old Alex using an avatar of an androgynous child. Avatars are a virtual representation of oneself in a digital space, although they are not limited to humanoid forms and can be anything from a tin can to a walking hot dog. In VR, they are controlled by the person wearing the HMD and their movements are operated by hand controllers and tracking from the headset. The invisible avatars allow the remaining audience in *Welcome to Respite* to move around the space, unseen to everyone in the digital environment. To help them feel that they are still present in the space, even though they appear transparent to themselves, these audience members can see five small blue spheres on each hand, which represent their fingers, visible only to them. We justify the invisible audience by casting them as alternative personalities of Alex, AKA 'Alters'. And their experience during the performance differs from Alex's, who remains visible to all during the show.

Employing different audience viewing experiences allows producers the ability to be sensitive to the audiences' needs and to accommodate all levels of participation from passive observers, to those who wish to be front and centre. This satisfies the desires of newly emerging types of audiences, shaped by growing up in a social media drenched world.

Proximity and intimacy

In *Welcome to Respite*, our invisible audience is given agency to move around the space and be as close to or as far away from the action as they prefer. Unobtrusive but integral to the story, they are given moments to assist and protect our story's hero, Alex, as well as engage in other interactions that Alex does not experience. The Alters encounter memory orbs, only visible to them, that reveal moments of Alex's family history. During certain parts of the performance, the Alters get to vote on specific responses to help Alex answer difficult questions; they even help shield Alex from danger when the scary 'Shadow' appears. The script was written in such a way that even if the audience member playing Alex is on the passive side and responds minimally, the show will still play out as intended. Additionally, these differing tiers of experience can allow for multiple pricing structures that are not based on how far away the audience is but, instead, on the amount of participation an individual would like to engage in.

Another unique and exciting feature of immersive theatre is the use of branching narratives, a storytelling device that is quite popular in gaming, visual novels and role-playing games, but is also well known from the *Choose Your Own Adventure* (Jamison 2022) books that were wildly popular in the 1980s, where readers go on different paths from one another. For example, in our 4th show *Gumball Dreams* (designed for three audience members and one actor), there is a moment when the main character, Onyx, a dying alien who needs help to transition from this life, sends a pair of audience members off to solve a puzzle, while the third stays behind and engages in a personal discussion with Onyx. These opportunities create moments of bonding between the audience and the actor, as well as between the two other audience members who are working together to complete the required task. This allows for unique interactions between the characters and the audience and encourages intriguing discussions afterwards. Branching narratives also provides opportunities for returning audiences who wish to experience the production again in new ways.

Intimacy and personal connection are the currency of both physical and VR immersive performances. Because of this, scaling up a show can be tricky, as the entire play space is the stage and both the cast and audience are on it together. Scaling up the size of a physical immersive production that accommodates more audience members can end up feeling too crowded, resulting in a less-than-satisfying experience for everyone. However, because VR allows for the use of invisible avatars, a much larger audience can be present in the space without distraction, as we did with *Welcome to Respite*.

Working within the bounds of current technology allows our imagination to step out of the limitations of what we know in the physical world, discovering innovative ways to add audiences. For example, an invisible camera can be placed in the environment and stream the show to a 2D platform, introducing more people to this medium. Or instead of having invisible avatars, audiences can inhabit small, unobtrusive avatars which preserve valuable megabyte space (memory) and remain part of the story. An example of this is the audience-embodied Eyebot robots in The Meta Movie's *Alien rescue*, which fly around other audience members who portray the primary humanoid characters. Audiences are no longer confined by a seat, limited by a physical space with only one viewpoint for an entire show.

Micro-expressions and body language

The fidelity of today's VR, particularly on the most accessible HMD, is rudimentary. When it comes to live performance, micro-expressions and subtle body language for audiences to take cues from either do not exist or are limited. Likewise, watching avatars perform from a distance, analogous to the proscenium theatre format, suffers because of this, while disregarding the affordances facilitated by the VR platform. As time passes, VR headsets will allow for faster computing power and Wi-Fi will become stronger, providing increased upload and download speeds, which will allow for a higher fidelity and emotionally impactful experience. As this evolutionary process plays out, VR theatre creators and audiences will benefit from ultra-expressive avatars and higher-poly environments with which to explore. When this happens, more traditionally staged theatre may become more engaging on a VR platform.

One way in which VR theatre makes up for the loss of micro-body language information of the performers is a phenomenon called the Proteus Effect. 'In virtual environments, it is known that synchronizing the actions of an avatar with the operator causes a change in the operator's self-perception, resulting in a change of behavior' (Obana, Hasegawa, and Sakuta 2017). In Greek mythology, Proteus was sometimes known as the god of elusive sea change because he transformed himself to evade capture. From Proteus we get the adjective *protean*, meaning *adaptable, versatile* or *capable of taking many forms* (Wigmore 2014). In their Stanford University paper entitled *The Proteus Effect: The Effect of Transformed Self-Representation on Behavior*, Yee and Bailenson (2007) describe experiments that show how individuals who change their self-representation can cause changes in their behaviour.

We discovered this during *Welcome to Respite* when performing with audiences. It is not uncommon to hear audience members who portray the role of Alex say how much they identified with and felt like the seven-year-old that they once were, getting to experience looking up at their parents, or being too short to see well over the counter. While our minds recognize that we are adults, our bodies remember what it was like to be a child, we are thus connected to memories of how we felt when we were young. The brain often fails to differentiate between virtual experiences and real ones.

> The patterns of neurons that fire when one watches a three-dimensional digital re-creation of a supermodel, such as Giselle or Fabio, are very similar – if not identical – to those that fire in the actual presence of the models. Walking a tightrope over a chasm in virtual reality can be a terrifying ordeal even if the walker knows it's virtual rather than physical.
>
> (Blascovich, J., & Bailenson, J. N. (2011) (see Plate 24)

From an acting perspective, we noticed that the performances of those audience members playing Alex, who strongly identified with the character, were the most fun to interact with. When they allowed themselves to relax into the role, they reacted in surprising and emotionally honest ways. While the show is scripted for the actors, performers never know what the audience will say or do when responding to a particular prompt or question. Will they sit and colour with VR crayons when asked to? What do they say when asked if they remember when they received their favourite toy? Those who performed Alex with abandon often take the story on exciting and unexpected tangents, where the actors can improvise with them before skilfully bringing them back to the next story point, continuing on with the narrative.

In *Gumball Dreams*, our avatars are aliens from another galaxy, allowing the audience to become other beings, when they look down at four fingered hands and see themselves in a mirror as something entirely different. This affords them the opportunity to experience 'maskenfreiheit', a German word that describes the freedom one feels when hiding our identities, originally behind a mask but now also behind the skin of an avatar. This is also known as 'Carnival License' (see Plate 25).

Our minds are incredibly powerful, and with the technology of VR, everywhere we look is a magical world populated by real and unique people. Through interaction, we gain a sense of their personalities, their feelings, their likes and dislikes. Everyone in the same instance is present, communicating from behind our HMD masks, and after a while, we stop paying attention to the mask. And somewhere within this knowledge, when we virtually hug, or reach out and caress Alex's face during a loving moment in *Welcome to Respite*; our mind fills in the memory of the same feelings we have when we hug someone in the physical world. An emotional-physical need for that loving touch is fulfilled, even though actual touch is not possible in VR.

Physical hugs release oxytocin and lower cortisol: 'While a digital hug may not achieve the same levels of oxytocin in the blood, we might assume the brain goes through similar processes' (Eichenseer 2017). In this way, immersive and interactive theatre offers something that proscenium theatre does not; the power of touch, in person and virtually. Touch in VR is certainly not as compelling as in physical life; it has been our experience that it is still incredibly powerful and allows a feeling of connection and intimacy that mimics physical experiences.

Implications for cast and crew

Every person performing or working behind the scenes in VR is taking up limited computing space within the digital world. World builders can control what is seen and not seen by the audience and the development team programs triggers that perform tasks, activated by the actor, but invisible to the audience. For example, in *Welcome to Respite*, the performer will activate a trigger that starts the radio, or a different trigger that starts a sequence of animations without the need for an additional stage manager or control-booth operator. This not only helps with the performance as it is beneficial for timing and limits the effects of latency that would occur by having someone else trigger an animation or event but allows another potential audience member to be in the world instead of a backstage crew member.

One of the biggest advantages of theatre in VR is that it can be performed and experienced from home. Shows are inherently pandemic-safe, available to those who do not live in the same locale as the production or have other challenges with accessibility. As long as audience members have a VR

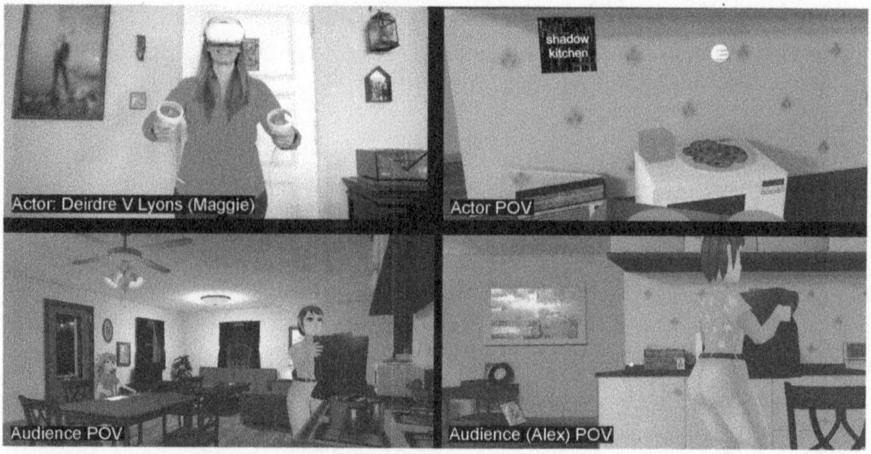

FIGURE 12.1 *Welcome to Respite*, Mom with Groceries, multiple views inside and outside of VR, 2021 (© Stephen Butchko).

headset and Wi-Fi, performances can be experienced from anywhere around the globe. VR has greatly increased our potential audience reach, and we regularly perform shows with audience members from all over the world. During performances of *Gumball Dreams*, we put SXSW attendees in Austin, Texas, into headsets to join an actor performing a show from her home in Bangkok, Thailand, followed by additional performances by other actors from Los Angeles, California. Actors have done shows in hotel rooms, or even in a trailer on set, in between filming scenes for a different production.

VR theatre allows for easier creation within our global storytelling community, bringing different cultures together to share stories, retelling them from differing perspectives for local communities and promoting understanding and encouraging collaboration. We were honoured when approached by GiiÖii Immersive Storytelling Studio (Gayet 2022), who licensed *Welcome to Respite* and worked with Ferryman Collective to adapt the play, translating it for Korean audiences. As cross-cultural working relationships continue to flourish, understanding will grow as we discover that we all have more in common than not, resulting in the potential for profound multicultural stories to be told (see Plate 26).

Lastly, there is an incredible opportunity for reimagining classical theatre in VR, showcasing important and time-honoured works like the plays of Shakespeare (there have already been a handful of VR adaptations) and a whole range of culturally diverse classics that have endured throughout the centuries and thrive when reinterpreted with new and exciting technology. This encourages exposure to today's young audiences and allows new generations to discover these historic tales.

Conclusion

Audiences who have multiple entertainment choices at their fingertips will be the ultimate arbiter of theatre in VR, whether proscenium or immersive productions are preferred, whether theatre will exist at all in VR, or become something completely different. While we are biased toward immersive and interactive theatre versus more traditional staging, both have their place. In either case, we encourage experimentation with the affordances of VR while thinking outside the limitations of one's previous physical experiences. In doing so, this new genre of theatre will continue to shine (see Plate 27).

It is doubtful that physical theatre will ever be replaced, but it is our belief that VR is such a powerful platform for live theatre that it will continue growing in popularity, while inspiring creators of all genres to find new and powerful ways of connecting with audiences far and wide. Broadway is now digital.

Note

1 Dissociative identity disorder is a severe form of dissociation, a mental process which produces a lack of connection in a person's thoughts, memories, feelings, actions, or sense of identity. Dissociative identity disorder is characterized by the presence of two or more distinct or split identities or personality states that continually have power over the person's behaviour. Although not everyone experiences DID the same way, for some the 'alters' or different identities have their own age, sex or race.

13

Scenography for VR: Procedural modelling, emergence and discovery in the creation of *Namuanki*

Kevin Mack

Introduction

Namuanki (Mack 2022) is an ancient aquatic oasis, a resort destination from the distant future and a virtual getaway to an otherworldly reality designed to encourage a transcendent experience of awe, mystery and imagination (see Plate 28).

In this chapter I discuss the ideas, techniques and processes that were used to create *Namuanki*, a virtual world I created for the cloud-based social VR platform VRChat. *Namuanki* was an Official Selection of Venice Immersive (at Venice International Film Festival 2022) and of Raindance Immersive 2022, where it was nominated for Best Immersive World, and an Official Selection and winner of the People's Choice and Technical Achievement Awards at (FIVARS) The Festival of International Virtual and Augmented Reality Stories 2022. Festival visitors (both physically present and remote) were given virtual guided tours of the world.

In this chapter, I present techniques in procedural modelling along with detailed examples of their application in the creation of *Namuanki*. I discuss emergence, discovery and the search for novelty in relation to the creative process of worldbuilding, including scenography, backstory and performance.

I include a step-by-step account of many of the conceptual and technical processes I used in the development of *Namuanki*, as well as a discussion of how the mythology, backstory, characters and performances emerged from the worldbuilding process. I also discuss how the first-person experience of spatial presence provided by virtual reality may incorporate narrative, but is fundamentally different from narrative and must be considered in the context of a new paradigm in order to realize its potential.

In addition, I present my approach to dealing with the limitations of procedural modelling and other methods which I call 'the hybridization of means'. Lastly, I provide some thoughts on how generative AI provides new opportunities for using emergence, discovery and the search for novelty in the creative process and its impact on the future of 3D scenography and the creation of virtual worlds.

Complexity and emergence

In discussing my work, I frequently refer to complexity and emergence. Complexity generally refers to intricate detail or the quality of having many different, connected parts. In science and complex systems theory, complexity characterizes the behaviour of a system or model whose components interact in multiple ways and follow local rules, leading to nonlinearity, randomness, collective dynamics, hierarchy and emergence (Turner and Baker 2019). In common usage, emergence means to come into view, come into being or become important or prominent. While a comprehensive examination of complexity and emergence is beyond the scope of this chapter, in my book *Emergent Visions: AI Art by Kevin Mack* (Mack 2022), I give the following definition of emergence, which attempts to convey its meaning and its vast and profound implications:

> Emergence occurs when properties arise unexpectedly due to the interaction between the parts of a system in which the parts cannot account for the properties that emerge. The whole is both greater than, and different from, the sum of its parts. Emergence is the essential ingredient in all creative processes, from the subatomic to the astronomic. Emergence is behind the primal mystery of existence and all that inspires awe.
>
> (2022)

I employ complexity and cultivate emergence in my creative process to enable discovery in the search for novelty. Procedural modelling provides a powerful framework for working with complexity and emergence to facilitate discovery and the search for novelty.

Procedural modelling

Procedural modelling refers to techniques in computer graphics that are used to create 3D models, textures and animation from sets of rules. Procedural modelling is an effective approach to building complex virtual worlds. Rather than having to design and create each individual object for a world one at a time, a procedural approach enables the creation of complex systems of objects using rules (Ebert et al. 2002). The procedural approach can also be used to produce textures, shaders, materials and even animation. Procedural rules can establish dependencies and relationships between different parameters and/or define them directly using patterns, randomness and procedural noise. For instance, the size of an object could be used to determine its speed in an animation, or to control an aspect of a material such as the colour or roughness. Objects and materials can also be animated based on time in combination with noise and/or other functions. Procedural noise and random functions are an effective way to introduce complexity and to cultivate and explore emergence. Procedural noise provides the ability to direct, constrain and control randomness in a multitude of ways and is fundamental to simulating all manner of complex natural phenomena in computer graphics.

Principles of procedural modelling are now employed in many off-the-shelf tools. Procedural methods are commonly built into terrain building tools, such as those used in game-engine software. Rather than using traditional manual modelling techniques to create the uneven ground of a terrain, procedural terrain tools use various types of procedural noise to create a heightmap and a greyscale image that is used to displace the surface of a polygonal mesh that forms the basis of a ground plane in a given 3D environment. The world-builder, or scenographer, can establish rules for the maximum variation of frequency and amplitude for the hills and valleys of a terrain. Additionally, functions that simulate erosion can be applied using procedural methods to give nuance and realism to surfaces. Many variations can be created and iterated on, allowing the scenographer to converge on a desired result. More importantly, experimentation with the rules can lead you to discover unanticipated results that exceed your original intention.

Most terrain tools employ heightmaps to generate terrains. This can be an effective technique; however, because they contain only height information, heightmaps cannot create overhangs. Various procedural functions including noise can also be applied directly to the geometry without the use of a heightmap. Volumetric representations that specify objects volumetrically rather than geometrically can be used to create terrains with overhangs, complex caves or any kind of form (see Plate 33). There are a variety of volumetric data formats that can be generated and manipulated procedurally based on density and other arbitrary attributes. Additionally, one can easily convert geometric representations into volumetric ones and vice versa enabling the benefits of each.

Another procedural modelling technique that is commonly employed in environment creation tools is scattering. This allows you to place large numbers of elements, such as rocks, plants and trees, in the terrain based on rules. These rules can define relationships and constrain randomness, and objects can be scaled and rotated as they are placed. For example, you could establish a relationship between tree size and elevation in the terrain such that the largest trees are placed at the lowest elevations and the smallest at the highest elevations, or you could make the size, rotation and placement of the trees entirely random, with perhaps a minimum distance between them. You could also combine these rules such that the largest trees are at the lowest elevations but with some random variation that would allow a few large trees at higher elevations. The possibilities are vast.

Most terrain tools have some limitations because they are purpose-built to make it easy to create familiar types of terrain. They are generally designed to scatter pre-made assets, so you need to either create or purchase libraries of assets for them to work with. However, if you are creating your own procedural systems through code, or using procedural software like Houdini,[1] you can create the assets and implement any rules you wish, not just for terrains but also for anything you can imagine and, more importantly, things you *cannot* imagine.

The search for novelty

Because of complexity and emergence, it is impossible to anticipate the precise results of even a few simple rules interacting, but through an iterative trial-and-error process akin to evolution, one can converge on a desired result systematically. Furthermore, during the iterative process, you may discover surprising results that take you in directions that are more interesting than your initial intention. Exploring the surprising complex emergent results that come from the interaction of procedural rules is an effective way to experiment and conduct a search for novelty. The search for novelty is another area with profound implications that are beyond the scope of this chapter. In their book *Why Greatness Cannot Be Planned, The Myth of the Objective* (2015), Kenneth O. Stanley and Joel Lehman argue:

> Objectives are well and good when they are sufficiently modest, but things get a lot more complicated when they're more ambitious. In fact, objectives actually become *obstacles* towards more exciting achievements, like those

> involving discovery, creativity, invention, or innovation – or even achieving true happiness. In other words (and here is the paradox), the greatest achievements become *less likely* when they are made objectives. Not only that, but this paradox leads to a very strange conclusion – if the paradox is really true then the best way to achieve greatness, the truest path to 'blue sky' discovery or to fulfil boundless ambition, is to have *no objective at all*.
>
> (Stanley and Lehman 2015: 7–8)

In summary, if you are seeking to accomplish a goal and the necessary steps to achieve it are known, then planning is fine, but for ambitious goals where the steps to achieve a goal are not known, a search for novelty is a more effective strategy than any plan you can come up with. Through a search for novelty, we can discover and accumulate what the authors refer to as 'stepping stones' (2015, 6). Eventually these stepping stones can be combined in ways that enable the achievement of ambitious goals that have not previously occurred. Experimentation, discovery and the search for novelty are fundamental to evolution and the creative process and I have employed these principles in my work for decades. I have found that having ambitious objectives and the search for novelty need not be mutually exclusive. For my own projects, I work with a variety of objectives – some broad, some specific, some ambitious, some modest. For example, I may decide to create a virtual reality project, as opposed to some other kind of project. Establishing the objective of creating a virtual reality project greatly constrains the space of possibilities, while remaining broad and undefined. Each step or choice in the creative process serves to further limit the possibility space and, at each undefined step, one can employ a search-for-novelty attitude, enabling emergence and discovery.

Namuanki – making a procedural virtual world

Namuanki is a virtual world that I created for the social VR platform, VRChat.[2] *Namuanki* is an ocean world with rocky isles, labyrinthine rock formations, bizarre lifeforms and subterranean caves. Visitors can explore the islands and complex rock formations above and below the water and encounter a variety of unique benevolent beings along the way, some of whom can provide mystical visions.

Namuanki began as an experiment to see what I could accomplish when building a world for VRChat. I love water and I wanted to see what I could do with water in real-time VR, so I started with that. I found a VRChat-compatible procedural water shader plugin, called 'Perfect Water Shader' by

RED_SIM.[3] It has a lot of parameters which makes it very flexible. Before setting up the water, I created a seafloor with five small isles. I tried some completely procedural versions, but decided I wanted more control over the size, shape and placement of the isles; therefore, I created them and other variations in the seafloor by deforming the seafloor with magnets.[4] I then added procedural noise to the islands and the entire seafloor to add more variation and complexity.

After I had established a seafloor with islands that ascended above sea level, I wanted to add lots of unique rocks. By isolating the islands from the rest of the seafloor, I was able to procedurally create rocks and scatter them separately on the surface of each island. I created three separate sizes of rock systems for each island: large, medium and small. To achieve interesting rock shapes, I copied boxes to the scattered points of each system to establish the approximate size and position of the rocks. Each box was randomly scaled and rotated within an appropriate range along each axis when copied to the scattered points.

When I was satisfied with the sizes and distribution of the boxes, I scattered points inside the boxes and copied randomly scaled and rotated metaballs[5] to those scattered points. Through trial and error, I quickly deduced the ideal quantity of points and size range for the metaballs so that, when they melded together, they made interesting shapes. Rotation was set to a random value to add further variation.

Next, I converted the metaballs to polygons. I started by making them very low-poly to get interesting faceted shapes. Then the low-poly rocks were deformed with noise and subdivided. This process of adding more noise deformation and more subdivision was repeated through several iterations which resulted in some very complex and detailed rocks. Then I reduced the polygon count procedurally to retain as much shape complexity as possible. Finally, about half of each rock was positioned below the island's surface, to give them a natural sense of rest (see how the rocks are bedded into the sand in Plate 28).

Setting these up may seem like a lot of work, but keep in mind that it was procedural; therefore, once the steps of the process were established, it was easy to make changes by tweaking parameters. Additionally, once the procedural network for this rock creation/scattering process was defined, I could just duplicate it, altering the input and parameters, and scatter unique rocks to the other islands and the ocean floor.

After I added the water and adjusted the parameters to match what I wanted, I added some basic shaders to the islands and rocks. I also added and set up a procedural volumetric cloud/sky plugin, also by RED SIM.[6] After testing the world in VR, I added some abalone-inspired creatures to the rocks along the shoreline. With a minor modification to the rock scattering process,

I was able to add hundreds of unique shelled creatures clinging to the rocks. I scattered them onto the surface of the rocks slightly above and below sea level all around the shoreline.

I also used a procedural approach to develop the shaders/materials for the islands, seafloor and rocks. This enabled complex detailed variation for the ground and rocks with only a few texture maps. I developed a procedural shader process that combined variations of the textures at different scales to provide a variety of detail without having to create large numbers of high-resolution textures. All the rocks and rock formations in *Namuanki* use the same modest set of textures (see Plate 29).

After spending some time refining what I had so far, I added a big rock formation jutting up from the deeper water, north of the islands. This provided a feature to explore above and under the water, allowing visitors to go rock-climbing. To make it possible to climb all the way to the top and to improve the overall design, I manually sculpted parts of the structure. Noise was used to add more detail and variation, and the geometry was converted to a volume, smoothed out a little and converted back to polygonal geometry for better topology. I made a copy of the rock material and adjusted the parameters to suit the larger formation, completing the feature. In VR, I explored the formation, found my way to the top and jumped off. This was so much fun it became a regular part of the guided tour itinerary.

I also added the 'SwimSystem 2.0' plugin for VRChat[7] to my world which lets visitors swim with buoyancy in the water. I enjoyed exploring the underwater rocks and features and discovering the abalone-like shells attached to them. This encouraged me to add more variety of life on the rocks. I created several 'coral-like' species and distributed them on the rocks in selected areas. These were created procedurally, using variations of the scattering/metaball approach along with extrusion and subdivision parameters. This involved producing a low-resolution polygonal shape, selecting a group of random polygons in a given area and then extruding them to random lengths. The entire mesh was then deformed with noise and subdivided to smooth it out before poly-reducing to optimize the topology (see Plate 30).

I added another rock formation to the west, and on the ocean floor next to the rock formation, I created a deep chasm. The chasm expands from the opening downward so that the bottom chamber is much larger than the opening. The shape was created procedurally with the scattered metaballs and noise approach and was then used to cut a hole in the ocean floor. Using similar procedural methods, I added a massive subterranean ice cave, and connector tunnels between the chasm, the ice cave and the bottom of the seafloor.

The underwater volume shader and the swim system were both able to have a bottom limit at which the underwater atmosphere and buoyancy effects would end. Therefore, I set the bottom-limit at the base of the ocean floor, at the junction to the tunnel that leads to the ice cave. I fashioned it as a swirling surface with bubbles rising from it, and as one passes through it, there is a sound effect signifying you are no longer underwater. Gravity takes over and you fall a short distance to the dry tunnel floor below, with the swirling bottom-limit of the ocean now visible above. From there one can hike down the rest of the way to the subterranean ice cave. To return to the ocean one can climb up the edge of the tunnel, to just beneath the swirling surface, and then jump up into it and go swimming underwater again. This feature extended to the chasm, so that only the very top portion of the chasm is underwater.

The hybridization of means

Sometimes a procedural approach can introduce unanticipated challenges. For example, the seafloor rocks of *Namuanki* are scattered on selected sets of polygons from the seafloor geometry. When I cut the hole in the seafloor to create the opening to the chasm, the polygonal topology of the seafloor was slightly changed which resulted in the rock scattering procedure being recomputed based on the newly generated seafloor geometry. In some cases, this change was insignificant because the new arrangement, though different, accomplished the same effect; however, in other cases, I preferred the previous arrangement. For this situation, I would temporarily go back to the old topology and export the geometry for the objects in question, then read them back in, disconnecting them from the procedural network so they were no longer subject to changes in the network. This combination of procedural methods and manual manipulation allowed me to achieve the benefits of the procedural approach while reducing the limitations. This is an aspect of my creative process that I refer to as 'The Hybridization of Means'. While it can be interesting, effective and elegant to emphasize purity when working with any creative system, medium or process such as procedural modelling, it is not mandatory. Some traditional photographers might consider Photoshop retouching to be 'cheating' and insist on the final work being unembellished. Similarly, with procedural and generative art, some prefer that their works be the pure unembellished output of the system, while others feel the need to manually tweak the output. When purity of process is important to the artist, the hands-off approach is valid. For myself, the end result, and the experience it conveys or elicits, is the most important thing, so I am willing to sacrifice purity in my creative process by *hybridizing the means* by which I achieve the end result. Hybridizing the creative process expands the creative possibilities and the potential for emergence, as well as providing more intentional control over the aesthetics, design and topology in general.

Cast of characters

Once I had built the world, I wanted to add more life to it. I created a variety of creatures, or 'benevolent beings', that inhabit the world. I started with 'Benti', a stationary blobby creature that sits in the sandy shallows of a lagoon. Her tentacled 'mouth' protrudes slightly above the water's surface and small, urchin-like creatures float out of it and fly around the surrounding area. Benti was modelled procedurally as was her performance. A procedural shader/material uses noise to animate the vertices of her geometry making her undulate naturally, like an undersea invertebrate such as an anemone. Her textures exhibit complex, coloured patterns that are also driven by noise to shift and flow like the skin of an octopus. I created a particle system to periodically emit the flying, urchin-like creatures from her 'mouth'. I imagined these as 'sensory nodes' that she uses to observe her surroundings.

Next, I created a giant air whale, named 'An', after the Sumerian god of the heavens (see Plate 31). An can be summoned using a trigger located on one of the large translucent stones on the main Isle. When the summons is triggered, the sound of a giant horn fills the air. At first, An appears as a small shape in the distant sky, but as the giant air whale slowly approaches, his 100-metre length and massive girth become apparent. An's body ripples and undulates and his textures slowly warp and change using procedural noise. As An approaches, he slows and descends, pausing at the shore of the main Isle. Visitors can peer into his large maw and see the hollow inner tube of his body that channels air (or water) to fly (or swim). An bellows a mighty greeting call that sounds like a foghorn. He bobs, floating at the shore, and bellows again, then ascends and flies slowly across Namuanki, departing with a farewell call.

I then added a unique human-scale creature to each of the two large rock formations, and one in each of the undersea rock gardens that lead to the formations. I thought of these beings as 'Sages' and gave them undulating forms with slowly shifting colours and textures. I added an interactive performance feature to each one. When you get very close to them an 'interact' box appears that reads, 'Request vision'. Pressing the controller trigger causes the world to disappear and a psychedelic, 3D-animated, mystical vision takes its place (see Plate 32). Each Sage provides their own unique vision and a musical performance. After ten to thirty seconds, the vision vanishes and the Namuanki world reappears.

I decided to add another very large creature to inhabit the giant chasm area. Since the chasm is a fissure deep beneath the ocean, I imagined a volcanic rock creature, partially molten and flowing slowly. I carved a large, natural alcove on one side of the chasm and modelled the creature as a huge rock formation protruding from the natural alcove using warped metaballs. I created a dedicated emissive texture for the procedural rock shader to create lava glow in and around the crevices and recessed areas of the form. I used a similar texture with a different 'falloff' to control the amount of vertex distortion in the rock creature. This made the glowing molten areas warp and flow while keeping the non-glowing rock areas more rigid, like how solidified rock moves on molten lava. I added a spatial audio composition with a primitive rhythm that emits from the space as well as sounds that emit from the creature itself. I named the massive lava creature, Ki, after the Sumerian deity of the earth. Ki's performance as a primordial deity relies on the hypnotic properties of her movement and soundscape, and the resonances she creates with the awe-inspiring massive scale of the space.

In the giant ice cave, I wanted something very different from the other creatures. To contrast with the physicality of the other beings, I created a large, slowly swirling cloud of glowing mist using multiple particle systems. This had the added benefit of providing a practical source of soft lighting for the ice cave and made the glowing mist a focal point in the space (see Plate 33). I composed a spatial-audio musical soundscape with different sonic parts emanating from different areas of the cave. Each sound source attenuates with distance. The various parts were designed to combine and attenuate dynamically, based on your movement through the vast space, creating a variable, evolving composition. As you approach the glowing mist, the various sonic sources mix together in balance and become background for the central melodic theme which emanates from the glowing mist itself. The deity took on the name, Feth Fiada, from Irish mythology, which means magical mist or veil. She performs her 'Song of Compassion' for those who make the pilgrimage to 'The Ice Cave of Feth Fiada'.

As the world of Namuanki was taking shape and I considered the paths that people might take as they explored, I found a good place for my next character. Namu, a tentacled sea creature named after the Sumerian Goddess of the primordial ocean. She swims in the upper (undersea) portion of the Chasm of Ki, greeting visitors and guiding them to descend into the chasm or ascend from below while singing a haunting melody.

I added a 3D map of the world to enable VRChat visitors to find their way to the different areas and features of the world, and I provided guided tours for the festivals and events where it was featured. Initially, I did not think of my tour-guide role as a 'performance', but as the design of the tour and the story of Namuanki emerged, I became a narrator and a central character. This character incorporated actual and imaginative versions of myself. As the creator of the world, I would point out features and discuss the technical and creative processes in the context of actual geological and biological phenomena, and I would introduce the various deities and benevolent beings as well as the story behind the world. Seamlessly interweaving the real with the imaginary created an interesting ambiguity for visitors.

Emergent story

As the world of *Namuanki* emerged, it began to align with, and expand on, an imagined mythology that I have developed since early childhood, which has inspired and informed much of my work. The mythology is built around *Ancient Elders from the Distant Future*, who were the first self-engineered benevolent beings that emerged from the symbiotic relationship between humanity and AI. This symbiotic relationship enabled the 'Great Transcendence', in which humanity transcended the struggle to survive. I created *Namuanki* at the behest of the Ancient Elders who reached back through time to provide me with visions of *Namuanki*, so that I could create it now, opening a causal loop connecting our time with their time and helping to ensure their eventual existence and the survival of humanity. Namu, An, Ki and Feth Fiada are some of these Ancient Elders.

The process of naming things is a powerful aspect of emergent narrative. Naming something imbues it with semantic representation, which is fundamental to narrative, language and meaning. I often choose names derived from Sanskrit. For me, Sanskrit and Hindu mythology have an ancient, mystical quality that suits my aesthetic intention. I combined Sanskrit words to create titles for my previous VR projects, *Anandala* (Mack 2021) and *Devalaya Rupinam* (Mack 2019). For *Namuanki*, I also chose to draw from ancient Sumerian and Irish mythology. Namu, An and Ki are named after Sumerian deities, and inspired the name of the world, *Namuanki*. I often discover words whose meaning informs and expands my own concept of the thing being named. For example, I named the tallest rock formation, Ikshana Rock. Ikshana is a Sanskrit word meaning sight, care and superintendence, and also refers to eye, looking, seeing, viewing, aspect, caring for, looking after and regarding. My initial idea was to look up the Sanskrit word for *vision*. This led me to the word, *Ikshana*, but when I saw the full definition of *Ikshana*, it inspired me to consider the Sage creatures as the 'stewards', or 'caretakers' of the areas they inhabit, and to have them share their names with their locations. The sage character I placed at that rock formation became Ikshana, the wise steward of Ikshana Rock, and this carried through to other creatures and locations.

The ice cave became 'The Ice Cave of Feth Fiada'. The chasm became 'The Chasm of Ki'. The undersea slope leading to Ikshana Rock became 'The Slope of Shanti', with Shanti (the local benevolent being) providing visions to visitors as they enter that area. Much of the backstory of *Namuanki* emerged from the process of naming things in the world.

I use the word *backstory* deliberately here because *Namuanki* is not a story. It is a virtual reality world with a backstory. Visitors may go on a guided tour of the world during which they can learn about the backstory of Namuanki, but their experience is a real-time, first-person, spatially present one. It is dynamic, interactive, participatory, unpredictable and experienced from their unique point of view. *Namuanki* can be an antecedent, a setting or an inspiration for countless possible stories, but it is not itself a story. This may be a subtle distinction, but it is an important one in relation to virtual reality.

The etymology of *story* is that it originally referred to the accounting of history. Over time it came to be applied to literature, mythology, theatre, journalism, cinema and so on. In a broad sense, anything we think or say can be considered a story, but stories are always after the fact. Our minds have evolved to infer meaning by telling ourselves, and each other, stories about our experience of reality, which helps us make sense of the world. Nonetheless, while reality and stories may have elements in common such as settings, events and characters, they are also fundamentally different. Reality provides a first-person, present-tense experience of spatial presence, whereas stories are the mediated accounting of real or imagined events and experiences. Reality is undetermined.

Many have characterized VR as a new medium for storytelling and stories can indeed be told in VR, but to consider VR as a storytelling medium diminishes the powerful, fundamental new capability that it provides. For the first time in history, we can directly communicate the first-person, dynamic, interactive experience of reality, independent of actual reality. The first-person experience of reality (virtual or actual) is dynamic, interactive and unpredictable, whereas narrative tends to be fixed and predetermined. Virtual reality, like actual reality, is fundamentally different from narrative. It is analogous to reality, but with different capabilities and limitations. It requires an entirely new paradigm. To consider it an extension of an existing paradigm is to diminish its powerful capabilities.

AI and the future of procedural emergence

As I write this chapter, developments in generative AI continue to create excitement and controversy. I have had a keen interest in neuroscience, neural networks, artificial life and artificial intelligence since the early 1990s. Artificial neural networks have enabled a variety of exciting creative applications, and over the last few years, huge leaps have been made. Diffusion models have enabled text-to-image and large language models have enabled chatbots like GPT 4o. These technologies provide vast new opportunities to employ emergence, discovery and search for novelty in the creative process.

I became deeply engaged in exploring the latest generation of AI in my work as soon as it became available. *Emergent Visions*, the book of art I made using generative Text-to-image AI, emerged from that exploration. These applications of AI are only the beginning. Efforts to create AI applications for generating 3D objects, textures and scenes from natural language, as well as for constructing procedural modelling networks, have already begun to emerge. While still nascent, they provide a glimpse of the incredible potential impact that AI could have on 3D scenography and the creation of virtual worlds.

Originally, we created things by describing them with physical materials. With digital 3D tools, we gained the ability to describe things parametrically, algorithmically and procedurally. With AI we can create things by describing them with natural language. The implications of AI are staggering and well beyond the scope of this chapter, but I encourage people to learn about neural networks, which are the basis of modern AI and our own minds. Computational neural networks are implemented differently from biological ones, but they employ the same fundamental mechanisms that enable the incredible emergent properties and behaviours that we have traditionally associated only with humans. While AI has vast potential applications and uses, it can also provide profound insight into how human minds work.

Conclusion

Procedural modelling shares many of the same ideas as artificial life, which simulates the behaviour and characteristics of living things. Artificial life employs procedural rules to create artificial living systems capable of emergent behaviour. Indeed, biological life and evolution, like everything in nature, are emergent processes. People tend to think of computers and programming as limited to predetermined (programmed) actions or behaviours, but programs can employ complex interactions between rules, parameters and randomness to generate emergent, unpredictable behaviour. Emergence is often spoken of in relation to life and other complex natural systems like the weather, but it can occur in any system where variable parameters interact; it is the essential phenomenon in all creative processes – hence the emergence of my performative role as a tour guide and mystagogue.

Procedural modelling greatly expands the possibilities for creating complex virtual worlds. Procedural rules can establish dependencies and relationships between different parameters and/or define them directly using patterns, randomness and procedural noise. Directed randomness and procedural noise are fundamental tools for working with emergence in procedural modelling. An examination of the creative process employed in the creation of *Namuanki* provides some specific examples of procedural modelling, discovery and the search for novelty.

A search for novelty is an effective strategy for achieving ambitious goals that require unknown steps. By combining broad ambitious objectives with a search for novelty in the creative process, we can adapt to discoveries along the way, optimizing our search. Incorporating this methodology in the pursuit of modest objectives enables the discovery and achievement of more ambitious objectives. The hybridization of means, or the combination of different creative processes, including manually modifying the results of procedural modelling, or any other emergent process, allows one to exercise greater control in accomplishing specific intentions when working with emergence. Furthermore, the advent of neural network generative AI greatly expands the creative possibilities for using emergence, discovery and the search for novelty in creative processes. These strategies, in combination with procedural modelling, are a powerful way to enhance the creative process of scenographing for extended reality.

Notes

1 Houdini, by SideFX™, is a 3D procedural software for modelling, rigging, animation, VFX, look development, lighting and rendering in film, TV, advertising and video gaming. See https://www.sidefx.com/.

2 VRChat is a social VR platform – see https://vrchat.com.

3 'Perfect Water Shaders' by RED_SIM – see https://www.patreon.com/posts/32252234.

4 A magnet operation allows for the deformation of geometry based on the field of influence, or weight, of a metaball, which is a type of isosurface.

5 In computer graphics, Metaballs (also known as blobby atoms, or blobs) are blobby looking isosurfaces that meld smoothly together when in close proximity to form contiguous organic forms. Metaballs define curved shapes implicitly from functions rather than by arranging many polygons. Metaballs are generally converted to polygonal geometry to enable shape manipulation and rendering compatibility.

6 'Beautiful Sky Shader' by RED_SIM. See https://www.patreon.com/posts/beautiful-sky-35667377.

7 'SwimSystem 2.0' for VRChat – https://booth.pm/ja/items/2127684.

References

Alice's Adventures Underground by Les Enfants Terribles (2015–20), [Performance] Dir. O. Lansley. & J. Seager, London, Shanghai.

Allen, J., K. Guillery, L. Hughes, J. Lopes Ramos, P. J. Maravala, B. Simon, and J. Stenros (2022), 'Understanding Liveness in Participatory Theatre, Larp and Games', DiGRA 2022 - Kraków. Jagiellonian University, 7–11 July.

Allison, R. S., L. R. Harris, M. Jenkin, U. Jasiobedzka, and J. E. Zacher (2001), 'Tolerance of Temporal Delay in Virtual Environments.' In *Proceedings IEEE Virtual Reality* 2001, 247–54. Yokahama: IEEE.

Amacker, A. (2019), 'Surrendering to the Now. Improvisation and an Embodied Approach to Serendipity', *The Design Journal*, 22 (sup1): 1841–51. https://doi.org/10.1080/14606925.2019.1595043.

An Unexpected Ally to Reclaiming Our Humanity: Virtual Reality | Victoria Bousis | TEDxMIT Salon (2023), https://www.youtube.com/watch?v=ljv1z7GpwSU.

Aronson, A. (2005), *Looking into the Abyss: Essays on Scenography*, Ann Arbor: University of Michigan Press.

Ascott, R. (2003), *Telematic Embrace: Visionary Theories of Art, Technology, and Consciousness*, Berkeley: University of California Press.

Aswad, J. (2021), 'Justin Bieber to Stage Interactive Concert with Wave'. *Variety*, 9 November. Available online: https://variety.com/2021/digital/news/justin-bieber-interactive-virtual-concert-wave-1235108070/ (accessed 18 February 2025).

Augmented Play (2019), [Augmented Reality Interactive Application] Dir. Nicholas Johnson, Dublin: V-SENSE, Trinity College Dublin. https://www.youtube.com/watch?v=ceZ9zfUkoUs.

Auslander, P. (2012), 'Digital Liveness: A Historico-Philosophical Perspective', *PAJ: A Journal of Performance and Art*, 34 (3): 3–11, DOI: 10.1162/PAJJ_a_00106.

Baía Reis, A., and M. Ashmore (2022), 'From Video Streaming to Virtual Reality Worlds: An Academic, Reflective, and Creative Study on Live Theatre and Performance in the Metaverse', *International Journal of Performance Arts and Digital Media*, 18 (1): 7–28, DOI: 10.1080/14794713.2021.2024398.

Bailenson, J. (2018), *Experience on Demand: What Virtual Reality Is, How It Works, and What It Can Do*, 1st edn, New York: W. W. Norton.

Baillargeon, J. Dr. 'VR, a Pod-cast VR Curator, Posted a Review of SAMS on Steam'. May 2024. Available online: https://store.steampowered.com/app/2806890/STAY_ALIVE_MY_SON/.

Bandersnatch: Netflix (2018), *Bandersnatch*. Netflix. https://www.netflix.com/title/80988062.

Barba, E. (1995), 'An Amulet Made of Memory: The Significance of Exercises in the Actor's Dramaturgy'. In P. B. Zarilli (ed.), *Acting Re-Considered*, 99–105. London: Routledge.

Barker, M., and M. Reason (2022), 'Martin Barker in conversation'. In M. Reason, L. Conner, K. Johanson, B. Walmsley (eds.), *Routledge Companion to Audiences and the Performing Arts*, London and New York: Routledge.

Barnard, D. (2022), 'History of VR – Timeline of Events and Tech Development', VirtualSpeech, 06 October. Available online: https://virtualspeech.com/blog/history-of-vr (accessed 19 April 2023).

Baugh, C. (2013), *Theatre, Performance and Technology: The Development and Transformation of Scenography*, London: Macmillan Education UK.

Bay-Cheng, S., C. Kattenbelt, A. Lavender, and R. Nelson (eds.) (2011), *Mapping Intermediality in Performance*, Amsterdam: Amsterdam University Press.

Beat Saber: Beat Games (2018), *Beat Saber*. Beat Games.

Beckett, S. (2006), 'Play'. In *The Complete Dramatic Works of Samuel Beckett*, 305–20. London: Faber & Faber.

Beckett, S., G. Devine (Dir.), and William Gaskill (1963), *Play*, London: National Theatre Programmes.

Behrendt, F. (2012), 'The Sound of Locative Media', *Convergence: The International Journal of Research into New Media Technologies*, 18 (3): 283–95.

Belfiore, E. and O. Bennett (2007), 'Rethinking the Social Impacts of the Arts', *International Journal of Cultural Policy*, 13 (2): 135–51. https://doi.org/10.1080/10286630701342741.

Benford, S. and G. Giannachi (2011), *Performing Mixed Reality*, Cambridge, MA: The MIT Press.

Bengler, B., and N. Bryan-Kinns (2013), 'Designing Collaborative Musical Experiences for Broad Audiences', *Proceedings of the 9th ACM Conference on Creativity & Cognition*, 234–42. New York.

Benkler, Y., R. Faris, and H. Roberts (2018), *Network Propaganda: Manipulation, Disinformation, and Radicalisation in American Politics,* Oxford: Oxford University Press.

Betz, B. (2020), 'Zoom Pops after Passing 300M Users', *Stocks and Shares Reporting*. SeekingAlpha, 23 April. Available online: https://seekingalpha.com/news/3563763-zoom-pops-after-passing-300m-users (accessed 19 November 2024).

Binaural Dinner Date by ZU-UK (2017), Dir. P. J. Maravala. [Stratford Centre, London].

Binaural Dinner Date by ZU-UK (2017–23), Dir. P. J. Maravala. [International Tours: Various Locations].

Binaural Dinner Date by ZU-UK (2018), Dir. P. J. Maravala. [Latitude Festival, UK].

Bindoff, S. (1949), 'Ket's Rebellion, 1549', *Historical Association, General Series*, G 12: 3–6.

BIOBOXES: Artifacting Human Experience (2007), Rochon, A., Cindy Mochizuki, Donna Soares, Una Memesevic, Marco Soriano and Paul Ternes. (2007). Dir. Maiko Yamamoto and James Long, Toronto, 30 April 2009.

Blascovich, J., and J. N. Bailenson (2011), 'Infinite Reality – Avatars, Eternal Life, New Worlds, and the Dawn of the Virtual Revolution', Stanford VR. Available online: https://stanfordvr.com/pubs/2011/infinite-reality/ (accessed 22 April 2023).

Bolt, B. (2010), 'The Magic is in the Handling'. In E. Barrett and B. Bolt (eds.), *Practice as Research: Approaches to Creative Arts Enquiry*. London and New York: I.B.Tauris.

Bolter, J. D., M. Engberg, and B. Macintyre (2021), *Reality Media: Augmented and Virtual Reality*, Massachusetts: The MIT Press.
Bousis, V., dir. (2021), *Stay Alive, My Son. Virtual Reality. Immersive Cinema, Biography, Historical.* Ume, Konvrge Entertainment, The Bousis Film Company. https://letterboxd.com/film/stay-alive-my-son/.
Bousis, V. (2023), 'The Digital Human Revolution', ACM Digital Library Publication. Available online: https://history.siggraph.org/experience/stay-alive-my-son-chapter-1-2-by-bousis/.
Bousis, V. (2023), 'TEDxMIT: An Unexpected Ally to Reclaiming Our Humanity', June 2023. Available online: https://www.youtube.com/watch?v=ljv1z7GpwSU.
Bradbury, A. (2018), *Vestige* [Virtual Reality].
Braidotti, R. (2013), *The Posthuman*, 1st edn, Cambridge; Malden, MA: Polity Press.
Braun, V., and V. Clarke (2006), 'Using Thematic Analysis in Psychology', *Qualitative Research in Psychology*, 3 (2): 77–101. Available at: https://doi.org/10.1191/1478088706qp063oa.
Breel, A. (2022), 'Agency'. In M. Reason, L. Conner, K. Johanson, B. Walmsley (eds.), *Routledge Companion to Audiences and the Performing Arts*, London and New York: Routledge.
Brejzek, T. (ed.) (2011), *Expanding Scenography: On the Authoring of Space*, Prague: Arts and Theatre Institute.
Briar & Rose (2024), [Far Throw AR Theatre] Glitch Studios. https://www.glitchstudios.co/projects-archive/the-theatre-reimagined-introducing-ar-to-the-stage/.
Broadhurst, S. (2007), *Digital Practices: Aesthetic and Neuroesthetic Approaches to Performance and Technology*, Basingstoke / New York: Palgrave Macmillan.
Broadhurst, S., and S. Price (2017), *Digital Bodies: Creativity and Technology in the Arts and Humanities*, London: Palgrave Macmillan.
Campbell, J. (2008). *The Hero with a Thousand Faces*, 3rd edn, Novato: New World Library.
Carey, J. (2010), *What Good Are the Arts?*, 1st edn, New York: Oxford University Press.
Carlton, B. (2020), https://vrscout.com/news/john-legend-live-vr-concert-wave/.
Carmigniani, J., and B. Furht (2011), 'Augmented Reality: An Overview'. In B. Furht (ed.), *Handbook of Augmented Reality*, 3–46. London: Springer.
Carson, E. (2018), 'The Princess Bride Performed Live – in a VR App', CNET, 20 November. Available online: https://www.cnet.com/tech/mobile/the-princess-bride-gets-the-vr-treatment/ (accessed 19 April 2023).
Cassam, Q. (2019), *Conspiracy Theories*, Cambridge: John Wiley & Sons.
Causey, M. (1999), 'The Screen Test of the Double: The Uncanny Performer in the Space of Technology', *Theatre Journal*, 51 (4): 383–94. https://doi.org/10.1353/tj.1999.0083.
Cegys, P., and J. Weijdom (2020), 'Mixing Realities: Reflections on Presence and Embodiment in Intermedial Performance Design of Blue Hour VR', *Theatre and Performance Design*, 6 (1–2): 81–101. https://doi.org/10.1080/23322551.2020.1785710.
Center, Columbia Business School-the Eugene Lang Entrepreneurship (2020), 'How the Coronavirus Crisis Will Shape the Future of Virtual Reality', Forbes, 21 May. Available online: https://www.forbes.com/sites/

columbiabusinessschool/2020/05/21/how-coronavirus-crisis-will-shape-future-of-virtual-reality/ (accessed 19 November 2024).
Chalmers, D. (2022), *Reality +: Virtual Worlds and the Problems of Philosophy*, London: Penguin Books.
Chesher, C. (1994), 'Colonizing Virtual Reality: Construction of the Discourse of Virtual Reality', *Cultronix*, 1 (1): 1–27.
Cockburn, A. (2004), *Crystal Clear: A Human-Powered Methodology for Small Teams*, Boston: Addison-Wesley Professional.
Coniglio, M. (2006), 'Materials vs Content in Digitally Mediated Performance'. In S. Broadhurst and J. Machon (eds.), *Performance and Technology: Practices of Virtual Embodiment and Interactivity*, 78–84. London: Palgrave Macmillan UK.
Connor, S. (1989), *Postmodernist Culture: An Introduction to Theories of the Contemporary*, New York: Blackwell.
Dahlbäck, N., A. Jönsson, and L. Ahrenberg (1993), 'Wizard of Oz Studies—Why and How', *Knowledge-Based Systems*, 6 (4): 258–66. https://doi.org/10.1016/0950-7051(93)90017-N.
Dalsgaard, P. (2010), 'Research in and through Design: An Interaction Design Research Approach', *Proceedings of the 22nd Conference of the Computer-Human Interaction Special Interest Group of Australia on Computer-Human Interaction*, 200–3. https://doi.org/10.1145/1952222.1952265.
Damiani, J. (2019), '"The Under Presents" Is a Novel Exploration of VR And Live Immersive Theatre', Forbes, 19 November. Available online: https://www.forbes.com/sites/jessedamiani/2019/11/19/the-under-presents-is-a-novel-exploration-of-vr-and-live-immersive-theatre/?sh=f4f4d3274556 (accessed 19 April 2023).
Dance Trail (2020), [Augmented Reality] Gilles Jobin. https://www.gillesjobin.com/en/creation/dance-trail-ar/.
Davies, C. (1998), 'OSMOSE: Notes on Being in Immersive Virtual Space', *Digital Creativity*, 9 (2): 65–74.
Dhonau, D. (2022), 'Interview with Sophy Smith, Relating to for Audience of the Future (Performance Demonstrator) Prototype Creation'.
Dickson, A. (2019), 'Love, Virtually', *Financial Times*, January 5, 13.
Dissociative Identity Disorder (Multiple Personality Disorder) (2023), WebMD. Available at https://www.webmd.com/mental-health/dissociative-identity-disorder-multiple-personality-disorder (accessed 20 April 2023).
Dixon, S. (2006), 'A History of Virtual Reality in Performance', *International Journal of Performance Arts and Digital Media*, 2 (1): 28–31. Available online: https://www.researchgate.net/publication/228625222_A_history_of_virtual_reality_in_performance (accessed 19 April 2023).
Draw Me Close (2021), Written and Directed by Jordan Tannahill [Interactive Experience] https://www.drawmeclo.se/ (accessed 23 July 2024).
Dunne-Howrie, J., J. Lopes Ramos, P. J. Maravala, and B. Simon (2020), 'The Post-Immersive Manifesto', *International Journal of Performance Arts and Digital Media*, 16 (2): 196–212.
Ebert, D. S., F. K. Musgrave, D. Peachey, K. Perlin, and S. Worley (2002), *Texturing and Modeling: A Procedural Approach*, San Francisco: Elsevier.
Echoes (n.d.), 'What Is Geolocated Sound and Audio AR?', Echoes. Available online: https://echoes.xyz/faq (accessed 2 December 2024).

Eckersley, M. (2014), 'Schechner and Environmental Theatre', Theatre Styles, 19 December. Available online: http://theatrestyles.blogspot.com/2014/12/schechner-and-environmental-theatre.html (accessed 19 April 2023).

Egliston, B., and M. Carter (2022), 'Oculus Imaginaries: The Promises and Perils of Facebook's Virtual Reality', *New Media & Society*, 24 (1): 70–89.

Eichenseer, M. (2017), 'Hugs in Virtual Reality. Online Social Connections Are Forever Changed.', Medium: VR Dojo, 10 June. Available online: https://medium.com/vrdojo/hugs-in-virtual-reality-online-social-connections-are-forever-changed-602d3d411d3f (accessed 21 April 2023).

Etiquette by Rotozaza (2007–23), Dir. A. Hampton & S. Mercuriali. [International Tours: Various Locations].

Fatherland (2018–2019), [performance] Dir. B. Samuels, Limbik, London, Portsmouth, Worthing, Brighton.

Fictum, C. (2016), *VR UX: Learn VR UX, Storytelling & Design*. Createspace Independent Publishing Platform.

'Final Fantasy' (2024), Final Fantasy Wiki. 21 July 2024. https://finalfantasy.fandom.com/wiki/Final_Fantasy.

Fisher, J. (2021), *Augmented and Mixed Reality for Communities*. Raton, FL/Oxon: CRC Press.

Fitness22 LTD (no date), 'Couch to 5K Runner (version 9.3420)' [Mobile App]. (accessed 4 May 2023).

Fleming, V. (1939), *The Wizard of Oz* [Film].

Francksen, K. (2021), 'Intensive Practice Research Labs: Music Performance in VR: New Immersive Environments for Performance and Composition', Reporting Document for Audience of the Future (Performance Demonstrator).

Francksen, K., and S. Smith (2018), 'Editorial', *International Journal of Performance Arts and Digital Media*, 14 (2): 127–9. https://doi.org/10.1080/14794713.2018.1528739.

Frayling, C. (1994), 'Research in Art and Design', *Royal College of Art Research Papers*, 1 (1): 9.

Fromell, A. (2018), 'Dramaturgical Possibilities within Virtual Realities: Notes from AΦE's VR-Performance Whist', *International Journal of Performance Arts and Digital Media*, 14 (2): 139–44. https://doi.org/10.1080/14794713.2018.1499386.

Gall, D., D. Roth, J. Stauffert, J. Zarges, and M. E. Latoschik (2021), 'Embodiment in Virtual Reality Intensifies Emotional Responses to Virtual Stimuli', *Frontiers in Psychology*, 12: 674179.

Gayet, M. (2022), 'Immersive Studio Giioii is Adapting Theater XR Performance WELCOME TO RESPITE for Korea', XR Must, 22 May. Available online: https://www.xrmust.com/xrmagazine/welcome-respite-korea/ (accessed 22 April 2023).

Gilmore, J. H., and B. J. Pine (2013), 'The Experience Economy: Past, Present & Future'. In J. Sundbo and F. Sørensen (eds.), *Handbook on the Experience Economy*, 21–44. Edward Elgar Publishing, UK & USA.

Goffman, E., *The Presentation of Self in Everyday Life*, Scotland: Doubleday, 1956.

Gow, N. (1809), *Lament for the Death of His Second Wife. Fifth Collection of Strathspey Reels for the Piano Forte, Harp, Violin and Violoncello*, Scotland, Edinburgh, Gow & Shepherd Music Sellers (No. 16 Princess St.) | John Gow (No. 31 Carnaby St., Golden Square).

Gerber, E. (2007), 'Improvisation Principles and Techniques for Design', *Proceedings of the SIGCHI Conference on Human Factors in Computing Systems*, 1069–72. https://doi.org/10.1145/1240624.1240786.

Gerber, E. (2009), 'Using Improvisation to Enhance the Effectiveness of Brainstorming', *Proceedings of the SIGCHI Conference on Human Factors in Computing Systems*, 97–104. https://doi.org/10.1145/1518701.1518718.

Giannachi, G., and N. Kaye (2011), *Performing Presence: Between the Live and the Simulated.* Manchester: Manchester University Press.

Gregory, J. (2014), *Game Engine Architecture*. New York: A K Peters/CRC Press.

Gob Squad (2021), *1984: Back to No Future*, [Theatre performance]. https://www.gobsquad.com/projects/1984-back-to-no-future/

Greenfield, A. (2017), *Radical Technologies: The Design of Everyday Life*, London/New York: Verso.

Groot Nibbelink, L. and S. Merx (2011), 'Presence and Perception: Analysing Intermediality in Performance'. In S. Bay-Cheng, C. Kattenbelt, A. Lavender, and R. Nelson (eds.), *Mapping Intermediality in Performance*, 218–29. Amsterdam University Press.

Guillery, K., P. J. Maravala, and J. Lopes Ramos (2022), 'The Significance of "Role-Play" and "Instruction-Based Performance" as Modes of Teaching, Collaborating and Performing with/for Participating Audiences'. In S. Bartley and W. W. Lewis (eds), *Experiential Theatres: Praxis-Based Approaches to Training 21st Century Theatre Artists*, 91–7. New York and Oxon: Routledge 1st edn.

Gumball Dreams (2022), [VR Theatre] Dir. David Lyons, USA: Ferryman Collective.

Gussow, M. (1970), 'Schechner's Performance Group in "Commune"', *The New York Times*, 21 December. Available online: https://www.nytimes.com/1970/12/21/archives/schechners-performance-group-in-commune.html (accessed 20 April 2023).

Hansen, S. (1999). 'Polarised in Tempe, Arizona'. *RealTime Arts – Magazine*.

Haraway, D. (1991), 'A Cyborg Manifesto: Science, Technology, and Socialist-Feminism in the Late Twentieth Century'. In D. Haraway (ed.), *Simians, Cyborgs and Women: The Reinvention of Nature*, 149–82. New York: Routledge.

Hayden, S. (2020), 'The Under Presents' Redefines Immersive Theater in Live VR Retelling of 'The Tempest', Road to VR, 6 July. Available online: https://www.roadtovr.com/the-under-presents-immersive-theater-tempest/ (accessed 19 April 2023).

Hayles, N. K. (1999), *How We Became Posthuman: Virtual Bodies in Cybernetics, Literature, and Informatics*, Chicago, IL: University of Chicago Press.

Heidegger, M. (2003), 'The Question Concerning Technology'. In M. Heidegger (ed.), *Philosophical and Political Writings*, 279–303. New York; London: Continuum.

Hitchcock, A. (1954) *Rear Window* [Film].

Höök, K. (2018). *Designing with the Body: Somaesthetic Interaction Design*, Cambridge, MA: MIT Press.

Hosokawa, S. (1984), 'The Walkman Effect,' *Popular Music*, 4: 165–80.

Hugill, Andrew. *The Digital Musician*, 3rd edn. New York; London: Routledge, 2018.

'Immersive Doc *Stay Alive My Son* Uses Compassion to Spur Action' by Ben Kroll. Variety, 24. Available at: https://variety.com/2024/digital/festivals/stay-alive-my-son-victoria-bousis-1235983152/.

Institute for Immersive Learning (2020), *VR/AR-Apps (Collaboration) Working / Learning*, Institute for Immersive Learning. https://www.immersivelearning.institute/solution-apps/.

Jamison, L. (2022), 'The Enduring Allure of Choose Your Own Adventure Books', *The New Yorker*, 12 September. Available online: https://www.newyorker.com/magazine/2022/09/19/the-enduring-allure-of-choose-your-own-adventure-books (accessed 20 April 2023).

Jarvis, L. (2019), *Immersive Embodiment: Theatres of Mislocalized Sensation*, Cham: Palgrave Macmillan.

Johnson, E. (2016), 'Oculus Rift Inventor Palmer Luckey: Virtual Reality Will Make Distance Irrelevant (Q&A)', Vox, 19 June. Available online: https://www.vox.com/oculus-rift-inventor-palmer-luckey-virtual-reality-will-make-distance-irrelevant (accessed 22 April 2023).

Johnson, N., Dir. (2017a), *Intermedial Play*, Dublin. [Live Webcast]. https://www.youtube.com/watch?v=R11IT65HCZg.

Johnson, N., Dir., (2017b), *Virtual Play*, [Virtual Reality Interactive Application], V-SENSE, Trinity College Dublin. https://v-sense.scss.tcd.ie/research/mr-play-trilogy/.

Johnson, N. (2022), 'Directing Play in Digital Culture'. In Rapcsak, B., M. Nixon and P. Schweighauser (eds.), *Beckett and Media*, 197–214. Manchester University Press.

Johnson, N. E., N. O'Dwyer and E. Bates (2021), 'Samuel Beckett's *Play* in Digital Culture: Technologies of Influence'. In Rákóczy, A., M. H. Tanaka and N. E. Johnson (eds.), Influencing Beckett / Beckett Influencing, 145–57. Budapest, and Paris: L'Harmattan.

Johnson, N., and N. O'Dwyer (2018), 'Virtual Play: Beckettian Experiments in Virtual Reality', *Contemporary Theatre Review, Interventions*, 28 (1): 1–10.

Jones, S. (2022), 'Communication Technology and the Suspension of Disbelief', *Communication+ 1*, 9 (2), Article 9. DOI: https://doi.org/10.7275/v5e3-5a27.

Kaplin, S. (1999), 'A Puppet Tree: A Model for the Field of Puppet Theatre', *TDR/The Drama Review*, 43 (3): 28–35. https://doi.org/10.1162/105420499760347306.

Kaptelinin, V. (2014), *Affordances and design*. The Interaction Design Foundation.

Kates, B. (2020), 'Incandescent Edges of the Future: Performance Creation with Virtual, Augmented and Carbon Realities,' Master's thesis, University of Calgary, Calgary, Canada, 8 September. Available online: http://hdl.handle.net/1880/112510.

Kelley, John F. (2018), 'Wizard of Oz (WoZ): A Yellow Brick Journey', *Journal of Usability Studies*, Usability Professionals' Association, 13 (3): 119–24. https://doi.org/10.5555/3294033.3294034.

Kendrick, L. (2017), *Theatre Aurality*, London: Palgrave Macmillan.

King, A. F. (2018), 'Moving Masks and Mobile Monkeys: The Technodramaturgy of Augmented Reality Puppets', *Theatre and Performance Design*, 4 (4): 324–41. https://doi.org/10.1080/23322551.2018.1558539.

Kitchin, R., and M. Dodge (2011), *Code/Space: Software and Everyday Life*, Massachusetts: The MIT Press.

Klich, R. (2017), 'Amplifying Sensory Spaces: The In- and Out-Puts of Headphone Theatre', *Contemporary Theatre Review*, 27 (3): 366–78, DOI: 10.1080/10486801.2017.1343247.

Kozel, S., R. Gibson, and B. Martelli (2018), 'The Weird Giggle: Attending to Affect in Virtual Reality', *Transformations* (31): 24.

Krampusnacht (2020), [VR Theatre] Dir. Tull, USA: Ferryman Collective.

La Biennale di Venezia, 'Biennale Cinema 2022 | Venice Immersive', 6 July 2022. https://www.labiennale.org/en/cinema/2022/venice-immersive.

Lai, C. (2017), 'Animation and Physics Engines in Game Development: Achieving Realism in Interactive Narratives', *Journal of Game Development*, 12 (4): 345–59.

Lecoq, J. (2001), *The Moving Body (Le Corps Poetique)*, London: Routledge.

The Legend of Zelda: Nintendo (1986), 'The Legend of Zelda', Nintendo. https://zelda.nintendo.com/.

Lehmann, H.-T. (2006). Postdramatic Theatre. Oxon/New York: Routledge.

Leman, M. (2007), *Embodied Music Cognition and Mediation Technology*, Cambridge, MA: MIT Press.

Lesaffre, M., P. M. Maes, and M. Leman (eds.) (2017), *The Routledge Companion to Embodied Music Interaction*, London/New York: Routledge.

Li, B. J., et al. (2013), 'Effects of a Multisensory Immersive Virtual Environment on Cognitive Load and Performance', *International Journal of Human-Computer Interaction*, 29 (6): 571–84.

Loke, L., and T. Schiphorst (2018), 'The Somatic Turn in Human-Computer Interaction', *Interactions*, 25 (5): 54–5863. https://doi.org/10.1145/3236675.

Lotker, S., and R. Gough (2013), 'On Scenography: Editorial', *Performance Research*, 18 (3): 3–6. https://doi.org/10.1080/13528165.2013.818306.

Mack, K. (2019), 'Devalaya Rupanam', Exhibition. Museum of Other Realities. https://www.museumor.com/artwork/devalaya-rupanam.

Mack, K. (2021), 'Anandala', Portfolio. Kevin Mack Art, http://www.kevinmackart.com/anandala.html.

Mack, K. dir (2022), *Namuanki*. http://www.kevinmackart.com/namuanki.html.

Mack, K. (2023), *Emergent Visions: AI Art by Kevin Mack*. USA. http://www.kevinmackart.com/emergent-visions.html.

Maclaurin, A. (2000), 'A Collective Approach to Designing for Devised Theatre', *Studies in Theatre and Performance*, 20 (2): 97–104. https://doi.org/10.1080/14682761.2000.10807028.

Madary, M., and T. K. Metzinger (2016), 'Real Virtuality: A Code of Ethical Conduct. Recommendations for Good Scientific Practice and the Consumers of VR-Technology', *Frontiers in Robotics and AI*, 3. https://doi.org/10.3389/frobt.2016.00003.

Mancewicz, A. (2024), *Extended Reality Shakespeare*, Cambridge: Cambridge University Press.

Márquez Segura, E., L. T. Vidal, and A. Rostami (2016), 'Bodystorming for Movement-Based Interaction Design', *Human Technology*, 12 (2): 193–251. https://doi.org/10.17011/ht/urn.201611174655.

Martens, T. (2022), 'Halloween Season Brings out the Best in L.A. Immersive Scene with "The Willows" and "Witch!"', *LA Times*, 14 October. Available online: https://www.latimes.com/entertainment-arts/story/2022-10-14/the-willows-spooky-immersive-theater (accessed 20 April 2023).

Mayer, R. E. (1997), 'Multimedia Learning: Are We Asking the Right Questions?' *Educational Psychologist*, 32 (1): 1–19. https://doi.org/10.1207/s15326985ep3201_1.

McCauley, J. (2016), 'The Evolution of Virtual Reality', *IGN*, 15 January. Available online: https://www.ign.com/articles/2016/01/14/the-evolution-of-virtual-reality (accessed 19 April 2023).

McKinney, J., and S. Palmer (2017), *Scenography Expanded*, London; New York: Bloomsbury Methuen Drama.

Melnick, K. (2018), 'Tribeca: VR Documentary "Vestige" Explores Love & Loss', VRScout, 27 April. Available at: https://vrscout.com/news/vestige-vr-documentary-love-loss/ (accessed 28 May 2021).

Melnick, K. (2020), 'Bizarre Interactive VR Performance "Scarecrow" Makes VRChat Debut', VR Scout, 2 November. Available online: https://vrscout.com/news/live-vr-theater-scarecrow-vrchat/ (accessed 19 April 2023).

Meyer, R. (2020), 'The Expansion of Scenography in Virtual Reality Theatre: Investigating the Potential of Double Scenography in Makropol's Anthropia', *Theatre and Performance Design*, 6 (4): 321–40, DOI: 10.1080/23322551.2020.1854929.

Milgram, P., and F. Kishino (1994), 'A Taxonomy of Mixed Reality Visual Displays', *IECE Transactions on Information and Systems*, 12 (12): 1321–9.

Milk, C. (2015). 'How Virtual Reality Can Create the Ultimate Empathy Machine', March 2015. https://www.ted.com/talks/chris_milk_how_virtual_reality_can_create_the_ultimate_empathy_machine?language=en.

Mirages & Miracles (2017), [Augmented Reality] Adrian Mondot and Claire Bardainne. https://www.am-cb.net/en/projets/mirages-miracles.

Montola, M., J. Stenros, and A. Waern, *Pervasive Games: Theory & Design - Experiences*, Elsevier, USA: 2009.

Mosco, V. (2019), *The Smart City in a Digital World*, Bingley: Emerald Publishing.

Museum of Austerity (2021), [Augmented Reality Experience] Dir. Sacha Wares, All Seeing Eye. https://ett.org.uk/our-work/museum-of-austerity/.

Nelson, R. (2013), *Practice as Research in the Arts: Principles, Protocols, Pedagogies, Resistances*, Basingstoke and New York: Palgrave Macmillan.

Nickel, T. (2020), 'Theatre Critique: Neverland', *AR/VR Journey: Augmented & Virtual Reality Magazine*, 26 December. Available online: https://arvrjourney.com/theatre-critique-neverland-4c21a052ec1 (accessed 19 April 2023).

Night Trap: Digital Pictures (1992), *Night Trap*, Digital Pictures. https://www.nintendo.com/us/store/products/night-trap-25th-anniversary-edition-switch/.

Nijs, L. (2017), 'The Merging of Musician and Musical Instrument: Incorporating, Presnece and Levels of Embodiment'. In M. Lesaffre, P. M. Maes, and M. Leman (eds.) (2017) *The Routledge Companion to Embodied Music Interaction*, London/New York: Routledge.

Nijs, L., P. Coussement, B. Moens, D. Amelinck, M. Lesaffre, M. Leman (2012), 'Interacting with the Music Paint Machine: Relating the Constructs of Flow Experience and Presence', *Interacting with Computers*, 24 (4), July 2012: 237–50.

Núñez-Pacheco, C. (2018), 'Reflection through Inner Presence: A Sensitising Concept for Design', *Multimodal Technologies and Interaction*, 2 (1): 5. https://doi.org/10.3390/mti2010005.

Obana, K., D. Hasegawa, and H. Sakuta (2017), 'Change in Subjective Evaluation of Weight by the Proteus Effect', HCI International 2017 – Posters' *Extended Abstracts*, 713: 1. Available online: https://www.researchgate.net/

publication/317174417_Change_in_Subjective_Evaluation_of_Weight_by_the_Proteus_Effect (accessed 20 April 2023).

O'Dwyer, N. (3 April 2015), 'The Scenographic Turn: The Pharmacology of the Digitisation of Scenography', *Theatre and Performance Design,* 1 (1–2): 48–63. https://doi.org/10.1080/23322551.2015.1023667.

O'Dwyer, N. (2021), *Digital Scenography: 30 Years of Experimentation and Innovation in Performance and Interactive Media*, London; New York: Bloomsbury Methuen Drama.

O'Dwyer, N., G.W. Young, N. Johnson, E. Zerman, and A. Smolic (2020), 'Mixed Reality and Volumetric Video in Cultural Heritage: Expert Opinions on Augmented and Virtual Reality'. In M. Rauterberg (ed.), *Culture and Computing*, 195–214. Cham: Springer. https://doi.org/10.1007/978-3-030-50267-6_16.

O'Dwyer, N., and N. Johnson (2019), 'Exploring Volumetric Video and Narrative through Samuel Beckett's *Play*', *International Journal of Performance Arts and Digital Media,* 15 (1): 53–69. https://doi.org/10.1080/14794713.2019.1567243.

O'Dwyer, N., N. Johnson, E. Bates, R. Pagés, J. Ondřej, K. Amplianitis, D. Monaghan, and A. Smolić (2017), 'Virtual Play in Free-Viewpoint Video: Reinterpreting Samuel Beckett for Virtual Reality'. In *2017 IEEE International Symposium on Mixed and Augmented Reality (ISMAR-Adjunct)*, 262–7. https://doi.org/10.1109/ISMAR-Adjunct.2017.87.

O'Dwyer, N., N. Johnson, E. Bates, R. Pagés, J. Ondřej, K. Amplianitis, D. Monaghan, and A. Smolic (2018), 'Samuel Beckett in Virtual Reality: Exploring Narrative Using Free Viewpoint Video', *Leonardo*, December, 1–10. https://doi.org/10.1162/leon_a_01721.

O'Dwyer, N., N. Johnson, R. Pagés, J. Ondřej, K. Amplianitis, E. Bates, D. Monaghan, and A. Smolić (2018), 'Beckett in VR: Exploring Narrative Using Free Viewpoint Video'. In *ACM SIGGRAPH 2018 Posters*, 1–2. Vancouver, British Columbia: ACM. https://doi.org/10.1145/3230744.3230774.

Pagés, R., K. Amplianitis, D. Monaghan, J. Ondřej, and A. Smolić (2018), 'Affordable Content Creation for Free-Viewpoint Video and VR/AR Applications', *Journal of Visual Communication and Image Representation,* 53: 192–201. https://doi.org/10.1016/j.jvcir.2018.03.012.

PARA (2020), [VR Theatre] Dir. Tull, USA: Ferryman Collective.

Pariser, E. (2011), *The Filter Bubble: What the Internet Is Hiding from You,* London: Penguin.

Parisi, T. (2021). 'The Seven Rules of the Metaverse. A Framework for the Coming Immersive Reality', [Blog]. Medium – Tony Parisi, October 22. https://medium.com/meta-verses/the-seven-rules-of-the-metaverse-7d4e06fa864c.

Pawlowicz, L. (2019), 'CoAct Productions Goes Dark with Severance Theory – An Interview', Become Immersed, 14 July. Available online: https://becomeimmersed.com/coact-interview-severance-theory/ (accessed 20 April 2023).

Peirce, C. S. (1991a), 'On a New List of Categories'. In J. Hoopes (ed.), *Peirce on signs: Writings on Semiotic by Charles Sanders Peirce*, 23–33. USA: University of North Carolina Press.

Peirce, C. S. (1991b), 'One, Two, Three: Fundamental Categories of Thought and of Nature'. In J. Hoopes (ed.), *Peirce on Signs: Writings on Semiotic by Charles Sanders Peirce*, 180–5, USA: University of North Carolina Press.

Peters, G. (2009), *The Philosophy of Improvisation*, Chicago, IL: University of Chicago Press.

Phelan, P. (1993). *Unmarked: The Politics of Performance*, London/New York: Routledge.

Philharmonia (2018), 'Immersive'. https://philharmonia.co.uk/what-we-do/digital-immersive/immersive/.

Pietrobon, A. (2020), 'The Metamovie Presents: Alien Rescue … aka the new frontier of fandom', Fanheart3, 24 February. Available online: https://www.fanheart3.com/alien-rescue-eng/ (accessed 19 April 2023).

Popat, S. (2016), 'Missing in Action: Embodied Experience and Virtual Reality', *Theatre Journal; Baltimore*, 68 (3): 357–78.

Precedence Research (2022), 'Extended Reality Market Size, Trends, Share, Report 2030', November 2022. https://www.precedenceresearch.com/extended-reality-market.

Rauschnabel, P., R. Felix, C. Hinsch, H. Shahaband, and F. Alt (2022), 'What Is XR? Towards a Framework for Augmented and Virtual Reality', *Computers in Human Behavior*, 133: 1–18.

Reaney, M. (1999), 'Virtual Reality and the Theatre: Immersion in Virtual Worlds'. *Digital Creativity*, 10 (3): 183–8. https://doi.org/10.1076/digc.10.3.183.3244.

Rebel Rabble (2022), [Performance] Dir. B. Samuels, & S. Johnson. Limbik, Norwich: UK.

Riggs, S. (2019), 'The End of Storytelling: The Future of Narrative'. In M. Hustad (ed.), *The Storyplex*. Illustrated edition. Beat Media Group.

Rizzo, A., A. Hartholt, M. Grimani, A. Leeds and M. Liewer (2014), "Virtual Reality Exposure Therapy for Combat-Related Posttraumatic Stress Disorder," *Computer*, 47 (7): 31–7, July, DOI: 10.1109/MC.2014.199.

Room Service – Gob Squad (2003), [Immersive Interactive Live Theatre–Film] Johanna Freiburg, Sean Patten, Elyce Semenec, Berit Stumpf, Sarah Thom, Bastian Trost and Simon Will, Berlin: Gob Squad. https://www.gobsquad.com/projects/room-service/.

Rouse, R., M. Engberg, N. Jafari Naimi, and J. D. Bolter (2015), 'MRX: An Interdisciplinary Framework for Mixed Reality Experience Design and Criticism', *Digital Creativity*, 26 (3–4): 175–81. https://doi.org/10.1080/14626268.2015.1100123.

Royal Shakespeare Company: The Tempest (2017), [Theatre Production] Dir. Gregory Doran, UK: Royal Shakespeare Company.

Royal Shakespeare Company (2021), *Dream* [Performance]. Available online: https://www.rsc.org.uk/support/members-room/exclusive-members-content/dream-q-a (accessed 15 June 2023)

Sainer, A. (1997), The New Radical Theatre Notebook. UK: Applause.

Sanchez-Vives, M. V., and M. Slater (2005), 'From Presence to Consciousness through Virtual Reality', *Nature Reviews Neuroscience*, 6 (4): 332–9. Available online: https://doi.org/10.1038/nrn1651.

Salter, C. (2010), *Entangled: Technology and the Transformation of Performance*, Cambridge, MA; London: MIT Press.

Sansom, C. (2018), *Tombland*, London: Mantle.

Sawyer, R. K. (2000a), 'Improvisation and the Creative Process: Dewey, Collingwood, and the Aesthetics of Spontaneity', *The Journal of Aesthetics and Art Criticism*, 58 (2): 149–61. https://doi.org/10.2307/432094.

Sawyer, R. K. (2000b), 'Improvisational Cultures: Collaborative Emergence and Creativity in Improvisation. Mind', *Culture, and Activity*, 7 (3): 180–5. https://doi.org/10.1207/S15327884MCA0703_05.

ScarecrowVRC. Sngmoo Lee (2020), Dir. Sngmoo Lee and Jihyun Jung. [Online. 19 June 2020 and 8 November 2020].

Schmalstieg, D., and T. Hollerer (2016), *Augmented Reality: Principles and Practice*, Addison Wesley.

Scott, J. (2022), *Wanders in the Wild, Smart City* [Sound Walk]. Available online: https://explore.echoes.xyz/collections/L5BiNwqm8EEGMaMP (accessed 02 December 2024).

Shusterman, R. (1999), 'Somaesthetics: A Disciplinary Proposal', *The Journal of Aesthetics and Art Criticism*, 57 (3): 299–313. https://doi.org/10.2307/432196

Sigur Rós (2018), *Tónandi* app, Magic Leap (accessed 5 June 2023).

Sirkin, D., and W. Ju (2015), 'Embodied Design Improvisation: A Method to Make Tacit Design Knowledge Explicit and Usable'. In H. Plattner, C. Meinel, and L. Leifer (eds.), *Design Thinking Research: Building Innovators*, 195–209. Cham: Springer International Publishing. https://doi.org/10.1007/978-3-319-06823-7_11.

Six to Start (2012), *Zombies, Run!* (version 11.0.3). [Mobile App]. (accessed 4 May 2023).

Skarbez, R., M. Smith, and M. C. Whitton (2021), 'Revisiting Milgram and Kishino's Reality-Virtuality Continuum', *Frontiers in Virtual Reality*, 2: 27. https://doi.org/10.3389/frvir.2021.647997.

Slater, M. (2018), 'Immersion and the Illusion of Presence in Virtual Reality', *British Journal of Psychology*, 109 (3): 431–3. https://doi.org/10.1111/bjop.12305.

Slater, M., and S. Wilbur (1997), 'A Framework for Immersive Virtual Environments (FIVE): Speculations on the Role of Presence in Virtual Environments', *Presence: Teleoperators and Virtual Environments*, 6 (6): 603–16.

Sleep No More (2011), [Theatre Production] Dir. Felix Barrett and Maxine Doyle, UK: Punchdrunk.

Smith, M. (2014), '"The Pit of Naturalism": Neuroscience and the Naturalized Aesthetics of Film'. In T. Nannicelli and P. Taberham (eds.), *Cognitive Media Theory*, London/New York: Routledge.

Snyder, G. (2020), *The Practice of the Wild: Essays* (30th anniversary edition), Berkeley, CA: Counterpoint.

Solirax (2018), 'Neos VR Metaverse. Neos VR Metaverse'. https://neos.com/.

SPACE (2018), Focus – Next: Art + Tech Residency Open Call. Available online: https://spacestudios.org.uk/artist-support-post/focus-next-art-tech-residency-open-call/ accessed 15 June 2023.

Sparks, M. (2019), 'Metafocus: Avoiding the Uncanny Valley in VR & Serious Games', Learning Solutions Magazine, Available at: https://learningsolutionsmag.com/articles/metafocus-avoiding-the-uncanny-valley-in-vr-serious-games (accessed 9 September 2020).

Stanley, Kenneth O., and Joel Lehman (2015), *Why Greatness Cannot Be Planned: The Myth of the Objective*, 2015 edn. Cham, Heidelberg, New York, Dordrecht, London: Springer.

Stiegler, B. (1998), *Technics and Time, 1: The Fault of Epimetheus*, trans. R. Beardsworth and G. Collins. Stanford, CA: Stanford University Press.

Stiegler, B. (2010), 'The Age of De-Proletarianization: Art and Teaching Art in Post-Consumerist Culture'. In K. Corcoran, C. Delfos, and F. Solleveld (eds.), *ArtFutures: Current Issues in Higher Arts Education*, 10–19. Amsterdam: ELIA.

Strange, A. (2017), 'Intimate Stories and Live Actors Show Just How Beautiful VR Can Be', *Mashable*, April 26. Available online: https://mashable.com/2017/04/26/tribeca-film-fest-virtual-reality-experiences/ (accessed 12 May 2018).

Svanæs, D., and L. Barkhuus (2020), 'The Designer's Body as Resource in Design: Exploring Combinations of Point-of-view and Tense', *Proceedings of the 2020 CHI Conference on Human Factors in Computing Systems*: 1–13. http://doi.org/10.1145/3313831.3376430

Sweeney, T. (2015), *The Unreal Engine: Real-Time Rendering and the Future of Immersive Storytelling*. GDC Conference.

Tarkovsky, A. (1975), *The Mirror* [Film].

Taylor, J. L. (2009), 'Proprioception'. In L. R. Squire (ed.), *Encyclopedia of Neuroscience*, 1143–9. Oxford: Academic Press. Available online: https://doi.org/10.1016/B978-008045046-9.01907-0.

TEDx Talks (2022), 'Hacking the Familiar | Jorge Lopes Ramos | TEDxUniversityOf Greenwich', https://www.youtube.com/watch?v=2QCFSEr4Dik (accessed 31 August 2022).

Tell No One by Secret Cinema (2016), [location n.k.].

Tender Claws (2020), Tempest [VR Performance].: https://tenderclaws.com/tempest (accessed 15 June 2023.

The Burnt City (2022), [Immersive Theatre] Dir. Felix Barrett and Maxine Doyle: Punchdrunk. https://www.punchdrunk.com/project/theburntcity/.

The Encounter (2016), [Theatre Production] Dir. Simon McBurney and Kirsty Housley, UK: Complicité, Gary Goddard Entertainment, and Marks-Moore-Turnbull Group.

The Grim by Quietly Fighting Theatre (2020), Dir. L. Fleming. [Vault Festival, London, UK].

The Lion King (1997), [Stage Musical] Dir. Julie Taymor, USA: Disney Theatrical Productions.

These Rooms: An Immersive Live Performance (2016), [Immersive Theatre] Dir. David Bolger and Louise Lowe, Ireland: Cois Céim and ANÚ Productions. https://theserooms.ie/room01/.

The Killing Fields. (1984). Dir. Roland Joffé, performances by Sam Waterston, Haing S. Ngor, and John Malkovich, Warner Bros.

The Making of *Queerskins: ARK* (2020), Available online: https://vimeo.com/456287749 (accessed 11 March 2021).

The Performance Corporation (2004), Dr Ledbetter's Experiment [Performance]. https://www.theperformancecorporation.com/portfolio-item/dr-ledbetters-experiment/ (accessed 14 June 2023).

The Performance Corporation (2006), *Drive-By* [Performance]. https://www.theperformancecorporation.com/portfolio-item/drive-by/ accessed 14 June 2023.

The Severance Theory: Welcome to Respite (2021), [VR Theatre] Dir. Lyndsie Scoggin, USA: CoAct Productions and Ferryman Collective.

Thrift, N. (2014), 'The "Sentient" City and What It May Portend', *Big Data & Society*, 1(1): 1–21.

Tree (2019), [Theatre Production] Dir. Idris Elba and Kwame Kwei-Armah, UK: Young Vic Theatre.

Tsiboulski, C., and I. Szilak (2020), *Queerskins: ARK* [Virtual Reality].
Tufekci, Z. (2017), *Twitter and Tear Gas: The Power and Fragility of Networked Protest*. New Haven, CT: Yale University Press.
Turner, John R., and Rose M. Baker (2019), 'Complexity Theory: An Overview with Potential Applications for the Social Sciences', *Systems*, 7 (1): 4, 19 January. https://doi.org/10.3390/systems7010004.
UNeditions (2014), [Web Browser Application] Creative Dir. Jon Spooner, UK: Unlimited Theatre.
Vader Immortal: Vader Immortal (2019), *Vader Immortal*, Meta. https://www.meta.com/experiences/2108775495884888/.
Verbeek, P.-P. (2008), Cyborg Intentionality: Rethinking the Phenomenology of Human–Technology Relations', *Phenomenology and the Cognitive Sciences*, 7 (3): 387–95. https://doi.org/10.1007/s11097-008-9099-x.
Vincent, C. (2021), *Digital Scenography in Opera in the Twenty-First Century*, London: Routledge. https://doi.org/10.4324/9781003093305.
Vindenes, J., and B. Wasson (2021), 'A Postphenomenological Framework for Studying User Experience of Immersive Virtual Reality', *Frontiers in Virtual Reality*, 2: 40. https://doi.org/10.3389/frvir.2021.656423.
Violette, A. D. (2018), 'Directed by Catherine Bourgeois', [Kingston, 21 June 2018].
WaveXR (2022). About Wave XR. Available online: https://wavexr.com/about/ (accessed 18 February 2025).
Weijdom, J. (2022), 'Performative Prototyping in Collaborative Mixed Reality Environments: An Embodied Design Method for Ideation and Development in Virtual Reality', *TEI '21: Proceedings of the Sixteenth International Conference on Tangible, Embedded, and Embodied Interaction*: 13. https://doi.org/10.1145/3490149.3501316.
Wigmore, I. (2014), 'Definition Proteus effect', *Tech Target*, 14 January. Available online: https://www.techtarget.com/whatis/definition/Proteus-effect (accessed 21 April 2023).
Wike, J. (2021), 'Inside Ariana Grande's *Fortnite* virtual concert', https://theface.com/music/ariana-grande-fortnite-rift-tour-performance-gaming-vr-mac-miller-travis-scott-lil-nas-x (accessed 4 October 2022).
Winters, T. (2019), 'The Speakeasy Society's The Portal Is a Fitting Conclusion to the Kansas Collection', Haunting, 20 June. Available online: https://www.haunting.net/portal-kansas-collection-review/ (accessed 20 April 2023).
Wise, K. (2021), Facades [Virtual Reality]. Available online: www.facades.info.
Witmer, B. G., and M. J. Singer (1998), 'Measuring Presence in Virtual Environments: A Presence Questionnaire', *Presence: Teleoperators and Virtual Environments*, 7 (3): 225–40. Available online: https://doi.org/10.1162/105474698565686.
Wu, T. (2017), *The Attention Merchants: The Epic Scramble to Get Inside Our Heads*. Vintage.
Xambó, A. (2017), 'Embodied Music Interaction: Creative Design Synergies between Music Performance and HCI', [PUBLISHED] [AAM]. In S. Price and S. Broadhurst (eds.), *Digital Bodies: Creativity and Technology in the Arts and Humanities*, 207–20. London: Palgrave Macmillan.
Yathay, Pin (2000), *Stay Alive, My Son*. Ithaca, NY: Cornell Press.
Yeats, W. B. (1934), 'A Dream of Death'. In *The Collected Poems of W. B. Yeats*, 47–8. Basingstoke: Macmillan.

Yee, N., and J. Bailenson (2007), 'The Proteus Effect: The Effect of Transformed Self-Representation on Behavior', *Human Communication Research*, 33 (3): 271–90. Available online: https://stanfordvr.com/mm/2007/yee-proteus-effect.pdf (accessed 21 April 2023).

Yee, N., J. N. Bailenson, and N. Ducheneaut (2009), 'The Proteus Effect: Implications of Transformed Digital Self-Representation on Online and Offline Behaviour', *Communication Research*, 36 (2): 285–312.

Zenk, L., N. Hynek, G. Schreder, and G. Bottaro (2022), 'Toward a System Model of Improvisation', *Thinking Skills and Creativity*, 43: 100993. https://doi.org/10.1016/j.tsc.2021.100993.

Zork: Infocom (1980), 'Zork', *Infocom*. Available online: https://www.pcjs.org/software/pcx86/game/infocom/zork1/.

ZU-UK (2022), *Binaural Dinner Date*. Available online: https://zu-uk.com/project/binaural-dinner-date/ (accessed 15 February 2022).

Index